PERSIA AND TORAH

SOCIETY
OF BIBLICAL
LITERATURE

SBL
SYMPOSIUM SERIES

Christopher R. Matthews, Editor

Number 17
PERSIA AND TORAH
edited by
James W. Watts

James W. Watts, editor

PERSIA AND TORAH

The Theory of Imperial
Authorization of the Pentateuch

Society of Biblical Literature
Atlanta

PERSIA AND TORAH

edited by
James W. Watts

Library of Congress Cataloging-in-Publication Data

Persia and Torah : the theory of imperial authorization of the Pentateuch / James W. Watts, editor.
    p. cm.— (SBL symposium series ; no. 17)
Includes bibliographical references and index.
ISBN 1-58983-015-6 (pbk. : alk. paper)
    1. Bible. O.T. Ezra VII—History of biblical events—Congresses. 2. Bible. O.T. Pentateuch—Criticism, interpretation, etc.—Congresses. 3. Judaism—History—Post-exilic period, 586 B.C.–210 A.D.—Congresses. 4. Achaemenid dynasty, 559–330 B.C.—Congresses. I. Watts, James W. (James Washington), 1960– II. Symposium series (Society of Biblical Literature) ; no. 17.
BS1355.52.P47 2001
296'.06'014—dc21   2001049197

09 08 07 06 05 04 03 02 01 5 4 3 2 1

Printed in the United States of America
on acid-free paper

CONTENTS

ABBREVIATIONS

Primary Sources

Aelian
    Nat an.   *De natura animalium*
AP   Aramaic Papyri
b.   Babylonian Talmud
DB   Darius, Behistun inscription
Diodorus Siculus
    Hist.   *Bibliotheca Historica*
DNa   Darius, Naqsh-i-Rustam A
DNb   Darius, Naqsh-i-Rustam B
Josephus
    Ant.   *Jewish Antiquities*
    J.W.   *Jewish War*
m.   Mishnah
Philo
    Mos.   *De vita Mosis*
Plato
    Ep.   *Epistulae*
    Leg.   *Leges*
Pliny the Elder
    Nat.   *Naturalis historia*
Plutarch
    Is. Os.   *De Iside et Osiride*
PT   Pyramid Texts
Šabb.   *Šabbat*
Sanh.   *Sanhedrin*
Tacitus
    Ann.   *Annales*
Xenophon
    Cyr.   *Cyropaedia*
    Oec.   *Oeconomicus*

Secondary Sources

    ABD   *Anchor Bible Dictionary*. Edited by D. N. Freedman. 6 vols. New York: Doubleday, 1992.
    ABRL   Anchor Bible Reference Library

AEL	*Ancient Egyptian Literature*. M. Lichtheim. 3 vols. Berkeley and Los Angeles: University of California Press, 1971–1980.
ÄF	Ägyptologische Forschungen
AH	Achaemenid History
AHw	*Akkadisches Handwörterbuch*. W. von Soden. 3 vols. Wiesbaden: Harrassowitz, 1965–1981.
AJP	*American Journal of Philology*
AJSL	*American Journal of Semitic Languages and Literature*
AMI	*Archäologische Mitteilungen aus Iran*
ANET	*Ancient Near Eastern Texts Relating to the Old Testament*. Edited by J. B. Pritchard. 3d ed. Princeton, N. J.: Princeton University Press, 1969.
AOSM	American Oriental Society Monographs
AS	Assyriological Studies
ASAÉ	*Annales du service des antiquités de l'Égypte*
ASAÉSup	Supplements to Annales du service des antiquités de l'Égypte
BAR	*Biblical Archaeology Review*
BBB	Bonner biblische Beiträge
BDB	Brown, F., S. R. Driver, and C. A. Briggs. *A Hebrew and English Lexicon of the Old Testament*. Oxford: Oxford University Press, 1907.
BEATAJ	Beiträge zur Erforschung des Alten Testaments und des antiken Judentum
BETL	Bibliotheca ephemeridum theologicarum lovaniensium
BHT	Beiträge zur historischen Theologie
Bib	*Biblica*
BibInt	Biblical Interpretation
BIFAO	*Bulletin de l'Institut français d'archéologie orientale*
BJS	Brown Judaic Studies
BKAT	Biblischer Kommentar, Altes Testament. Edited by M. Noth and H. W. Wolff
BO	*Bibliotheca orientalis*
BWANT	Beiträge zur Wissenschaft vom Alten und Neuen Testament
BZAW	Beihefte zur Zeitschrift für die alttestamentliche Wissenschaft
CAD	*The Assyrian Dictionary of the Oriental Institute of the University of Chicago*. Chicago: University of Chicago Press, 1956–.
CAH	*Cambridge Ancient History*. 14 vols. Cambridge: Cambridge University Press, 1970–2000.
CANE	*Civilizations of the Ancient Near East*. Edited by J. Sasson. 4 vols. New York: Scribner, 1995. Reprinted in 2 vols., Peabody, Mass.: Hendrickson, 2000.

CAP	Cowley, A. E. *Aramaic Papyri of the Fifth Century B.C.* Oxford: Clarendon, 1923.
CBQ	*Catholic Biblical Quarterly*
CBQMS	Catholic Biblical Quarterly Monograph Series
CCG	Cairo Musem, *Catalogue generale*
CHI	*Cambridge History of Iran.* 7 vols. Cambridge: Cambridge University Press, 1968–1991.
CHJ	*Cambridge History of Judaism.* Edited by W. D. Davies and Louis Finkelstein. Cambridge: Cambridge University Press, 1984–.
ChrEg	*Chronique d'Égypte*
CRAI	*Comptes rendus de l'Académie des inscriptions et belles-lettres*
DMOA	Documenta et monumenta Orientis antiqui
DNWSI	*Dictionary of the North-West Semitic Inscriptions.* J. Hoftijzer and K. Jongeling. 2 vols. Leiden: Brill, 1995.
EB	Étude Biblique, Nouvelle Série
Edfu	*Le Temple d'Edfou.* Edited by Maxence Marquis de Rochemonteix, Emile Chassinat, Sylvia Cauville, and Didier Devauchelle. 15 vols. Cairo: Institut français d'archéologie orientale, 1897–1985.
EVO	*Egitto e Vicino Oriente*
FAT	Forschungen zum Alten Testament
FRLANT	Forschungen zur Religion und Literatur des Alten und Neuen Testaments
GM	*Göttinger Miszellen*
HAL	Koehler, L., W. Baumgartner, and J. J. Stamm. *Hebräisches und aramäisches Lexikòn zum Alten Testament.* 5 vols., with supplement. Leiden: Brill, 1967–1995.
HALOT	Koehler, L., W. Baumgartner, and J. J. Stamm, *The Hebrew and Aramaic Lexicon of the Old Testament.* Translated and edited under the supervision of M. E. J. Richardson. 4 vols. Leiden: Brill, 1994–1999.
HAR	*Hebrew Annual Review*
HAT	Handbuch zum Alten Testament
Hellenica	*Hellenica: Recueil d'épigraphie, de numismatique et d'antiquités grecques*
JARCE	*Journal of the American Research Center in Egypt*
JBL	*Journal of Biblical Literature*
JCS	*Journal of Cuneiform Studies*
JEA	*Journal of Egyptian Archaeology*
JESHO	*Journal of the Economic and Social History of the Orient*
JETS	*Journal of the Evangelical Theological Society*

JNES	*Journal of Near Eastern Studies*
JSOT	*Journal for the Study of the Old Testament*
JSOTSup	Journal for the Study of the Old Testament: Supplement Series
JSS	*Journal of Semitic Studies*
KRI	*Ramesside Inscriptions: Historical and Biographical.* Edited by K. A. Kitchen. Oxford: Blackwell, 1969–.
LÄ	*Lexikon der Ägyptologie.* Edited by W. Helck, E.Otto, and W. Westendorf. Wiesbaden: Harrassowitz, 1972–.
LAPO	Littératures anciennes du Proche-Orient
LCL	Loeb Classical Library
LD	Lepsius, K. R. *Denkmäler aus Ägypten und Äthiopien.* Berlin: Nicolaische Buchhandlung, 1849.
LSJ	Liddell, H. G., R. Scott, and H. S. Jones, *A Greek-English Lexicon.* 9th ed. with revised supplement. Oxford: Oxford University Press, 1996.
LXX	Septuagint
MDAIK	Mitteilungen des Deutschen archäologischen Instituts, Kairo
MT	Masoretic Text
MVAG	Mitteilungen der Vorderasiatisch-ägyptischen Gesellschaft. Vols. 1–44. 1896–1939.
NAB	New American Bible
NCB	New Century Bible
NICOT	New International Commentary on the Old Testament
NJPS	*Tanakh: The Holy Scriptures: The New JPS Translation according to the Traditional Hebrew Text*
NRSV	New Revised Standard Version
OBO	Orbis biblicus et orientalis
OLA	Orientalia lovaniensia analecta
OP	Old Persian
Or	*Orientalia* (NS)
OTL	Old Testament Library
OTS	Old Testament Studies
OtSt	*Oudtestamentische Studiën*
P.	Papyrus
PM	Porter, B., and R. Moss. *Topographical Bibliography of Ancient Egyptian Texts, Reliefs and Paintings.* 7 vols., the first three in 2d ed. Oxford: Oxford University Press, 1927–1978.
PW	Pauly, A. F. *Paulys Realencyclopädie der classischen Altertumswissenschaft.* New edition G. Wissowa. 49 vols. Munich: Druckenmueller, 1980.
RB	*Revue biblique*
RdE	*Revue d'Égyptologie*

REA	*Revue des études anciennes*
RÉS	*Répertoire d'épigraphie sémitique*
RIDA	*Revue internationale des droits de l'antiquité*
SAOC	Studies in Ancient Oriental Civilizations
SBAB	Stuttgarter biblische Aufsatzbände
SBLDS	Society of Biblical Literature Dissertation Series
SBLSymS	Society of Biblical Literature Symposium Series
SCO	*Studi classici e orientale*
SEG	*Supplementum epigraphicum graecum*
SHANE	Studies in the History of the Ancient Near East
SIG	*Sylloge inscriptionum graecarum.* Edited by Wilhelm Dittenberger. 4 vols. 3d ed. Leipzig: S. Hirzelium, 1915–1924.
SJLA	Studies in Judaism in Late Antiquity
SPAW	Sitzungsberichte der preussischen Akademie der Wissenschaften
StIr	*Studia Iranica*
TAD	Porten, Bezalel, and Ada Yardeni. *Textbook of Aramaic Documents from Ancient Egypt.* 4 vols. Jerusalem: Hebrew University, 1986–1999.
TB	Theologische Bücherei: Neudrucke und Berichte aus dem 20. Jahrhundert
TCS	Texts from Cuneiform Sources
TLG	*Thesaurus linguae graecae: Canon of Greek Authors and Works.* Edited by L. Berkowitz and K. A. Squitier. 3d ed. Oxford: Oxford University Press, 1990.
TOB	*Traduction oecuménique de la Bible.* Paris: Editions du Cerf - Société Biblique française, 1991.
Transeu	*Transeuphratène*
TRu	*Theologische Rundschau*
Urk.	*Urkunden des ägyptischen Altertums.* Edited by G. Steindorff. Leipzig: Hinrichs; Berlin: Akademie-Verlag, 1903–.
VF	*Verkündigung und Forschung*
VT	*Vetus Testamentum*
VTSup	Supplements to Vetus Testamentum
WÄS	*Wörterbuch der ägyptischen Sprache.* Edited by A. Erman and H. Grapow. 5 vols. Leipzig: Hinrichs, 1926–1931.
WBC	Word Biblical Commentary
WMANT	Wissenschaftliche Monographien zum Alten und Neuen Testament
ZABR	*Zeitschrift für altorientalische und biblische Rechtgeschichte*
ZÄS	*Zeitschrift für ägyptische Sprache und Altertumskunde*
ZAW	*Zeitschrift für die alttestamentliche Wissenschaft*

INTRODUCTION

James W. Watts

Syracuse University

In 1984, Peter Frei revived an old theory about the influence of the Persian Empire on the promulgation of Jewish law in the time of Ezra.[1] Citing ancient references to codifications of Egyptian law under Darius, Persian involvement in the founding of local cults in Asia Minor and at Elephantine in Upper Egypt, and Persian permission for the promulgation of Jewish legal texts in the biblical books of Ezra, Nehemiah, and Esther, Frei argued that the Persians authorized local legislation in various parts of the empire. Such "imperial authorization" created a federal arrangement by which the local communities gained a degree of legal autonomy while remaining under imperial rule. Thus he depicted Artaxerxes' authorization of Ezra's law book (Ezra 7), presumably the Pentateuch more or less, as an action typical of Persian, and only of Persian, policies.

In the past decade, this theory of Persian imperial authorization of the Pentateuch has been cited frequently in discussions of the composition and form of pentateuchal literature.[2] There has been extensive critical

---

[1] "Zentralgewalt und Lokalautonomie im Achämenidenreich," in Peter Frei and Klaus Koch, *Reichsidee und Reichsorganisation im Perserreich* (OBO 55; Fribourg: Universitätsverlag, 1984; 2d ed., 1996), 8–131.

[2] E.g., Erhard Blum, *Studien zur Komposition des Pentateuch* (Berlin: de Gruyter, 1990), 346–56; Joseph Blenkinsopp, *The Pentateuch: An Introduction to the First Five Books of the Bible* (ABRL; New York: Doubleday, 1992), 239–42; Frank Crüsemann, *The Torah: Theology and Social History of Old Testament Law* (trans. W. Mahnke; Minneapolis: Fortress, 1996), 260–61; trans. of *Die Torah: Theologie und Sozialgeschichte des alttestamentlichen Gesetzes* (Munich: Kaiser, 1992); Rainer Albertz, *From the Exile to the Maccabees*, vol. 2 of *A History of Religion in the Old Testament Period* (trans. J. Bowden; OTL; Louisville: Westminster/John Knox, 1994), 467–68; trans. of *Vom Exil bis zu den Makkabäern*, vol. 2 of *Religionsgeschichte in alttestamentlicher Zeit* (ATD 8.2; Göttingen: Vandenhoeck & Ruprecht, 1992); Jon L. Berquist, *Judaism in Persia's Shadow: A Social and Historical Approach* (Minneapolis: Fortress, 1995), 138–39; David M. Carr, *Reading the Fractures of Genesis: Historical and Literary Approaches* (Louisville: Westminster/John Knox, 1996), 324–33; James W. Watts, *Reading Law: The Rhetorical Shaping of the Pentateuch* (Biblical Seminar 59; Sheffield: Sheffield Academic Press, 1999), 137–44.

discussion of Frei's proposal in German and French.[3] English language discussion, however, has for the most part been limited to brief descriptions and evaluations in works surveying the Pentateuch or Judea in the Persian period or dealing primarily with other specialized subjects.

In order to stimulate further evaluation of this theory in English, the Society of Biblical Literature's Pentateuch Section joined with the Biblical Law Section and the Literature and History of the Persian Period Section to sponsor a joint panel on the subject at the 2000 SBL Annual Meeting in Nashville. Panelists were invited to evaluate, in whole or in part, the theory of Persian imperial authorization and its application to the Pentateuch. In addition, the Biblical Law Section issued an open call for papers on law in the Persian period. Joseph Blenkinsopp, Lisbeth Fried, Lester Grabbe, Gary Knoppers, Donald Redford, and Jean Louis Ska presented papers on various aspects of the theory in these two sessions. These papers are being published here, preceded by a translation of Frei's 1995 article summarizing his theory, to make this discussion available to a larger audience.

Joseph Blenkinsopp concludes that, on balance, imperial authorization of the Pentateuch remains a possibility, though perhaps not in as strong a form as Frei suggested. He argues that the initiative for consolidating Judean law may well have come from Persian authorities, but there is no evidence for whether or how their oversight may have influenced the content of the Pentateuch.

Lisbeth Fried argues that Ezra's commission from the Persian king Artaxerxes was limited to appointing Persian judges in the province of Yehud. They would have acted in accord with Persian law, not the Pentateuch or other Jewish legal traditions, though local rulers with Persian

---

[3] The critical discussion has included: Joseph Wiesehöfer, "'Reichsgesetz' oder 'Einzelfallgerechtigkeit'? Bemerkungen zu P. Freis These von der Achämenidischen 'Reichsautorisation,'" *ZABR* 1 (1995): 36–46; Udo Rüterswörden, "Die persische Reichsautorisation der Thora: Fact or Fiction?" *ZABR* 1 (1995): 47–61; Hans-Christoph Schmitt, "Die Suche nach der Identität des Jahweglaubens im nachexilischen Israel: Bemerkungen zur theologischen Intention des Pentateuch," in *Pluralismus und Identität* (ed. J. Mehlhausen; Munich: Kaiser, 1995), 259–78; Eckart Otto, "Die nachpriesterschriftliche Pentateuchredaktion im Buch Exodus," in *Studies in the Book of Exodus: Redaction-Reception-Interpretation* (ed. M. Vervenne; BETL 126; Leuven: Peeters, 1996), 61–111; Jean Louis Ska, *Introduction à la lecture du Pentateuque: Clés pour l'interprétation des cinq premiers livres de la Bible* (Le livre et le rouleau; Paris: Cerf, 2000), 310–21; Pierre Briant, "Histoire impériale et histoire régionale: À propos de l'histoire de Juda dans l'empire achéménide," in *Congress Volume: Oslo, 1998* (ed. A. Lemaire and M. Sæbø; VTSup 80; Leiden: Brill, 2000), 235–45.

backing, like Nehemiah, may well have issued edicts based on Judean legal traditions on their own authority.

Lester Grabbe confirms the claim that the Pentateuch appeared in more or less its present form by the end of the Persian period. He questions, however, the historicity of the Ezra traditions and therefore of any imperial authorization of Ezra's law.

Gary Knoppers notes that in Jewish literature of the Persian and Hellenistic periods, the distinction between royal and sacred law is applied to a variety of settings, not just to imperial and temple laws. He suggests that local leaders under the Persians enjoyed much more autonomy than Frei's theory had allowed.

Donald Redford surveys the references to law and the uses of law in Egyptian texts, and especially the Egyptians' concern in the two centuries prior to the Persian conquest for collecting and consulting old texts, including laws. Redford concludes that Darius's interest in collecting Egyptian laws was in continuity with previous Egyptian practices and served only to inform the Persians of existing traditions.

Jean Louis Ska surveys the debate over imperial authorization, noting in particular the Pentateuch's poor fit as a constitutional document of the Persian era. He argues that there is no need to invoke Persian intervention to explain the emergence of the Pentateuch. It may have achieved normative status in Persian-period Judea simply because it was the official archive/library of the Second Temple community.

Taken together, these articles suggest that the available evidence will not support Frei's comparison of Persian policy with modern federal arrangements governing the relationships between local and national governments. The examples of Persian influence on local laws seem too diverse and sporadic to be the product of a systematic "federal" policy. Nevertheless, the extant evidence does show some Persian involvement in local legal affairs.

I wonder if a better analogy for understanding such Persian interventions in local cults and laws may be the modern practice of designating various symbols, commodities, and events as "the official X" of a city, state, or nation. Such designations have little or no benefit to the issuing authority nor much effect on its conduct, but are granted to benefit constituents for whom they provide valued prestige, legal privileges, and/or commercial advantages. Thus the Persians may have designated the Pentateuch as the "official" law of the Jerusalem temple community simply as a token favor, with little or no attention to that law's form or content. Their only concern would have been that such designation not be resisted by influential proponents of alternative laws and thus inflame resentment of the empire rather than mollifying it. The possibility of Persian designation of an official law would then have encouraged Judean leaders to produce a single compromise document but would not have had any other significant effect on the Pentateuch's form or contents.

I appreciate Peter Frei's permission in allowing me to translate and publish his article, and even more his careful correction of the drafts of my translation. I am grateful to William S. Morrow, chair of the Biblical Law Section, and John W. Wright, co-chair of the Literature and History of the Persian Period Section, for their counsel and support in organizing the conference program, and to Christopher R. Matthews, editor of the SBL Symposium Series, for making this volume possible.

PERSIAN IMPERIAL AUTHORIZATION:
A SUMMARY*

Peter Frei
University of Zürich

Persian imperial authorization was the topic of a paper I presented at a conference of the Schweizerische Gesellschaft für orientalische Alter-tumswissenschaft (Swiss Society for Ancient Oriental Studies) on November 27, 1982. In 1984 it was published in a book together with Klaus Koch's exposition presented on the same occasion.[1] When this went out of print, the publisher proposed a new edition containing the unaltered text with supplements and corrections. The new revision of the part to be discussed here was completed around 1991. Working through all this material again for the Frankfurt conference in the fall of 1994 cast several items in a new light, and the discussion during the symposium was fruitful in many respects.

So there is pressing need for a presentation that can summarize what has become a somewhat disparate whole. To a great extent, the formulations in this short version lean wherever possible on the work in the two editions of the book. One should as a rule consult the more extended versions for specifics and references to the secondary literature.[2] This essay

---

* Translated by James W. Watts from Peter Frei, "Die persische Reichsautorisa-tion: Ein Überblick," *ZABR* 1 (1995): 1–35. The author thanks Udo Rüterswörden for the opportunity to read the manuscript of his Frankfort conference paper, "Die persische Reichsautorisation der Thora: Fact or Fiction?" (published in *ZABR* 1 [1995]: 47–61). He is grateful to Erik Hornung and Elisabeth Staehelin for biblio-graphic help and for advice on Egyptian matters.

[1] Peter Frei and Klaus Koch, *Reichsidee und Reichsorganisation im Perserreich* (OBO 55, Fribourg: Universitätsverlag, 1984).

[2] The second revised and expanded edition appeared in 1996. The text of the first edition was reprinted unaltered in the second, with new page numbers. In what follows, references to pages of the first edition will be marked with a super-script 1, after which in brackets the page numbers of the second edition will be marked by a superscript 2. References to the new material in the second edition will also be marked by a superscript 2.

should, however, be understandable by itself. Previously undiscussed issues naturally require more explicit justification. But for reasons of space new literature can only be treated selectively.

1. TERMINOLOGICAL PRESUPPOSITIONS

The following considerations involve the general problem of the state and its regional subunits, insofar as these are matters of public law. The structure of every government is based on such subunits and must for practical purposes leave them a certain range of responsibilities in which to regulate their affairs for themselves. This holds good in all periods and cultures. At any given time two basic systems of administration exist beside each other, that of the central government and that of the subunits. These latter can necessarily only be effective in the immediate area of a distinct group. They have only local jurisdiction but are autonomous within their areas and within the boundaries of the legitimate responsibilities granted by the central government. Therefore I designate its characteristic status as "local autonomy"[3] and understand that to mean the right of the subunit to regulate its own interests to a lesser or greater degree. I call local units, which in their political structure may be organized along very different lines, "local self-organized bodies" or, shorter and more simply, "communities." These two terms are used here synonymously.

Naturally, these communities remain under the central government's supervision and threat of intervention. The limits of autonomy are not strictly defined in advance; in particular cases they can be tightly circumscribed or even annulled almost entirely. But it is just as likely that intervention is negligible and comes into play only when essential interests of the central government are at stake.

This holds good on the one hand especially in states with a federal structure, such as the Federal Republic of Germany or Switzerland, and this topic has immediate relevance in contemporary European politics, as is widely known. The same bifurcation appears just as impressively in imperial organizations. I will limit the following discussion to the latter, specifically to the ancient empire. Its ruling classes were usually not in a position to build quickly a complex and efficient administration that could be managed by its own members. In order to consolidate their rule, it was imperative to concede administrative responsibilities to the conquered. The

---

[3] For a justification for using the term *autonomy* in this context, which corresponds completely to ancient usage, see *Reichsidee,* 28^1 (10^2) n. 5; and Mauro Corsaro, "Tassazione regia e tassazione cittadina dagli Achemenidi ai re ellenistici: alcune osservazioni," *REA* 87 (1985): 82–83.

administrative system consisted then at any given time of the rulers—the central administration—and the subjects—the local administration.

They should all be understood as subsystems of a comprehensive, higher-ranking system—the empire. The contact points between the central and local systems through which the channels of communication flow are essential to the organization. It is important for the central government to supervise, but also to protect, local regulations. Various methods exist for this purpose, even in the modern state. How such interfaces are worked out is an important criterion qualifying the whole system in an imperially structured state. My intention will therefore be to observe the cooperation between the systems more closely and to investigate how they influence each other.

This is the context within which the phenomenon described below should be understood. It occurs only in the Achaemenid Empire. By definition it is a process by which the norms established by a local authority are not only approved and accepted by a central authority but adopted as its own. The local norms are thereby established and protected within the framework of the entire state association, that is, the empire, as higher-ranking norms binding on all. The phenomenon thus clearly involves a specific kind of organization of legal norms. Its concrete significance will be explained in the concluding section. I have named this situation where the central government guarantees local norms "imperial authorization."[4] Obviously, the term does not rule out the possibility that this institution can (also) serve to help the higher authority control the lower. The higher authority would guarantee only what corresponds with its own norms and intentions.[5]

---

[4] I thereby avoid problematic terms such as *sanction,* which today is tied up with implications of disciplinary interventions, or *ratification,* which today is used predominantly for the confirmation of a foreign policy agreement. Hans G. Kippenberg (*Die vorderasiatischen Erlösungsreligionen in ihrem Zusammenhang mit der antiken Stadtherrschaft* [Suhrkamp Taschenbuch Wissenschaft 917; Frankfurt am Main: Suhrkamp, 1991], 181–82) decided on the term "imperial sanction." His definition does not coincide in every respect with the one used here.

[5] See *Reichsidee,* 13[1] (15[2]) with n. 17. Modern federal republics also know of comparable regulations. According to article 15 of the Swiss constitution, the confederation "guarantees" (German: *"gewährleistet,"* French: *"garantit,"* Italian: *"garantisce"*) the constitutions of the cantons, so long as these cantonal constitutions satisfy specific requirements; see, e.g., the commentaries of Jean-François Aubert, *Traité de droit constitutionnel Suisse* (3 vols.; Neuchatel: Editions ides et calendes, 1967–1982), 1:216ff. §§567ff.; Yvo Hangartner, *Grundzüge des schweizerischen Staatsrechts* (2 vols.; Zürich: Schulthess, 1980–1982), 1:60–61.

2. Survey of the Evidence

The discussion should include a summary of all the attested cases, and a wide circle will purposely be drawn.[6] The order does not follow the heuristic relevance of the individual pieces of evidence—in that case the stela from the Letoon[7] would receive the greatest emphasis—but is arranged primarily from regional/ethnic and secondarily from chronological points of view.[8] For each piece of evidence, three sets of issues will be distinguished, which cannot always be separated neatly:

A. external circumstances, dating, contents of the regulation, how it is attested in the sources;
B. description of the process of authorization; and
C. political background of the authorization, insofar as it can be discovered from the (usually poorly known) context.

Methodologically, one must point out in advance that some of the evidence appears in contexts that must certainly be regarded as fictional, that is, literary depictions that do not wish to or cannot claim to describe historical reality. In some cases, their historical authenticity is also in dispute. Obviously, that is not to say that the institutions depicted in them are fictional. Stories that fabricate past events can, precisely in order to appear more believable, describe accurately situations, and thereby institutions and conditions, that are typical of the plot's environment. Naturally, the plots of fictional stories do not provide authentic accounts in every detail of administrative behavior, and sometimes they are, from a historical perspective, not at all plausible. But even then they appear only distorted, either because of narrative technicalities or because of the text's intended message. This holds true especially for the evidence from the Old Testament.[9]

----

[6] Included for clarity is the inscription from Sardis (section 2.4.2.2 below), which certainly cannot count as evidence, yet which is nevertheless significant, as will be shown. The example postulated (incorrectly) by Rütersworden ("Reichsautorisation," 47–61) of an imperial authorization in connection with the petition from the Jewish community in Elephantine to Bagavahya will be touched on briefly in n. 110.

[7] See 2.3.2 below.

[8] Obviously a chronological order in the strict sense is not possible, because on the one hand the temporal position is not always clearly recognizable and on the other hand evidence can be gathered from fictional narratives (see further below). At any rate, the arrangement is not intended to indicate my position on chronologically controversial cases (such as the problem of Ezra-Nehemiah).

[9] See 2.2 below.

2.1. EGYPT

2.1.1. The Legislation of Darius in Egypt.[10]

A. One third-century demotic text, that together with other texts was found on the reverse side of the papyrus whose obverse contains the famous so-called Demotic Chronicle,[11] reports that Darius I in 519–503 B.C.E carried out a codification of extant Egyptian laws through an expert commission composed of Egyptian soldiers, priests, and scribes. The collection was written down in two different scripts, which naturally means in two different languages: in "Assyrian script" which means Aramaic, on the one hand, and in "book script" which means demotic, on the other.[12] Darius's legislative work is also known from Diodorus, who counts Darius as the sixth lawgiver of the Egyptians.[13]

B. The commission's inclusion of representatives from various groups shows that the collection should cover the whole range of extant laws. The linguistic situation is the same as in the trilingual stela from the Letoon: we have a legal text in the native language and a translation in the administrative language of the empire. One can therefore posit a similar course of events. An important question is whether the Persian king functioned as a legislative authority himself and so was named in the collection as lawgiver. That is suggested by Diodorus's comments: if Darius was known in later times as a great lawgiver alongside genuine Egyptian kings, then people in those later periods must have immediately associated his name with this work of legislation. This is easiest to imagine if the collection carried his name[14] and is perhaps supported by the

---

[10] Cf. *Reichsidee,* 14–15[1] (16–18[2]), 47[2]. Unfortunately, the second edition of Erwin Seidl, *Ägyptische Rechtsgeschichte der Saïten- und Perserzeit* (2d ed.; AF 20; Glückstadt: Augustin, 1968), remains unavailable to me.

[11] The text was published by Wilhelm Spiegelberg, *Die sogenannte demotische Chronik des Pap. 215 der Bibliothèque Nationale zu Paris* (Leipzig: Hinrichs, 1914), 30–32. Of the other documents on the reverse, one should especially note an excerpt from Cambyses' regulations for the finances of the Egyptian temples.

[12] The historicity of this account has, so far as I know, never been seriously doubted. Cf. recently also Shafik Allam, "Traces de 'codification' en Égypte ancienne (à la basse époque)," *RIDA* 40 (1993): 25–26. The arguments that Rüterswörden ("Reichsautorisation") raises against it (the legitimization of Egyptian native law in Ptolemaic times by appeal to the Persian period) are not convincing.

[13] Diodorus, 1.95.4: ἕκτον δὲ λέγεται τὸν Ξέρξου πατέρα Δαρεῖον τοῖς νόμοις ἐπιστῆναι τοῖς τῶν Αἰγυπτίων κτλ.

[14] The reference appears in an excursus about the six lawgivers of Eygpt (1.94–95). Rüterswörden ("Reichsautorisation," 52–53) has for various reasons raised doubts about the historicity of this account. He thought that in the above

reference to the "command of Darius" in Pherendates' letter about the selection of a *lesonis* (chief) priest.[15]

C. It is possible to regard the codification of the laws governing Egypt as only one part of Darius's wider politics of reform, but this cannot be proven.[16] Historians voice very different opinions on the details of this issue.

---

quoted sentence Darius was not explicitly described as a lawgiver, and neither was Amasis. Neither of them were credited with legislative works. But to the latter are attributed new regulations (διατάξαι, 95.1; cf. διατάξαι, 94.3 for the activities of Sasychis, 94.5 for those of Bocchoris). The demotic text's portrait of the codifier of extant laws claims that Darius made no innovations. By the way, the formulas used (ἐφίστασθαι ["give one's attention to"] for Darius and προσελθεῖν ["apply oneself to"] for Amasis) do not detract from the fact that both are counted as νομοθέται (cf. 94.1 and 95.6). On possible evidence for the law collection of Darius, see 2.4.1.2 below. The rest of the comments about Darius in this context betray Greek coloring but are consistent with the statements of the demotic source. According to 95.4 (the continuation of the above quoted sentence), Darius intended in this way to reverse the illegal status of the temples occasioned by Cambyses (μισήσαντα ... τὴν παρανομίαν τὴν εἰς τὰ ... ἱερὰ γενομένην ὑπὸ Καμβύσου). But the composition of the commission shows that this statement is too narrow: see above and also E. Bresciani ("The Persian Occupation of Egypt," *CHI* 2:508 n. 1), who rightly notes that according to Diodorus's opinion, Darius's legislation did not primarily repeal the measures of Cambyses but rather reestablished legalities that he had violated. Diodorus's claim that he dealt (ὁμιλῆσαι, 95.5) with the priests may reflect the summoning of the commission, and the interest in the practices described in the holy books (μεταλαβεῖν αὐτὸν ... καὶ τῶν ἐν ταῖς ἱεραῖς βίβλοις ἀναγεγραμμένων πράξεων) refers to the codification. For the alleged divine worship (ὥσθ' ὑπὸ τῶν Αἰγυπτίων ζῶντα μὲν θεὸν προσαγορεύεσθαι κτλ), one may refer to the statue described by Alan B. Lloyd that portrays a figure kneeling before a falcon-shaped Darius. Lloyd emphasized that the monument originated "at a relatively humble level in society" ("The Inscription of Udjaḥorresnet: A Collaborator's Testament," *JEA* 68 [1982]: 174–75). If Diodorus's whole portrayal, or rather that of his source, has an anti-Ptolemaic thrust (as the conclusion 1.95.6 shows), this in no way casts doubt on the historicity of his description. I concur with Oswyn Murray, that "the sentiment attributing decline specifically to Macedonian rule" was Diodorus' particular addition ("Hecataeus of Abdera and Pharaonic kingship," *JEA* 56 [1970]: 149 n. 1).

[15] See 2.4.1.2 below.

[16] See *Reichsidee,* 31[1] nn. 22 and 24 (17[2] n. 22, 18[2] n. 24), 47[2] n. 41. Thierry Petit (*Satrapes et satrapies dans l'empire achéménide de Cyrus le Grand à Xerxes Ier* [Liège: Bibliothèque de la Faculté de Philosophie et Lettres de l'Université de Liège, 1990], 164) regarded the Egyptian codification as part of a comprehensive program by Darius in the various parts of the empire.

2.2. JUDAISM

As mentioned above in the introduction, the problem posed by fiction applies to some of the evidence found in the Old Testament: to Dan 6, Esther, and perhaps the decree of Artaxerxes in Ezra. This does not, however, mean that these accounts were wholly invented or that they were taken from some completely different, for example, Hellenistic, milieu.[17] The authors of the canonical or immediately precanonical form of Daniel, like those of the book of Esther, possessed for the most part a good picture of the internal structure of the Persian government. We may appeal to their stories as valuable testimonies to the legislative processes of the Achaemenid Empire.

Further, one must take into account that these Old Testament texts are connected to fundamental historical problems in the development of Judaism in the Persian and Hellenistic periods.[18] As a rule, they are also the result of complicated compositional and redactional histories. In interpreting them, it is clear that none of these wider points can be neglected, but neither can they be dealt with in detail here. The relevant complexes will be investigated in what follows only insofar as the subject under consideration requires or even allows. The larger discussion for its part cannot do without a consideration of the questions raised here.

2.2.1. Ezra's Credentials[19]

A. The Jewish priest Ezra was sent to Judea by the Persian government by a King Artaxerxes (whether it was the first or second of that name is debated). At any rate, he was ordered, among other things, to introduce a religiously based law book. It is self-evident that the introduction of a lawbook by a commissioner empowered for that purpose was not possible unless the central government approved of its contents. The only question is: What form did this approval take? Did the emperor permit in a general way the introduction of the law book, or did he make these norms his own, as would be suggested by what we have called imperial authorization?

B. The critical passage is found in the so-called firman of the emperor (Ezra 7:12–26) by which Ezra was fully empowered for his task.[20] Verses

---

[17] The stories would retain their worth even if they did first appear in Hellenistic times. That accurate knowledge of Achaemenid conditions was retained into the third century is not a bold opinion. See further *Reichsidee*, 51[2].

[18] See also 3.1 and n. 93 below.

[19] See *Reichsidee*, 17[1] (20–21[2]), 51–61[2].

[20] The authenticity of the letter is much debated. See on this ibid., 17[1] (21[2]) with n. 35, 54–60[2]. Kenneth G. Hoglund (*Achaemenid Imperial Administration in Syria-*

25–26 in particular contain instructions for the use of the law book and threats of punishment against those who disobey. The threats are aimed against those who do not follow exactly "the law of your God and the law of the king" (7:26, רתא די־אלהך ורתא די מלכא). Does the dichotomous construction "law of your God" and "law of the king" describe one and the same law, the law that Ezra brought with him to Jerusalem? Are the "law of your God" and the "law of the king" identical? Does the "and" express the identity of the two laws,[21] or are we dealing with two laws, the Jewish (the Torah) and a law of the king that legitimated the Torah but is formally distinct from it? This question cannot be decided definitively, yet likely considerations may be offered in favor of their identity. Namely, since the "law of your God" (i.e., the law of Yahweh) applies only to the Jews even though there is no mention in the whole context of a separate law of the king addressed to the Jews, it is reasonable to accept their identity. In that case, the king through imperial authorization sanctioned Ezra's law book that was composed by Jews.[22]

C. The historical background of Ezra's mission, like everything else, is controversial, but here the question is simply what interest the Achaemenid regime had in the mission as such. The relevant point is that, due to the initiative of members of a subordinate community, an important intervention in the structure of that community was undertaken by means of imperial authorization.

Palestine and the Missions of Ezra and Nehemiah [SBLDS 125; Atlanta: Scholars Press, 1992], 47–48, 226–31) reckons with at least a basis in fact. It is not necessary to go into the controversy here since, as was noted above, fictitious witnesses can also preserve genuine traditions. Even if the emperor's letter is a forgery, one can see from it that some of its inventors had concrete insights into the Persian government's political and administrative behavior, and the world they portray has a place for what we have called imperial authorization.

[21] This is grammatically possible. In the immediate context (v. 25) is a statement that Ezra should name שפטין ודינין. Clearly the aramaized Hebrew term is placed first, since the functionaries are supposed to work in the Judean sphere, and then it is explained by the Aramaic word. The Greek versions have γραμματεῖς for the Hebrew term, which is an attempt to translate the syntagma "judges and judges" (Jerome translated *iudices et praesides,* which is not awkward from a Roman perspective). The use of the conjunction in the sense "namely" is also attested elsewhere, though more commonly for connecting sentences (cf. the examples of Ernestus Vogt, *Lexicon Linguae Aramaicae Veteris Testamenti* [Rome: Pontifical Biblical Institute, 1971], 53–54).

[22] Hoglund (*Achaemenid Imperial Administration,* 230–31) speaks of "close ties between Ezra's 'inquiry' and the imperial order."

2.2.2. Nehemiah's Regulations[23]

A. Nehemiah's task (the temporal relationship between his work and that of Ezra is debated) was according to general opinion of a more political/organizational kind. Among other things, he issued a decree regarding the service duties of the temple personnel and the duties of the community to the temple; he probably received authorization for both from the king.

B. Nehemiah says (13:30–31) that he issued regulations governing the duties of the priests and the Levites. In 11:23, the subject is the ritual ordering of the Levitical singers for which there was "a rule of the king and a duty."[24] In the following verse (v. 24) "the king" appears again: Pethahiah the son of Meshezabel was "at the king's hand in all matters concerning the people."[25] In this respect, both verses certainly belong together since they appear in an insertion (vv. 21–24) into a list of the inhabitants of Jerusalem and Judah. According to 1 Chr 23–26, the organization of the temple personnel was accomplished by David.[26] But if 11:23 is supposed to refer to David, one would, on the basis of customary usage, expect the name and not just the simple title.[27] Wherever Pethahiah fits in history, one must at any rate reckon with the fact that his father Meshezabel has an Akkadian name and so hardly belongs in pre-exilic times.[28] Furthermore, it is hard to understand why the Israelite king needed an adviser "in all matters concerning the people." It is much more likely that the king referred to here was the Persian king, in whose court an appropriate adviser makes good sense. Since the insertion (vv. 21–24) is a unified whole, verse 23 must also refer to the Persian king. One should note that when Nehemiah speaks of his own edict in 13:30–31,

---

[23] See *Reichsidee,* 17–18¹ (21–22²), 98–99². The whole context is assessed there a bit differently.

[24] ‏כי־מצות המלך עליהם ואמנה על־המשררים דבר־יום ביומו‎.

[25] ‏ליד המלך לכל־דבר לעם‎.

[26] The unquestionably Chronistic passage in Neh 12:45–46 names David and his son Solomon as the founders of the regulations governing the singers: (45) ‏וישמרו‎ ‏משמרת אלהיהם ומשמרת הטהרה והמשררים והשערים כמצות דויד שלמה בנו‎. Verbal echoes of 11:23–24 and 13:30 are evident: cf. ‏מצות‎ for the decree of the king (11:23) and the general term ‏משמרת‎ corresponding to the plural ‏משמרות‎ in 13:30. That the Chronicler borrows verbally from the book of Nehemiah is easier to understand than the contrary assertion that the book of Nehemiah uses Chronistic terminology. See *Reichsidee,* 55² n. 85, 56–58².

[27] See ibid., 33¹ (22²) n. 41.

[28] See ibid., 33¹ (22²) n. 40. On Akkadian names, see Johann Jakob Stamm, *Die akkadische Namengebung* (MVAG 44; Leipzig: Hinrichs, 1939), 221 with n. 1.

there is no suggestion that he adopted or altered traditional regulations credited to David governing the service of the temple officials, although in his arguments he does not otherwise hesitate to use historical references throughout.[29] From the context, it is clear that he reacted to abuses, and it is these abuses that prompted his regulations. But then one must understand Nehemiah's document as the referent for the statement in 11:23–24. Since it explicitly refers to a norm of the king, a real imperial authorization must have taken place. Nehemiah issues his regulations through the king's authorization. We must leave open the question of what path led from the original document to the extant book of Nehemiah.

An opportunity to reveal an authorization is found in the regulations described as a duty (אֲמָנָה) of the people in Neh 10:1, which de facto represents a communal decree.[30] The rulings materially correspond in part with the orders of Nehemiah in 13:31 regarding one of the general regulations he had issued (provision of firewood for the altar [10:34], regulations regarding firstlings [10:36]). It is very significant that the term אֲמָנָה can otherwise be found only in the reference to the service duties of cult personnel in the text discussed above (11:23–24), which strong reasons suggest was derived from a legislative document of Nehemiah's. The term, whose precise meaning cannot be established,[31] must in some way have been connected with Nehemiah's legislative acts.[32] Nehemiah's mention of both regulations, the one for the cult personnel and the general one, in the same breath in 13:30–31 fits this conclusion. The terminological correspondence is an argument in support of the interpretation of the sequence in 11:23 and extends the fact of imperial authorization to the regulations of Neh 10. It is nevertheless disturbing that the more important duties of the people enumerated in 10:30–32 go unmentioned in 13:30–31, and the redactional process is again completely unclear.

---

[29] So 13:18 and 13:26–27. Cf. Wilhelm Rudolph, *Esra und Nehemia samt 3. Esra* (HAT 20; Tübingen: Mohr Siebeck, 1949), 211.

[30] Questions of redaction and, connected with it, historicity naturally appear here also, and again they receive very different answers. We cannot go into the problem. See *Reichsidee,* 98–99² with nn. 250–53.

[31] We may well ask whether the meaning "duty" arose precisely in this context. אֲמָנָה really means "strengthening" and so was perhaps the Hebrew term for "authorization." Since it concretely concerned duties laid on the temple personnel, or rather the whole people, the meaning "duty" was an appropriate modification.

[32] Cognate with it is perhaps the use of the also otherwise attested אֱמוּנָה in the sense of "official duty" in 1 Chr 9:22, 26, 31 and perhaps in the hard-to-understand line at the end of 2 Chr 31:18. Is the Chronicler dependent on the wording of Nehemiah here as well?

On the whole, one cannot speak of a proven fact because first of all, as just noted, the development of the text from the original document to the present arrangement of the book of Nehemiah cannot be reconstructed. It seems evident, however, that all the now-separated individual statements fit together best under the assumption of an imperial authorization. The mention of the relevant adviser provides a glimpse of the usual course of business in granting an authorization. The allusion to this official in this context makes sense only if he in fact took part in the procedures.

C. Here authorization can only have meant a guarantee of local norms through imperial authority. It is easy to understand why the governor, who under the circumstances presided de facto over the local corporate body and as such did not find unanimous agreement, wanted to safeguard his orders by invoking royal authority against the influence of his opponents.[33] Because of the regulation of the temple taxes, the whole issue had a financial-political aspect, as can be seen from the completely parallel situation in the trilingual stela from the Letoon.[34]

2.2.3. The So-Called Passover Letter from Elephantine[35]

A. The document contains instructions that are clearly connected with the celebration of the Passover festival. The text is a letter written by a certain Hananiah son of Yedonia, one of the community's leaders, and his colleagues.

B. Only the first four lines are relevant for us.[36] After the greeting, the writer in line 3 refers to a decree that a King Darius, no doubt the second of that name, issued in his fifth year (419/418 B.C.E) to Arsames, the satrap over Egypt. What immediately followed (the end of line 3 and approximately half of line 4) has been lost. When the text resumes, the letter's main section already begins with instructions for the performance of the Passover-Matzot festival, the contents of which are not inconsequential for the interpretation of the whole[37] but which cannot be gone into further here.

On textual grounds it cannot be doubted that the Passover instructions were also part of the royal decree. Something must have stood

---

[33] See also 2.4.2.3.4 and 3.2.3 below.

[34] See 2.3.2 below.

[35] See *Reichsidee*, 15–16¹ (18–20²), 48–49². The text can be found as AP 21 in CAP, 60–65; Pierre Grelot, "Le Papyrus pascal d'Éléphantine: essai de restauration," *VT* 17 (1967): 201–7; *TAD* 1:54–55, no. A.4.1.

[36] See, among other places, *Reichsidee*, 16¹ (19²) with n. 31.

[37] See, among others, ibid., 16¹ (19²) with nn. 30–31.

immediately before the instructions that explained or introduced the transmission of these orders. There is, however, not enough room for a separate royal decree on a different subject. Royal decree and festival instructions must be closely and immediately connected. Since the subject is an order from the king to the satrap Arsames, one suspects that in the missing piece he was asked to pass on the king's decree to the Jews in Elephantine. So I would like to supply: [מני שים טעם זי אנת ארשם תאמר לחילא יהוד]יא "I have given the order that you, Arsames, should say to the Jewish garrison." Naturally there can be no certainty about the contents of the text, but when one looks at the proportionate space in the gap together with the possible amendments, there remains hardly any other option, at least in substance, except the one just proposed.[38]

There is no reason to doubt that an intervention by the king took place, and it in fact has not been questioned. The only issue that affects the discussion here is whether the king himself was formally the lawgiver of the Passover regulations and thus authorized norms formulated by a Jewish body. The widespread notion that the Persian king would hardly concern himself in this detailed way with such things and that his adoption of Jewish regulations is not believable can, however, be ruled out precisely by the parallel examples. This is not a circular argument[39] but rather a case in which the unambiguous examples appropriately increase the likelihood of the more ambiguous examples, as a kind of circumstantial evidence.

C. Ideas about the concrete causes and objectives of the king's intervention are extremely varied.[40] In view of all the represented opinions, it is most likely that legal security was the fundamental motive for the royal establishment of norms.

2.2.4. The Endorsement of the Purim Regulations by Esther[41]

A. The novelistic, certainly fictional story in the book of Esther is set in the Persian royal court in the time of King Xerxes: the Jews succeed in avoiding their threatened annihilation because a Jewish young woman has become the chief wife of the king and so is able to influence him. The young woman's guardian and adviser, her cousin Mordecai, is awarded the

---

[38] Ibid.

[39] So H. G. M. Williamson in his review of the first edition of *Reichsidee* (review of Peter Frei and Klaus Koch, *Reichsidee und Reichsorganisation im Perserreich*, *VT* 35 [1985]: 379–80).

[40] See, among other places, *Reichsidee*, 48–49[2] with nn. 46–51.

[41] See ibid., 18–19[1] (22–23[2]), 82[2].

position of grand vizier. He establishes a special festival, the so-called Purim festival, to memorialize the rescue of the Jews and issues festival rules for it (9:20–28). Queen Esther endorses this decree in 9:29–32.[42]

B. I mention here only 9:29, "and Queen Esther ... wrote a complete endorsement [literally, "all power"] to make ... this Purim letter binding,"[43] and 9:32, "and Esther's word made this practice of Purim binding, and it was written in the book."[44] One should naturally note certain deviations from imperial authorization's "normal form" as we find it in the trilingual: Mordecai, the Jewish author of the regulations, can act as grand vizier and so takes on imperial authority himself, and it is not the king but the queen who pronounces the authorization. It is also not explicitly said that the empire's representative adopts the Jewish regulations as such. It nevertheless remains the fact that a norm that should apply only to a particular group in the empire's population and was produced by this group itself received royal confirmation and was fixed in written form.

The formulations used here are colored by Aramaic and reoccur in a similar fashion in Dan 6, there clearly referring to the legislative acts of the king.[45] They could therefore be influenced by that text. The author has not, however, shaped the course of events without any knowledge of the realities of imperial law. At most, he received inspiration from Dan 6, which after all does not report anything about an authorization.

C. This fictional story permits us a conclusion about the way its author viewed the institution of imperial authorization. It was a literary device for lending weight to the institution of Purim. On that basis, one should consider if this offers an explanation for Esth 9:29–32: knowledge of this legal institution gave the author of the book of Esther, for whom careful motivation of the plot was a matter of concern,[46] the opportunity to plausibly involve the main character of the book in establishing the Purim regulations.

---

[42] The book's complicated prehistory can be dealt with here only selectively (on this see also n. 93 below). Especially the literary-historical and text-critical uncertainties that impair interpretation of the passages will be dealt with here only insofar as they are immediately relevant. The fact that the whole situation is fictional and that perhaps the story in its present form originated first in the post-Persian period carries no weight at all. What the story shows us is the impression that Persian rule and Persian legal forms made in Jewish circles.

[43] ותכתב אסתר המלכה בת־אביחיל ומרדכי היהודי את־כל־תקף לקים את אגרת הפורים הזאת השנית. Cf. *Reichsidee,* 33[1] (22[2]) n. 43.

[44] ומאמר אסתר קים דברי הפרים האלה ונכתב בספר.

[45] See *Reichsidee,* 33[1] (23[2]) n. 45, 79–80[2].

[46] Cf. Gillis Gerleman, *Esther* (BKAT 21; Neukirchen-Vluyn: Neukirchener Verlag, 1973), 30–31.

2.3. ASIA MINOR

2.3.1. The Border Dispute between Miletus and Myus[47]

A. An inscription found in Miletus describes a border dispute around 390 B.C.E that the cities of the Ionian League had to decide between Miletus and Myus, both members of the league. The proceedings were carried out before a law court made up of delegates from the individual cities of the league but did not conclude with an actual verdict, since Myus had already given up the case. The satrap Struses (Struthas) was informed of the situation and formally pronounced the final decision that the disputed territory should remain in Miletus's possession.[48]

B. This situation differs from the others since it involves deciding a conflict between local bodies, rather than establishing norms that a local body writes for itself. If, however, one considers the Ionian League (the "Ionians") as a unit that takes the place of a local body, the course of events corresponds throughout to the process of imperial authorization: the local authorities made their decision independently, and the satrap authorized the contents of the decision through his own decree. The Greek syntagma τέλος ποιεῖν[49] corresponds in substance almost exactly to the κύριον εἶναι in the Greek version of the trilingual inscription from the Letoon (Greek line 35). The immediately following reproduction of the outcome of the judges' proceedings in an infinitive construction ("that the land should belong to the Milesians") shows that the satrap issued an explicitly formulated decree.

C. The inscription's poor state of preservation hinders our understanding of the political and legal presuppositions of the proceedings. The king was involved in the affair in some way.[50] It is conventionally assumed that the cities appealed the dispute to him and that he entrusted its settlement to the satrap in charge of the area.[51] Presumably its basis

---

[47] See *Reichsidee*, 96–97². The inscription is published as *SIG* 134; cf. also Marcus N. Tod, *A Selection of Greek Historical Inscriptions* (2 vols.; Oxford: Oxford University Press, 1948), 2:36–39, no. 113 (with commentary).

[48] Lines 42–44: Στρούσης ἀκούσας τῶν Ἰώνων τῶν [δ/ι]καστέων ἐξαιτράπης ἐὼν Ἰωνίης [τ/έ]λος ἐποίησε τὴν γῆν εἶναι Μιλησ[ί]ων.

[49] The word τέλος means in various constructions "power of decision, supreme power"; cf. the examples in LSJ under nos. 2 and 4, but not all the examples collected under no. 4 belong here, and the division between 2 and 4 should be reexamined. The connotation of ratifying the decisions of another authority appears in Greek material at most in Plato, *Leg.* 761e, 767a, but this is due to the Greek cities' general political presuppositions that very rarely acknowledged ratification rights by higher authorities.

[50] Line 9 β]ασιλεῖ καὶ σ[... in a very disturbed context.

[51] See in *SIG* the reconstructions of the beginning, which cannot be reproduced here.

was the ordering of the reciprocal relations among the Ionian cities brought about by Artaphernes at the end of the Ionian revolt.[52] The authorization carried out by Struses arose from the need for legal security, but the government's wish to monitor territorial divisions for reasons of taxation may have played a role as well.[53] The union between the intentions of the subordinate and the central governments fits the character and meaning of imperial authorization.

2.3.2. The Trilingual Inscription from the Letoon[54]

A. The stele that carries the inscription was found in 1973 in the shrine of the goddess Leto in the Xanthus Valley in Lycia, the southwestern peninsula of Asia Minor. The contents deal with a decree issued by the community of Xanthus in the first year of a King Artaxerxes, that is, either 358 or 337 B.C.E. At that time, Lycia belonged to the principality established by the Carian dynasty of Mausollus under Persian hegemony. The decree concerns the founding of a cult for two Carian gods. Detailed regulations govern the provisions for the cult and the management of the cult site, and then oaths and curses guarantee the contents of the regulations. The law is published on the stela in the Lycian language and also in a Greek version on the same stone. The Persian satrap at the time, Pixodarus, a Carian and the youngest brother of Mausollus, takes the community's decree as his own by having it registered on the front of the stela in Aramaic, the official language of the empire.

B. In the Aramaic portion, the Persian satrap adopts the community's decree and, with reference to its creators (line 6: אתעשתו בעלי אורן ["the citizens of Xanthus have proposed"]),[55] promulgates it in the administrative language of the empire as if it were his own. That is clarified by the poorly preserved verb [אמ]ר ("[Pixodarus] said") that immediately precedes the body of legal regulations, and by the text of line 19, כתב דך דתה ("he wrote this law"), that directly follows it. In this way the decree issued by the subordinate community of Xanthus within the boundaries of its legitimate responsibilities was absorbed into the empire's legislation, so to speak: it became locally applicable imperial law. This course of events is

---

[52] See 2.4.2.1 below.

[53] So Josef Wiesehöfer in discussion. See 3.2.2 below.

[54] See *Reichsidee*, 12–14¹ (12–16²), 39–47². The text can be found in Henri Metzger et al., eds., *Fouilles de Xanthos 6: La stèle trilingue du Létôon* (Paris: Klincksieck, 1979); cf. also Günter Neumann, *Neufunde lykischer Inschriften seit 1901* (Ergänzungsbände zu den Tituli Asiae Minoris 7; Vienna: Verlag der Österreichischen Akademie der Wissenschaften, 1979), 44–47, n. N.320.

[55] On the semantics of this verb, see below in 3.1.

reflected in the final lines of the Lycian and Greek versions. The Greek (line 35) says Πιξώταρος [*sic*] δὲ κύριος ἔστω, which must mean "let Pixodarus be legally responsible." The Lycian text contains a somewhat longer statement (lines 40–41) that unfortunately cannot be translated.

C. The formula's appearance at the end of the decree makes it likely that the community itself solicited this confirmation. One suspects that economic factors, that is, regulations for provisioning the new cult by the Xanthus community, triggered this request for authorization.[56] Other documents that all stem from Caria may illuminate this situation. Despite some uncertainties, it is clear that they distinguish between taxes levied at local discretion and those determined by the imperial government alone. The structure of the trilingual's charter of authorization, which is the Aramaic text, shows that it was based on this same legal-administrative situation and uses identical categories of tax law. In this text there are a series of omissions compared to the Lycian and the Greek parts (which mostly parallel each other), and it seems that the missing regulations are those that had little or no impact on the "king's" taxes.

The mention in the satrap's decree (lines 10–14) of the surrender of an estate and the assignment of a fixed sum from the city treasury shows that this could affect the taxes owed the king, since these would usually be collected by the city and handed over collectively. In certain situations, this process might lead to conflict. On the other hand, no such risk was associated with the manumission tax which, according to the public action, was apparently devised to finance the newly constituted cult, and so it is understandable that the Aramaic text does not take it into account. Nevertheless, mention is made of a general *ateleia* (exemption from public responsibilities) for the priests, if only as an afterthought (lines 17–18). It might collide with royal interests and so could not simply be left out.

So it is probable that within the interaction between a subordinate community and the imperial government, the process of authorization had its actual background in the arena of taxation and tribute. The community was presumably most concerned to guard against future interventions of various kinds by the imperial government.[57] But it should not be forgotten

---

[56] See *Reichsidee,* 39–44².

[57] Rüterswörden ("Reichsautorisation," 58–59) would like to explain the entire event by comparison with Greek endowment laws. These include the so-called δόσις, a decree by the individual donor, and the δόγμα, a decree by the community that receives or guarantees the endowment. The δόγμα regulates the details of administering the endowment, especially when the receiver is the community. (For this legal arrangement in the Hellenistic period, see among others Anneliese Mannzmann, *Griechische Stiftungsurkunden: Studien zu Inhalt und Rechtsform* [Fontes et Commentationes 2; Münster: Aschendorff, 1962], 51–55.) The law of the

that authorization undoubtably improved the prospects for the decree's enforcement among the affected citizens of the city of Xanthus.

2.4. OTHER POSSIBLE EXAMPLES OF AUTHORIZATION

We must also consult other examples of the norms and regulations of local administrative bodies from the Achaemenid period. In their legal form and/or in their contents, these texts suggest a background in imperial authorization, but they do not mention the process itself nor can it be deduced from the context.

---

city of Xanthus then contains the δόσις, and the דתה of Pixodarus contains the δόγμα. The context, however, will not support this. First of all, one must note that nowhere in the Greco-Roman world is there an example of the state authority adopting the regulations of a donor and proclaiming them as its own. This is the distinguishing characteristic of imperial authorization. It is also inherent to endowments that the donor is always an individual; the community is usually the receiver, less often the guarantor for the receiver (cf. the survey of Bernhard Laum, *Stiftungen in der griechischen und römischen Antike: Ein Beitrag zur antiken Rechtsgeschichte* [2 vols.; Leipzig: Teubner, 1914], 1:218–21). The situation in the Letoon inscription is completely different. The community of Xanthus, an authority under public law, is itself the author of the "cult foundation." It issues the regulations in a formal law and guarantees them itself in the same way ipso facto, like a Greek πόλις of Hellenistic times would guarantee the endowment regulations of a private donor. Technically, the "law" corresponds to the δόγμα. Neither can there be any thought of Pixodarus regulating the details of the law's execution. He adopts only a few of the regulations from the "foundation document" as such, and his decree is shorter, while in the third-century text cited as an example by Mannzmann (*Griechische Stiftungsurkunden,* 51–55), the δόγμα is approximately three times as long as the δόσις. Really more comparable, however, are the confirming decrees of the Roman emperors, which were obtained by the donors, perhaps together with the beneficiary community (for details about this see Michael Wörrle, *Stadt und Fest im kaiserzeitlichen Kleinasien: Studien zu einer agonistischen Stiftung aus Oinoanda* [Munich: Beck, 1988], 172–82: "Kaiser und Stiftung"). Even here the emperor does not guarantee the endowment regulations and details of administration; he simply makes his approval known in a relatively global way. But at any rate, the effect is comparable to the results of imperial authorization: "*Confirmatio* by Caesar's authority ... generally made an endowment more binding, not only against those ... city functionaries, officials and public gatherings whose dependability was suspect, but also against the interventions of Roman authorities" (Wörrle, *Stadt und Fest,* 181). The reason for these parallels lies in the legal situation of a subordinate community in an imperial union, whether Achaemenid or Roman.

2.4.1. Egypt

2.4.1.1. The Activities of Udjahorresne[58]

A. When the Persians invaded Egypt, the Egyptian official Udjahor-resne, whose biography appears on his statue,[59] took the side of the invaders and became a member of Cambyses' personal staff. One of his activities is relevant here: he ensured that the Persian king drove out the "foreigners" who had settled in the temple precincts of Neith in Sais and that he provided resources and regulated the functioning of the cult there.

B. The wording suggests that Cambyses commanded ($w\underline{d}$) that the temple's affairs be appropriately ordered. Udjahorresne was certainly behind it.[60] This is the situation that makes imperial authorization possible in principle and implies that it is even normal: the wielder of Persian power, in this case the king, authorized norms that were formulated by local authorities, in this case Udjahorresne and/or the local priesthood of the temple, promulgating them as his own. The wording ("his majesty commanded") suggests that this scenario could have been in the background. An actual authorization in the formal sense would, however, presuppose that the king referred explicitly to the author of the regulations and adopted these as his own. Since we do not have an original document, but simply a report of the event, we cannot know for sure. It is possible, perhaps even likely, that the formulation simply followed Egyptian tradition[61] in which the king was the author of all

---

[58] The essential literature can be found listed in Anthony Spalinger, "Udja-horresnet," *LÄ* 6:823–24 and in Joseph Blenkinsopp, "The Mission of Udjahorresnet and Those of Ezra and Nehemiah," *JBL* 106 (1987): 409 n. 1. The most important contribution is the detailed interpretation by Lloyd, "Inscription of Udjahorresnet." Cf. also Torben Holm-Rasmussen, "Collaboration in Early Achaemenid Egypt: A New Approach," in *Studies in Ancient History and Numismatics Presented to Rudi Thomsen* (ed. Aksel Damsgaard-Madsen; Aarhus: Aarhus University Press, 1988), 29–38. On the recently discovered grave of Udja-horresne and the problem of dating it, see Miroslav Verner, "La tombe d'Oudjahorresnet et le cimetière saïto-perse d'Abousir," *BIFAO* 89 (1989): 288–90; and idem, "Excavations at Abousir, Season 1988/89: A Preliminary Report," *ZÄS* 118 (1991): 162–67.

[59] Georges Posener (*La première domination perse en Égypte* [Bibliothèque d'Étude 11; Cairo: IFAO, 1936], 1–26) published the text, the most important part of which are pp. 15–17, above all lines 22–23.

[60] Lines 23–24. See Eberhard Otto, *Die biographischen Inschriften der ägyptischen Spätzeit: ihre geistesgeschichtliche und literarische Bedeutung* (Probleme der Ägyptologie 2; Leiden: Brill, 1954), 116; Bresciani, "Persian Occupation," 2:506–7.

[61] The relevance of the terminology remains an open question. In Udjahorresne, the root $w\underline{d}$ ("command") is used for the royal command. Other royal decrees from

norms,[62] especially since Udjahorresne found it important to portray Cambyses in the role of Pharaoh.[63] Assessment is complicated by the fact that we know hardly anything about the process of decision making in Egyptian tradition.[64] One can assume that the king had advisers who were involved in the problem's resolution. Even less is known about the opportunities and procedures for local bodies, especially priesthoods, to make their requests known to the head of government. So here the matter is presented as only a potential example.

C. If an authorization occurred, no doubt its purpose was to provide state guarantees for arrangements vital to the temple's existence, presumably not least against agents of the occupying power.[65]

2.4.1.2. Darius's Regulations for the Selection of Priests[66]

A. In a demotic copy of a letter from the satrap Pherendates to the priests of the Khnum temple in Elephantine on April 21, 491

---

the late period also use *ḏd* ("say"; "his/my majesty said"), as in the so-called Naucratis stela (cf., for example, Miriam Lichtheim, "The Naucratis Stele Once Again," in *Studies in Honor of George R. Hughes* [SAOC 39; Chicago: Oriental Institute, 1976], 140). Finally, *ḥn* ("command") is also attested in the demotic letter of Pherendates to the priests of the Khnum temple (lines 5, 7); see 2.4.1.2 below.

[62] The king appears in the so-called Copenhagen donation stela from the time of Apries as possessing the right of disposal, although the donor Nśw-Ḥr was the owner of the donated property (Hermann Kees, "Die Kopenhagener Schenkungsstele aus der Zeit des Apries," *ZÄS* [1936]: 40–44; and idem, *Zur Innenpolitik der Saïtendynastie* [Nachrichten aus der Altertumswissenschaft 1; Nachrichten von der Gesellschaft der Wissenschaften zu Göttingen, Philologisch-historische Klasse, N.F. Fachgruppe 1; Göttingen: Vandenhoeck & Ruprecht, 1935], esp. 101). Kees credited the king's leverage to the fact that the land in question was really "king's land."

[63] On this, see especially Lloyd, "Inscription of Udjaḥorresnet," 170–73.

[64] Nevertheless, see A. Théodoridès, "Dekret," *LÄ* 1:1038.

[65] Cf. the situation prior to the intervention of Cambyses (Otto, *Die biographischen Inschriften,* 113–14; Bresciani, "Persian Occupation," 2:505).

[66] The text was published by Wilhelm Spiegelberg, *Drei demotische Schreiben aus der Korrespondenz des Pherendates, des Satrapen Darius I., mit den Chnumpriestern von Elephantine* (SPAW; Berlin: Akademie der Wissenschaften, 1928), 605–11. S. P. Vleming has provided a recent commentary that includes discussion of the larger historical context ("Een lang uitgestelde benoeming," *Phoenix* 27 [1981]: 82–91). George R. Hughes provided a more philological exposition ("The So-Called Pherendates Correspondence," in *Grammata Demotika: Festschrift für Erich Lüddeckens* [ed. H.-J. Thissen and K.-T. Zauzich; Würzburg: Zauzich, 1984], 75–86). Both authors agreed that the letter is a translation of an Aramaic original.

B.C.E.,[67] the satrap refers to a "command of Pharaoh Darius" that must be taken into account in the selection of *lesonis* (chief) priests (lines 5, 7).

B. We learn nothing as to how the regulation came about. Perhaps it was part of Darius's general codification of laws that was discussed above.[68] It could also have been formulated in a separate decree, but certainly with the participation of Egyptian specialists. Due to the nature of the source, the question must remain open as to whether it presupposes the scenario of imperial authorization. At any rate, it remains possible.

C. From the context it can be assumed that up to now the priests had not been paying attention to the rule. This fact does not necessarily weigh against using the text as evidence for a particular case of imperial authorization. It is possible that the initiative behind this rule originated with the king. It is equally possible, however, that due to a particular case the priests approached the king with their wish that he authorize one of their rules, and that in a later situation, they no longer liked the rule and ignored it.

2.4.2. Asia Minor
2.4.2.1. The Legal Obligation of the Ionians by Artaphernes[69]

A. After the Ionian rebellion, the satrap of Sardis, Artaphernes, gathered the Ionian ambassadors and induced them to make agreements governing

---

[67] On the dating, see Vleming, "Een lang uitgestelde benoeming," 84, 88; Hughes, "Pherendates Correspondence," 77.

[68] See 2.1.1 above.

[69] On this, see Jack Martin Balcer, *Sparda by the Bitter Sea: Imperial Interaction in Western Anatolia* (BJS 52; Chico, Calif.: Scholars Press, 1984), 247–48; Christopher Tuplin, "The Administration of the Achaemenid Empire," in *Coinage and Administration in the Athenian and Persian Empires* (ed. Ian Carradice; BAR International Series 343; Oxford: B.A.R., 1987), 148. Corsaro ("Tassazione regia," 75 with n. 4) suspects that the land survey was conducted not only for fiscal reasons, but rather "anche per metter fine alle contese territoriali fra le città greche" (similarly p. 82). See also Pierre Briant, "Pouvoir central et polycentrisme culturel dans l'Empire achéménide," in *Sources, Structures and Synthesis: Proceedings of the Groningen 1983 Achaemenid History Workshop* (ed. H. Sancisi-Weerdenburg; AH 1; Leiden: Nederlands Instituut voor het Nabije Oosten, 1987), 3–4; Jack Martin Balcer, "Ionia and Sparta under the Achaemenid Empire: The Sixth and Fifth Centuries B.C. Tribute, Taxation and Assessment," in *Le tribut dans l'empire Perse: Actes de la Table ronde de Paris 12–13 Décembre 1986* (ed. P. Briant and C. Heffenschmidt; Travaux de l'Institut d'Études Iraniennes de l'Université de la Sorbonne Nouvelle 13; Paris: Peeters, 1989), 6–7, 8, 9; Mauro Corsaro, "Autonomia cittadina e fiscalità regia ecc.," in Briant, ed., *Le tribut dans l'empire Perse,* 66–67; Peter Frei, "Zentralgewalt und Lokalautonomie im achämenidischen Kleinasien," *Transeu* 2 (1990): 162.

the regulation of conflicts between cities.[70] Then followed a survey of the land, which also served as a basis for assessing tribute payments.[71]

B. There is nothing explicit here that points to imperial authorization. It is nevertheless clear that the central government intervened in order to oblige local communities to observe a regional security agreement that apparently they themselves composed. Some kind of ratification by the central power's representative must be assumed, though whether it followed the usual path of imperial authorization cannot be determined. The survey was intended to delineate the territories once and for all and simultaneously to serve the need for tax assessments, thus probably allowing the central government to address both concerns in the same way.

C. This case certainly provides a parallel to the codification in Egypt.[72] The central government ordered the establishment of norms with local application that were put forward by representatives of local bodies. The example deserves attention for this reason alone. Its goals clearly included legal security, as well as avoiding conflict and providing a basis for taxation.

2.4.2.2. The Inscription from Sardis[73]

A. In 1974 in Sardis, the old capital of Lydia, a second-century C.E. inscription was found consisting mostly of a copy of an older cult law that must have originated in the Persian period. It was enacted in the thirty-ninth year of an Artaxerxes, so 426 or 365 B.C.E., depending on whether it means the first or second of that name. The document begins with a dedication stating that Droaphernes, son of Barakes, hyparch of Lydia, set up a statue for the Zeus of Baradates.[74] Then, introduced by προστάσσει ("he

---

[70] So Herodotus 6.42.1: Ἀρταφρένης ὁ Σαρδίων ὕπαρχος μεταπεμψάμενος ἀγγέλους ἐκ τῶν πολίων συνθήκας σφίσι αὐτοῖσι τοὺς Ἴωνας ἠνάγκασε ποιέεσθαι, ἵνα δωσίδικοι εἶεν καὶ μὴ ἀλλήλους φέροιέν τε καὶ ἄγοιεν.

[71] So Herodotus in the immediately following 6.42.2: ... τὰς χώρας σφέων μετρήσας ... φόρους ἔταξε ἑκάστοισι.

[72] See 2.1.1 above, and Petit, *Satrapes et satrapies,* 164.

[73] Cf. *Reichsidee,* 19–21[1] (23–26[2]), 90–96[2]. The inscription was published by Louis Robert, "Une nouvelle inscription grecque de Sardes: Règlement de l'autorité perse relatif à un culte de Zeus," *CRAI* (1975), 306–30; Fritz Gschnitzer has made an important contribution to its clarification in "Eine persische Kultstiftung in Sardeis," in *Im Bannkreis des Alten Orients: Studien ... Karl Oberhuber zum 70 Gebürtstag gewidmet* (ed. W. Meid and H. Trenkwalder; Innsbrucker Beiträge zur Kulturwissenschaft 24; Innsbruck: Institut fur Sprachwissenschaft der Universität Innsbruck, 1986), 45–54.

[74] On the meaning of Βαραδατεω Διί (lines 4–5), see Gschnitzer, "Eine persische Kultstiftung," 46–48.

commands," line 5), it includes a command to the temple staff who enter the sanctuary and crown the god, that is, the statue of Zeus: they must not participate in the mysteries of Sabazios, Angdistis, and Ma, local gods of Asia Minor. The final sentence (lines 11–13), which asks one Dorates to keep his distance from these mysteries, seems to be an actual application of the old command. It apparently belongs to the time when the inscription was carved; presumably this application was the occasion for recording the whole affair. At least the date formula of the extant Greek text presupposes an Aramaic original.[75] So a version existed in the administrative language of the empire, and one cannot doubt that the edict was published in several languages. This shows that it had general validity.

B. The "Zeus of Baradates" is the divinity of a privately endowed cult established by an otherwise unknown Iranian named Baradates, and so a kind of family god. Presumably, it is either the Greek god or an Anatolian divinity identified with it. There are parallels to this: that Iranians living in Asia Minor made offerings to Greek or grecofied local divinities is attested elsewhere. The assumption that an Iranian would found a private cult for a Greek or local divinity is therefore permissible, especially when the cult terminology is clearly Greek.

Purity regulations for those who enter the *adyton* (inner sanctuary) are nothing special. A prohibition on taking part in other cults, namely mysteries, is otherwise not well attested in Greek areas, if not altogether without parallels. One should leave open the possibility that this special rule could be of Iranian origin and that it should be credited to the god's Iranian worshipers. The local divinity and the ideas associated with it formed the basis of the cult, but regulations stemming from Iranian religiosity could have been attached to it. So separation from the mystery cults can be understood as the essential restriction placed in this cult's regulations by Baradates or perhaps by later sponsors of the cult he founded.[76]

C. A clear explanation of the course of events is hardly possible, because we have in the copy from the Roman period no doubt only an

---

[75] See *Reichsidee,* 35[1] (26[2]) n. 56, 92[2] with nn. 221–23.

[76] Thomas Corsten ("Herodot I 131 und die Einführung des Anahita-Kultes in Lydien," *StIr* 26 [1991]: 163–80, esp. 176) takes a completely different view of the situation. According to him, Zeus here represents Ahura Mazda because he stands "in a completely Persian context." His worship became a "kind of state cult for the satrapy or one of its parts." In my opinion, this is unlikely, but a full discussion is not possible here. Only: I have never challenged the reliability of the evidence from Clement of Alexandria (so Corsten, "Herodot I 131," 175 n. 20) but have pointed out that he speaks only of statues of Anaitis (not of *Oromasdes).

excerpt from the original text. The chance is nevertheless slight that we are dealing here with an example of imperial authorization, since from what we know of the decree the hyparch can hardly have been using a request from a subordinate community as a basis. Nevertheless, this legal situation has significance for us, and we will come back to it.[77]

2.4.2.3. Documents from Western Asia Minor, especially Caria[78]

Not a few documents stem from western Asia Minor, all from the time when Caria was ruled by the Hecatomn dynasty, whose most famous member was Mausollus.[79] There is no proof that imperial authorization lay behind any of them; on the other hand, the composition of almost all of these texts is so ambiguous and our understanding of their real political context so imprecise that it cannot be ruled out either. They therefore bring to a discussion of the institution nothing of certainty, yet they should be kept in mind, and they are important here and there for assessing details, such as the question of material parallels to the trilingual's regulations.[80]

2.4.2.3.1. Three communal decrees of the Carian city Mylasa originated under Persian rule, since they are dated by the regnal years of Artaxerxes II and Artaxerxes III (the years 367/366, 361/360 and 355/354) and Mausollus is named as satrap. They deal with the sentencing of Mylasian citizens who had been unmasked as Mausollus's enemies and had acted against him.[81] To complete the picture one must note that a similar decree from Iasus existed at the same time that makes no reference to the satrapy of Mausollus and the Persian king.[82]

2.4.2.3.2. A boundary stone of the Dionysus temple of Tralles in the Meander Valley stems from the first century C.E. but carries a decree by the community of Tralles dated to the seventh, possibly the ninth, year of Artaxerxes III (350 B.C.E in the latter case) when Idrieus was satrap. Perhaps the unusual Greek form of the king's name ('Αρταξέσεω, genitive)

---

[77] See 3.1 below.

[78] See *Reichsidee*, 35¹ (27²) n. 58, 99–101².

[79] This evidence is one-sided not because of the subject but because the specific cultural situation has left its mark on it. This area was highly hellenized, and as a result the use of inscriptions to publish public documents was widespread.

[80] See 2.3.2 above.

[81] See *Reichsidee*, 35¹ (27²) n. 58, 99². For the text, see *SIG* 167, Tod, *Greek Historical Inscriptions*, 2:112–16, no. 138.

[82] See *Reichsidee*, 99². For the text, see *SIG* 169.

reflects an Aramaic version. A multilingual decree would point to the existence of an imperial authorization.[83]

2.4.2.3.3. An inscription from the year 323 found in Lagina reports that the community of Koarendeis together with Mausollus once granted an *ateleia* (tax exemption) to a person whose name is illegible and to his descendants. Since the text comes from the early Hellenistic period, it is of no use to us.[84]

2.4.2.3.4. More informative is the decree of the συγγένεια of Pelekos found in the temple of Sinuri at Mylasa.[85] Between 351/350 and 344/343, this body honored one Nesaius, bringing him into the association and granting him an *ateleia*. The analogy with the trilingual stele suggests that this measure could have been followed by an authorization process. Nothing of the sort is said, however, and since we have the bottom edge of the inscription and can judge the text's tenor in its complete context, one can assume that it did not take place.[86] This can probably be explained by the fact that the (unfortunately disturbed) context of line 6 mentions a command from Idrieus and Ada. One can conclude that the local body acted in Nesaius's favor because of a command from the dynasts, who performed the function of satrap in that land. Then it is understandable that no further confirmation of the local legislation was necessary. One should note the contrast with the actions of Nehemiah, who as satrap held a comparable station to that of the local Carian princes but arranged for authorization of one of his decrees.[87]

---

[83] See *Reichsidee*, 35[1] (27[2]) n. 58, 100[2]. For the text, see Franciszek Sokolowski, *Lois sacrées de l'Asie mineure* (École française d'Athènes. Travaux et mémoires 9; Paris: de Boccard, 1955), 173–74, no. 75, repeated by Simon Hornblower (*Mausolus* [Oxford: Clarendon, 1982], 365) as M4. A new edition has been provided by Fjodor B. Poljakov, *Die Inschriften von Tralleis und Nysa, Teil 1* (Inschriften griechischer Städte aus Kleinasien 36.1; Bonn: Habelt, 1989), 8–9, no. 3.

[84] See *Reichsidee*, 99–100[2]. For the text, see *SIG* 311, repeated by Hornblower (*Mausolus*, 364) as M2, and also by M. Çetin Şahin, *Lagina, Stratonikeia und Umgebung*, part 2.1 of *Die Inschriften von Stratonikeia* (Inschriften griechischer Städte aus Kleinasien 22.1; Bonn: Habelt, 1982), 1–2, no. 501.

[85] See *Reichsidee*, 41[2], 101[2]. For the text, see Louis Robert, *Le sanctuaire de Sinuri près de Mylasa: Première partie: Les inscriptions grecques* (Mémoires de l'Institut Français d'Archéologie de Stamboul 7; Paris: de Boccard, 1945), 94–97, no. 73; and decidedly improved in idem, "Décret d'une syngeneia carienne au sanctuaire de Sinuri," *Hellenica* 7 (1949): 59–68, esp. 63–64; repeated by Hornblower (*Mausolus*, 365) as M5.

[86] See the reproduction in Robert, *Sinuri*, pl. 13, no. 73.

[87] See 2.2.2 above and 3.2.3 below.

2.4.2.3.5. Another grant of *ateleia* found in the same temple at Sinuri mentions Idrieus and Ada and so should probably be dated to the Persian period. Its condition, however, is so fragmentary that it can add nothing to our discussion.[88]

2.4.2.3.6. In the Achaemenid period, the community of the Plataseis agreed to grant a *proxenia* (friendship between a state and a foreigner) and citizen's rights to a citizen of Cos and in connection with this also a partial tax exemption. The contents provide no insight into the Achaemenid Empire's administrative practices, since the decree is known only from a reference contained in an early Hellenistic document.[89]

2.4.2.3.7. An inscription from Lagina cannot be used because of the uncertainties caused by its poor state of preservation.[90]

2.4.2.3.8. The city of Erythrae's decision is not from the region ruled by Mausollus. It honors Mausollus and his descendants by granting citizen's rights, the *proxenia,* the *ateleia,* and the like. Statues of him and his wife Artemisia were erected and garlands of fifty or thirty darics dedicated. Here it would be important to know to what degree Erythrae was dependent on the Persians. That the worth of the garlands is measured in darics, a Persian unit, is not conclusive proof that the city was under actual Persian rule at the time. An authorization would have been unnecessary if it was legally or de facto free.[91]

3. EVALUATION: THE INSTITUTION OF IMPERIAL AUTHORIZATION

Before we can appreciate imperial authorization as such, several questions regarding its form and use must still be discussed.

---

[88] See *Reichsidee,* 101². For the text, see Robert, *Sinuri,* 98, no. 75.

[89] See *Reichsidee,* 40², 101². For the text, see Jonas Crampa, *The Greek Inscriptions,* vol. 3, part 2 of *Labraunda: Swedish Excavations and Researches* (Stockholm: Svenska Institut i Athen, 1972), 42–47, no. 42.

[90] See *Reichsidee,* 40–41², 101². For the text, see *SEG* 36:1229; Hornblower, *Mausolus,* 368–69, M13; Şahin, *Inschriften von Stratonikeia,* 2–3, no. 502. For its interpretation, see also I. Hahn, "Zur Frage der Sklavensteuer im frühen Hellenismus," in *Antike Abhängigkeitsformen in den griechischen Gebieten ohne Polisstruktur und den römischen Provinzen* (ed. H. Kreissig and F. Kühnert; Schriften zur Geschichte und Kultur der Antike 25; Berlin: Akademie-Verlag, 1985), 56–64.

[91] See *Reichsidee,* 100². For the text, see *SIG* 168; Tod, *Greek Historical Inscriptions,* 163–65, no. 155.

3.1. THE ORIGIN AND DEVELOPMENT OF IMPERIAL AUTHORIZATION

So far as I can tell, the institution is one of a kind. It did not exist in the Assyrian Empire nor in the Neo-Babylonian, for their responses to petitions by confirming the ancient privileges of Mesopotamian cities lie on a different level: Persian imperial authorization was concerned not with renewing old prerogatives but rather with guaranteeing new norms.[92] That justifies the question of whether we can explain the institution on the basis of the Persian context. In other words, is it connected to other Persian imperial institutions or can it even be derived from them?

Several passages in Dan 6 and the book of Esther provide some relevant insights.[93] It is evident that the relevant scene from the book of Daniel (6:7–10 [Eng. 6:6–9]) depicts customary Persian acts of sentencing and legislating at high levels.[94] The king's advisers bring a proposal for a norm to their lord, who possesses the power to make law. The request is introduced by the comment that all the high officials of the empire have "taken counsel together" (אתיעטו) that the king should make a law legally binding. They ask him to fix it in writing, "if it seems good to him" (6:9: "so establish now, O king, a ban and write a writing that may not be violated, in accordance with [or: "like" = "as a"?] the law of the Medes and the Persians[95] that

---

[92] Neither were similar actions normal in later imperial systems, such as the Seleucid or the Roman. On this, see *Reichsidee,* 103–7[2], and 36[1] (29[2]) n. 63 specifically for the *Imperium Romanum.* At any rate, these later empires are irrelevant for investigations of the origin of imperial authorization.

[93] In evaluating the two sources, one should remember my previous observations about the Jewish literary evidence and its problems (see the discussion above under 2.2). Both texts reveal an immediate connection to the Achaemenid period by their literary *genos*—the story of a Jewish dignitary at the court of a great Oriental monarch (cf. *Reichsidee,* 61–62[2]; and Richard D. Patterson, "Holding On to Daniel's Court Tales," *JETS* 36 [1993]: 445–54, who rightly points out the antiquity of the story type but who admittedly has different opinions than those represented here). A closer analysis shows that the story of Dan 6 transmits authentic elements of the Achaemenid state (see *Reichsidee,* 62–78[2], 83–86[2]). The same applies to the book of Esther (see *Reichsidee,* 79–80[2], 86–88[2]), though its prehistory is not simple and there are arguments for the Esther story in its present form presupposing Dan 6. Again and again, it is evident that the author of the relevant parts proceeds quite independently and appropriately, which is not conceivable simply on the basis of literary dependence. So one cannot deny a familiarity with Achaemenid institutions to those who wrote or edited the texts in question (see above 2.2.4 and below n. 97).

[94] See *Reichsidee,* 23–24[1] (30[2]), 25–26[1] (33–34[2]), 80[2].

[95] Whether the "law of the Medes and the Persians" (on this concept, see ibid., 69–70[2]) represents the higher norm that regulates the qualification of the royal

cannot be lost").[96] The norm takes effect when it is fixed in writing: it "cannot be lost, cannot be overlooked," expressed by the Aramaic verb עדה.

The corresponding scene in Esth 1:12–22 shows this more clearly.[97] Because of an offense, the king's chief wife is disowned. The corresponding decree of the king is written down at the suggestion of the royal advisers and incorporated into the laws of the Persians and the Medes (1:19: "if it seems good to the king, let him issue a royal decree and have it written among the laws of the Persians and the Medes, so that it will not be overlooked").[98] The explicit purpose of this action is to prevent the other women of the Persian Empire from offending their husbands in the same way. So a royal decree directed at an individual case is, by being fixed in writing, turned into a precedent and takes on the quality of a generalized, abstract norm.[99] This is so formulated that it will not "be lost," not "pass away." The Hebrew verb used here, עבר ("pass away"), is apparently a translation of the Aramaic term עדה.[100] The norm promulgated to deal with a specific situation does not disappear with the resolution of the specific problem but continues to exist for appropriate situations in the future. It applies to everyone who behaves similarly, and so becomes permanent.[101]

---

decree, or whether the latter is itself described this way, can be left undecided here. The story told by Herodotus 3.31 about Cambyses also knows of a higher norm that regulates the implementation of lower rules, which may be better characterized as administrative acts. It is to the credit of Onorato Bucci ("L'attività legislativa del sovrano achemenide e gli Archivi reali persiani," *RIDA* 25 [1978]: 14, 18–19) to have brought this example into the discussion. On the problem, see *Reichsidee,* 88–90².

[96] כען מלכא תקים אסרא ותרשם כתבא די לא להשניה כדת־מדי ופרס די־לא תעדא. On the Haphel of שנה meaning "violate" (not "alter"!), see n. 101 below.

[97] See *Reichsidee,* 23–24¹ (30–31²), 83². The interpretation offered here follows in the main that of Gerleman, *Esther,* 68–69. Even if the Esther story has been influenced by the corresponding scene in Dan 6, the author has not shaped the events without bringing to bear his own knowledge of the circumstances of imperial law. This may show the independence and appropriateness with which the book of Esther distinguishes these things.

[98] אם־על־המלך טוב יצא דבר־מלכות מלפניו ויכתב בדתי פרס־ומדי ולא יעבור.

[99] On the significance of textuality in Persian administrative affairs, see *Reichsidee,* 24¹ (31²) with n. 69.

[100] That this passage in the book of Esther is dependent on an Aramaic text is shown by the Aramaism על for ל in the conditional clause ("if it seems good to the king").

[101] The point is not that the law is unchangeable, as has often been maintained. Anyway, outside of these two biblical books there are no references to the irrevocable

Comparable observations can be made about the trilingual stela from the Letoon.[102] In the Aramaic decree of the satrap, the corpus of regulations apparently ends with line 18. That is why the line is indented at both ends, to mark the end graphically. Line 19 then says that he (Pixodarus) had the law written down.[103] A syntagma follows, introduced by זי, that unfortunately cannot be completely clarified. In place of the incomprehensible מהצצן of the extant text, Dupont-Sommer suggested a small graphic alteration to מההסן, the H-causative of the root חסן, which in this stem means "take possession, possess, keep, etc." At any rate, it is possible that we have here a concluding relative clause introduced by זי that stipulates the obligation to observe the law, as Dupont-Sommer suggested in his first translation ("Cette loi-ci, il l'a inscrite pour qu'on la garde").[104] If that is right, then the example of the trilingual inscription shows that the satrap did not simply accept the local norm but above all had it written

---

nature of Persian law. What Diodorus 17.30.4–6 reports certainly does not have to do with this; see *Reichsidee*, 23[1] (29–30[2]) with note 64. At least two characteristics of a royal decree must be distinguished to understand this phenomenon. One has to do with its origins, the other with its execution, and I differentiate them terminologically (see *Reichsidee*, 82–84[2]). A general compulsory norm is promulgated by being fixed in writing and affixed with the royal seal. This legislative event is expressed in Aramaic by the negated verb עדה ("pass by, vanish, be lost"), which is translated by the root עבר in Hebrew. Since permanence and universal validity is ascribed to the norm, I call this expression a "validation formula." The second characteristic of a royal norm concerns its execution. There was a problem with carrying out the will of the central administration in all ancient empires because of technical difficulties with communications. For this reason it was necessary to impress on all subordinate authorities that a legitimate edict from the central government must be followed without reservations. This was formulated by saying that it might not be altered, because every "violation" of the edict by a subordinate might be understood exactly as an "alteration." This is expressed in Aramaic by the negated causative from שנה (cf. Dan 6:9, די לא להשניה). I would like to name this phrase the "execution formula." It postulates actual obedience to the royal norm. This premise explains the corresponding events in Dan 6 and Esther (1:12–22, esp. 19) without difficulty. The passage from Esth 8:3–8 should probably be interpreted differently. On this see *Reichsidee*, 37[1] (31[2]) n. 68 and especially (and probably more plausibly) 82–83[2].

[102] See *Reichsidee*, 24–25[1] (32–33[2]), and also, with differences in details, André Dupont-Sommer, "La stèle trilingue récemment découverte à Xanthos: Le texte araméen," *CRAI* (1974): 138–39.

[103] The inscription says: דתה דך כתב זי מהצצן.

[104] See "La stèle trilingue," 135, though Dupont-Sommer later withdrew this suggestion (in Metzger et al., *Fouilles*, 152–53), wrongly it seems to me. On the semantic issues and the syntactic problems, see *Reichsidee*, 24–25[1] (32–33[2]) with nn. 72–73.

down. As a result, the law of the community of Xanthus would not be "lost" but became permanent because of the empire.

Authorization then means that the imperial authority issues in writing a norm proposed by subordinates. In this way, a normal act of high-level legislation would be transferred to the area of the local norms. So like the king's advisers, subordinates could apply to the king or to the easier-to-reach satrap and ask him for an authorization fixed in writing. This is the first starting-point for the institution of imperial authorization.

A closer examination of terminology confirms this. In Daniel, the request is introduced by the remark that all the high officials of the empire "have taken counsel together" (אתיעטו).[105] As far as semantics is concerned, this reading is certainly plausible: in this particular situation, "they have taken counsel together (and therefore now have the same advice)" carries the self-evident connotation of a proposal to a superior. In the trilingual inscription, the body of the *lex sacra* is introduced in a very comparable way: "the citizens of Xanthus have proposed" (אתעשתו).[106] So in both examples we find an introductory reference to a resolution by the subordinate authority that implicitly suggests that the higher authority is acting on a request from lower down. This reference was probably a part of the written authorization formula.

The verb אתעשתו used in the trilingual inscription from Xanthus (Aramaic lines 6–7) must be examined more closely.[107] Its basic form is attested since the eighth century and means generally "think, plan," which would fit well in this context. One must note, however, that the verb occasionally carries the nuance "to think about someone and worry about him," and this meaning is the usual one in the *ʾitpaʿal* stem (like Hebrew *hitpaʿel*) found in the inscription: in this derivation, the verb means "to be worried about, to be concerned about," and in fact the subject is always a superior who "concerns himself" with an inferior's request.[108] But how can one produce the meaning "propose" that is required by the trilingual?

---

[105] Dan 6:8: אתיעטו כל סרכי מלכותא ... לקימה קים מלכא. See *Reichsidee,* 25–26[1] (33–34[2]), 80[2].

[106] Lines 6–7: אתעשתו בעלי אורן כרפא למעבד.

[107] See *Reichsidee,* 80–82[2]. The references can be found in nn. 183–86.

[108] Note these examples: אתעשת לי ינתנו לי ("bear me in mind [and command that] they assign it to me") from a letter of petition from an Egyptian to Arsames asking him to assign his father's lost property to him (Godfrey R. Driver, *Aramaic Documents of the Fifth Century B.C.* [abridged and rev. ed.; Oxford: Clarendon, 1957], 8.3) and in Hebrew אולי יתעשת האלהים לנו ("perhaps God will concern himself with us") from Jonah 1:6, when the captain approaches Jonah in the middle of the storm and asks him to pray to his God. See also *Reichsidee,* 81[2] nn. 185–86.

The clearest example can be found in the famous letter from the Jewish community in Elephantine to Bagavahya, the governor of Judea (the same request was sent to Daliyeh and Shelamiah, the sons of the governor of Samaria): אתעשת על אגורא זך למבנה ("take thought of that temple to [re]build [it]").[109] The addressees are asked to be concerned that something be done in the petitioners' favor. They are certainly not in a position to bring about the restoration of the temple at Elephantine. But they could support the request within the imperial administration to the appropriate satraps for Egypt[110] and perhaps even to the king himself. If this is the case, when someone who is superior to the addressee, ultimately the king, is the target of the intervention, the connotation "put forward a request" arises immediately: the "concern for" someone lower down is the reason for a petition directed to a higher-up, ultimately to the king. If all goes well, the responsible authority then issues a relevant decree. Within the framework of actual government procedures for establishing law, such a course of events must not have been infrequent. This is the second possible source of imperial authorization.

We may have an example of this in the inscription from Sardis.[111] If one asks who may have had a special interest in seeing that the decree in question was issued, the answer must be either the cult founder, Baradates, himself or his descendants or other influential worshipers of the Zeus cult that he founded. One of them applied to the hyparch, Droaphernes, a Persian official residing in Sardis,[112] who was apparently favorably disposed toward the cult (hence the donation of the statue), to

---

[109] AP 30 in CAP, 108–19; *TAD* 1:68–71, no. A.4.7, line 23 (the translation follows *TAD*).

[110] The petitioner was counting on this (see the continuation in lines 23–25), and this is the course that Bagavahya and Daliyeh chose. See the messenger's note about the answer received, AP 32 in CAP, 122–24; *TAD* 1:76, no. A.4.9, lines 2–3: "Memorandum: you may say in Egypt before Arsames about the altar-house of the god..." (translation from *TAD*). It is clear that Arsames would be responsible for any rebuilding of the temple, and the community from Elephantine was advised to appeal to him. They were advised to go, as it were, through official channels, with the support of the governors of Jerusalem and Samaria, who were probably Jews. Because those consulted lacked legal responsibility, there can be no question of their answer granting an authorization, as Rütersworden ("Reichsautorisation," 60) has proposed. On the whole course of events, see Bezalel Porten, *Archives from Elephantine: The Life of an Ancient Jewish Military Colony* (Berkeley and Los Angeles: University of California Press, 1968), 282–96, esp. 291–94; also Kurt Galling, *Studien zur Geschichte Israels im persischen Zeitalter* (Tübingen: Mohr Siebeck, 1964), 164.

[111] See 2.4.2.2 above and, for the interpretation that follows, *Reichsidee*, 91–96².

[112] On the official rank of the hyparch, see *Reichsidee*, 92² with n. 237.

obtain this decree from him. That it made sense to get a governmental authorization would be easier to understand if the prohibition on taking part in the mystery cults was really a considerable restriction of previously available liberties, a new regulation that naturally needed to be brought to the attention of all (including Greek-speaking) participants in the cult, though it applied only to cult personnel in the narrow sense. The inter-- ested group (or individual) asked the official to "concern himself" with this matter, and since he had legal responsibility, or at least thought that he did, he reacted with his decree. Strictly speaking, of course, the intro- ductory dedication to Zeus does not belong to the actual decree. It was included in the Roman-period quotation, however, because it alone listed the name of the author and the date of the document. So we have before us evidence for the imperial authorization's starting point within Persian administration, comparable *mutatis mutandis* to the petition to Bagavahya and to the proceedings within the central imperial government portrayed in the book of Daniel.

The situation postulated here (intervention with a higher authority on behalf of someone of lower status) does not apply to the trilingual stela, though. But this could simply mean that the Itpaʿal of עשׁת had become in the administrative language of that time a general term for an application by a subordinate.

Thus a variety of evidence shows that the institution of imperial authorization fits easily within Achaemenid administrative practices and can be explained well historically. Obviously, laws were made at the emperor's court in this way: after discussing it among themselves, advisers proposed the relevant norm to the king and he approved (authorized) it. Interventions by influential individuals were possible in the same way, and of course the initiative could also come from the king. Once openness toward subordinates is taken for granted, one can easily understand that their proposals could be made to the king or the appropriate governor through an embassy or a trusted middle- man and then written down as the edict of the addressed ruler and thus authorized.

Many witnesses reflect the fact that it was possible for subordinates to reach the Persian government with a request.[113] In the actual center, the royal court, there were probably some particular experts on the affairs of locally autonomous groups who were the natural starting points for such attempts, as Nehemiah's edicts seem to show.[114]

---

[113] See ibid., 102² with nn. 276–77.

[114] See above 2.2.2.

3.2. The Scope of Imperial Authorization

The problems enumerated here are, as we will see, interconnected with regard to their contents.

3.2.1. The Question of Constraint[115]

Whether authorization was obligatory or voluntary for the subordinate bodies is an important question for assessing the political significance of the institution. Unfortunately, there is no certain answer. Decisive testimony could come only from those local regulations stemming from the Achaemenid period that contain no references to authorization, though by their nature it is possible that an authorization lay behind them. As far as I can see, the only evidence of this kind are the documents described above that all stem temporally and culturally from the rule of the Hecatomn dynasty in Caria.[116] As we noted, they permit no certain judgments.

Perhaps one can settle the issue by referring to the clause at the end of the Greek (and almost certainly the Lycian) text of the trilingual inscription: the desire to obtain an authorization is part of the community's decree. This phrase refers to imperial authorization explicitly and even in a hortative form ("let Pixodarus be legally responsible," according to the Greek version). Taken literally, that means that the attempt to have an authorization issued was neither taken for granted nor obligatory. The settlement of the border dispute between Miletus and Myus points in the same direction if the cities approached the king to decide the issue, which is a possible scenario.[117]

There were naturally situations that made an authorization essential, for example, when the situation required the partial or complete reconstitution of a self-governing body, as with Ezra's efforts. Obviously imperial officials could also order that these procedures be followed, as is shown by the codification of Egyptian law where the king himself commanded that the laws be collected,[118] and probably also by the Ionians' peace settlement issued by the satrap Artaphernes.[119]

---

[115] See *Reichsidee,* 14[1] (15–16[2]), 22[1] (27[2]), 26[1] (34[2]), 102[2].

[116] See 2.4.2.3 above.

[117] Naturally one must take into account the possibility that the procedure was strictly regulated by the settlements of Artaphernes. In that case, we cannot know if an authorization was required in a particular situation.

[118] The whole picture painted here would be seriously altered if the theory of a systematic codification of local laws by the Persian government is correct (see above n. 16). This impulse toward codification would then be the starting point for authorization of individual norms by Persian authorities.

[119] See 2.4.2.1 above.

General considerations, namely, that subordinate communities could provide legal security for themselves through imperial authorization,[120] also suggest that authorization was optional.

3.2.2. Categorizing the Subjects[121]

Almost all the examples we possess deal with religious concerns, not least the trilingual inscription itself. Was imperial authorization limited to the sphere of religious legislation? The answer partly depends on whether authorization was obligatory or not. If it was not obligatory, then there is no reason to suppose that there was any limitation of content. In view of the quite low number of reasonably convincing pieces of evidence, again no clear answer can be given.[122] Nevertheless, I want to suggest that there was a more extensive application of the institution. This is supported by the settlement of the border dispute of Myus, which obviously lies outside the religious sphere, as clearly does the codification of Egyptian law.[123] Some religious documents suggest a thoroughly realistic administrative background for authorization in financial politics: so the trilingual inscription,[124] perhaps also Nehemiah's regulations and the decree of Cambyses arranged by Udjahorresne. In other cases, the driving force could have been legal security: so in the conflict between Myus and Miletus,[125] and as one essential factor for Nehemiah, Ezra, Udjahorresne, and others.

Most of all, it is important to remember that in the ancient Near East, any law was based on divine legitimation and so involved religion. The best example of this is the Jewish legislation, which includes all areas of life and law. The Egyptian codification of law also belongs in this category, since it was not limited to religious affairs alone.[126] After all, if one includes funerary inscriptions, a predominant number of our epigraphic traditions from all regions and periods of the ancient world are concerned for the

---

[120] See 2.3.2 above and 3.3 below.

[121] See *Reichsidee,* 22¹ (27–28²), 103².

[122] On the basis of the Mausollus documents (see 2.4.2.3 above), which deal with purely secular issues and neither mention imperial authorization nor an intention to gain it, one could be *e contrario* inclined to suppose a limitation to religious affairs. However, this single collection of evidence is burdened, as has been shown, with such uncertainties about its tradition and its political and legal contexts are so little understood that wide-ranging conclusions cannot be derived from it.

[123] See 2.1.1 above.

[124] See 2.3.2 above.

[125] See 2.3.1 above.

[126] See 2.1.1 above.

most part with religiosity: it was very important to preserve a religious act in a permanent form. That is why we encounter it especially often.

3.2.3. The Legal Implications of Imperial Authorization[127]

The important question about the concrete effects and legal implications of imperial authorization can also not be immediately answered. That would only be possible if we were able to situate each example of authorization within its political context. Once again, we do not have nearly enough basis in the sources for this. It is apparent, however, that through it, the legal norms of a local body with subordinate status were elevated to the status of imperial legislation and so enjoyed corresponding authority. The formulation of the relevant text in Ezra 7:26 supports this.[128] Ezra's law book is simultaneously "the law of Ezra's God" and "the law of the king." One is subject to it in the same way that one is subject to royal law, and the corresponding sanctions are therefore also listed (Ezra 7:26). The validity of local norms thereby withstands every challenge, and legal security within the imperium is strengthened. Perhaps the actions of Nehemiah[129] can be informative here in comparison with the decree of the συγγένεια of Pelekos in Caria.[130] In both cases, the governor's authority supported from the beginning the community decrees in question. Nehemiah in his difficult situation requested the authorization; this was apparently not necessary in Caria. Authorization could also be effective against organs of government, as the regulations in the trilingual inscription make clear: the satrap expressly proclaimed as his own norms the financial consequences of the Xanthians' agreement, insofar as they concerned the empire. That means that in case of a conflict, officials of the central government must also take them into account.

Just as authorization necessarily implied the central government's approval of local norms, the process also provided the central government a chance to control a self-governing body in a constitutional manner. The subjects were promised legal protection on the condition that their plans did not contradict imperial interests.

3.3. The Political Meaning of Imperial Authorization[131]

Finally, we must appreciate the function of imperial authorization within the political system of the empire.

---

[127] See *Reichsidee,* 22–23[1] (28–29[2]).

[128] See 2.2.1 above.

[129] See 2.2.2 above.

[130] See 2.4.2.3.4 above.

[131] See *Reichsidee,* 26–27[1] (35[2]), 107–13[2].

Of course, the Persian system of government showed strong feudal features and was characterized by personal relationships between those holding power at various levels.[132] However, in such a feudal (that is, shaped most of all by personal loyalty) political and social system, the mechanisms of transmission, the institutions that manage communication, acquire particular significance. Among them belongs imperial authorization as set forth above. It mediated a connection between the rulers and the ruled quite apart from any possible changes in mentality.[133]

Regarding the empire's structure, we can conclude from this that it contained institutionalized crossing points from local systems to the central system. Some of them enabled an interaction between the two that gave subordinates legal security while providing the center a check on them, so that in certain contexts it served both their interests. These methods of communication were produced at various levels of the Persian bureaucracy, by the king or by a satrap, and they functioned without regard to the constitution of the subordinate group that determined the form of the local decision-making process.[134] In the case of Xanthus, it can be described as democratic (in a broad sense); in Egypt and among the Jews, experts or expert committees formulated the local norms. They were all compatible with the procedures used in the higher-ranking Achaemenid legislation.

It was certainly within the realm of possibility for the Persians to impose the will of the king or of an official upon a subordinate community in any way at all. But just the opposite situation, at least formally, is manifested by Pixodarus's actions in the trilingual inscription from the Letoon.[135] The satrap's decree shows a definite understanding for the inter-penetrating interaction between two unequally ranked political systems. The special thing revealed by the trilingual inscription is the fact that between the central government and the dependent community there was

---

[132] See ibid., 111².

[133] Regarding chronology, it must be stressed that the earliest example, the Egyptian collection of laws (2.2.1), belongs to the time of Darius I, while the latest, the trilingual inscription (2.3.2), belongs in the last decades, perhaps even the last few years, of the empire. Due to the scarcity of the material both quantitatively and in terms of its references to what we know of the context of every concrete example, we cannot discern any institutional development in the applications of imperial authorization nor any change in mentality. See *Reichsidee,* 110².

[134] See ibid., 109–10².

[135] See ibid., 107–9² with n. 305. In many articles on the interpretation of the trilingual inscription, too much importance is attached to the difference in the relevant terminology of the Lycian and Greek versions, on the one hand, and the Aramaic version, on the other.

an institutionalized form of cooperation. It was so tight that the satrap adopted the curses of the local agreement and apparently issued them in his own name. From this we can perhaps derive some broader conclusions about the inner conditions of the Achaemenid Empire.[136] For one thing, it demonstrates that constitutional elements, or at least the aim of pursuing them, existed in the Persian administration. It also shows that the central government paid attention to the phenomenon of local autonomy, even though there was no term for it. It seems evident that the Achaemenid government was conscious of the principle of local autonomy as such.[137] That this fundamental position had its limits in practice (e.g., in case of a revolt) does not change anything and on the contrary appears to confirm its existence.

So the Achaemenid Empire can be regarded as the first supranational empire of the Mediterranean cultural sphere that deserves this name not just because of its size, but because it manifested to some degree an imperial way of thinking. We cannot pursue here the degree of consensus and loyalty attained in non-Iranian areas, in comparison with the centrifugal tendencies that did not derive from the Iranian upper strata.[138]

Whenever these problems are raised, one cannot ignore the institution that we have named imperial authorization if one wishes to go deeper into fundamental questions of the structure of the Persian Empire that include aspects of universal history.

---

[136] See ibid., 111–13².

[137] See ibid., 110².

[138] See the somewhat more detailed discussion in ibid., 111–13².

WAS THE PENTATEUCH THE CIVIC AND RELIGIOUS CONSTITUTION OF THE JEWISH ETHNOS IN THE PERSIAN PERIOD?

Joseph Blenkinsopp
University of Notre Dame

1. THE PERSIAN CONCEPT AND PRACTICE OF LAW

A. T. Olmstead, one of the early maximalists, argued in *A History of the Persian Empire* that Darius I, following on the military successes of his *annus mirabilis,* set about drawing up a law code called The Ordinance of Good Regulations to be enforced throughout the empire. The compilation of this document was accomplished in record time, since it was already being implemented, Olmstead claimed, in a transaction recorded in 519 B.C.E. Such unusual expedition would compare well with the work of compiling the Egyptian laws that was getting under way about the same time and which the Demotic Chronicle tells us lasted sixteen years. According to Olmstead, this remarkable achievement of Darius was made possible by a deliberate and systematic borrowing, in style and substance, from the ancient Mesopotamian legal traditions and the Code of Hammurabi in particular, perhaps even (he speculated) from the original stela in Susa, now in the Louvre, rather than from one or other of the copies that were produced in the course of the sixth and fifth centuries B.C.E.[1] Olmstead therefore enthusiastically endorsed the high opinion of Darius as lawgiver, alongside Hammurabi and Solon, prevalent among the Greeks, including Plato, Xenophon, and Diodorus Siculus.[2]

Since caution is in order when dealing with issues between maximalists and minimalists, I begin by recording the judgment of T. Cuyler Young Jr.,

---

[1] A. T. Olmstead, *A History of the Persian Empire* (Chicago: Chicago University Press, 1948), 119–34; idem, "Darius As Lawgiver," *AJSL* 51 (1934–1935): 247–49. The 519 B.C.E. document that mentions "the king's law" (*dātu šarri*) is the record of the sale of a slave (Olmstead, *History,* 119).

[2] Plato, *Ep.* 7.332b; Plato, *Leg.* 695c; Xenophon, *Oec.* 14.6; Diodorus Siculus, *Hist.,* 1.94–95.

in *The Cambridge Ancient History,* that evidence for legal codification and legal reform in the early Achaemenid period remains elusive.[3] The state was based on the foundation of law and the administration of justice, and royal inscriptions abound in such terms as *aršta* (justice), *arṭa* (good order, truth), and, of course, *dāta*. This Old Persian term (Akkadian *dātu*) is generally translated "law," but the translation calls for no less explanation and qualification than the Hebrew word תורה. Where it occurs in Achaemenid royal inscriptions, it refers either to a specific decree or a general condition of law and order imposed by the will of the sovereign. In the Behistun inscription Darius I speaks of his *dāta* and adds, in lapidary fashion, "as was said to them by me, thus was it done." Similar expressions occur in connection with the royal *dāta* in the funerary inscriptions at Naqsh-i-Rustam and in one of the Susa inscriptions from the reign of Darius. In a Persepolis text Xerxes enjoins on his subjects respect for the law established by Ahura Mazda.[4] The firman of Xerxes, ostensibly the most religious of Achaemenid rulers, forbidding the worship of demons or false gods (*daiva*) and enjoining the worship of Ahura Mazda and Arta, was also a projection of that *dāta* rooted in the will of the cosmic creator-deity Ahura Mazda and expressed as the will of the ruler.[5]

Thus far, therefore, there is no evidence for Olmstead's thesis, and we know of no Persian compilation of laws prior to the collection of instructions in the *Vidēvdāt* or *Vendidat* (Antidemonic Law) from the Parthian period. This is not to say that the dominant ethnic class would not have brought elements of customary law with them from their tribal and nomadic

---

[3] "The Early History of the Medes and the Persians and the Achaemenid Empire to the Death of Cambyses," *CAH*² 4:94.

[4] Behistun (B) I:23; Naqsh-i-Rustam A,B 20–21; Susa E I:37; Persepolis H lines 49–52 in R. G. Kent, *Old Persian: Grammar, Texts, Lexicon* (AOSM 33; New Haven, Conn.: American Oriental Society, 1953), 119, 138, 140–41, 152.

[5] *Arṭa,* represented as an archangel or spirit attendant on Ahura Mazda, embodied the idea of justice and legal order and was an element in several theophoric names, e.g., Artaxerxes (= "possessing a kingdom of justice"); cf. Sanskrit *ṛta* ("cosmic order"). Moral and legal order, which it was the responsibility of the ruler to impose and maintain, is rooted in the will of the creator-deity and therefore in the created order. Naqsh-i-Rustam A begins in a manner somewhat reminiscent of Isa 40–48: "A great god is Ahuramazda, who created this earth, who created yonder sky, who created humanity, who created happiness for humanity, who made Darius king, one king of many, one lord of many" (Kent, *Old Persian,* 138). This must have been a more or less standard formula, since it appears on several inscriptions, including the inscription on the statue of Darius discovered in 1972 at Susa, on which see F. Vallat, "Les Inscriptions cunéiformes de la statue de Darius," *Cahiers de la délégation française en Iran* 4 (1974): 161–70.

past and from Median or Elamite borrowings that could have combined or coalesced with elements from the ancient Mesopotamian legal tradition. That tradition was still pervasive, as can be shown from private and family law reflected in the Elephantine and Daliyeh papyri.[6] But what was lacking, on evidence currently available, was a legal code compiled for use throughout the empire. Furthermore, it seems that Olmstead's Ordinance of Good Regulations depends on a mistranslation of Naqsh-i-Rustam B lines 21–24: "What a man says against a man, that does not convince me, until he satisfies the Ordinance of Good Regulations." The term *ha[n]duqām,* translated "record" or "statute" by Kent, apparently refers primarily to an *oral* affirmation or attestation.[7] But even if a written text were involved, the context in which the word occurs does not imply more than procedures for verifying the testimony of hostile witnesses, for example, by ordeal or oath.

Where cuneiform texts from the same period allude to "the law of the king" (*dātu ša šarri*), here too the reference is to a decree or royal command having the force of law.[8] More often than not such texts have to do with fiscal matters, of primary concern to the Achaemenids; one recalls Darius I's nickname "the Huckster" (κάπηλος) as recorded by Herodotus (3.89).[9] In one of the Persepolis Fortress Tablets *datam* (Elamite for *dāta*) refers to regulations to be followed by those in charge of the storerooms.[10] Another example of common usage would be the statement in the Aramaic, that is, the official version of the Xanthus inscription line 19 that "he [the satrap Pixodarus] wrote this decree" (רתה דך כתב), with reference to a specific disposition of the local community.[11]

On the basis of the available evidence, therefore, the legal terminology in use in the early Achaemenid period either refers to a particular edict

---

[6] See Jonas C. Greenfield, "The Aramaic Legal Texts of the Achaemenian Period," *Transeu* 3 (1990): 85–92, with further references.

[7] See Richard N. Frye, *The Heritage of Persia* (Costa Mesa, Calif.: Mazda, 1993), 113, following Émile Benveniste, *Bullétin de la Societé Linguistique* 47 (1951): 37.

[8] *CAD* D:122 translates *dātu* as "decree, royal command." See also A. L. Oppenheim, "The Babylonian Evidence of Achaemenian Rule in Mesopotamia," *CHI* 2:547.

[9] Raymond Descat, "Darius, le roi kapēlos," in *Continuity and Change: Proceedings of the Last Achaemenid History Workshop, April 6–8, 1990, Ann Arbor, Michigan* (ed. H. Sancisi-Weerdenburg et al.; AH 8; Leiden: Nederlands Instituut voor het Nabije Oosten, 1994), 161–66.

[10] Pierre Briant, *Histoire de l'Empire Perse de Cyrus à Alexandre* (Leiden: Nederlands Instituut voor het Nabije Oosten, 1996), 527.

[11] Peter Frei and Klaus Koch, *Reichsidee und Reichsorganisation im Perserreich* (2d ed.; OBO 55; Fribourg: Universitätsverlag, 1996), 39–47.

backed by the absolute authority of the ruler or is expressive of a broad, globalizing concept of a legal order. All legal enactments of any kind and originating in any part of the empire are therefore theoretically "law of the king," and this would also have been the case with Ezra's law ("the law of your God and the law of the king," Ezra 7:26). And since the king ruled by favor of the creator deity Ahura Mazda, this royal law could be said to be ultimately rooted in the cosmic order, though no evidence is extant that law was the object of theological reflection. In any case, evidence is lacking for a compilation or code of law in use throughout the empire.[12] A caveat is also in order with respect to the related term *dātabara,* literally "law bearer," often translated more precisely than the contexts warrant, for example in Dan 3:2, as "judge" or "magistrate." We must also take care not to be misled by Herodotus, whose occasional allusions to Persian laws (νόμοι, θεσμοί) generally refer to local customs. An example would be the custom that Persian boys are brought up with the women for the first five years of life (1.137). Herodotus's typical mixture of the plausible and the implausible is illustrated by a brief story he tells about Cambyses, who, wishing to marry his sister, inquired of the royal judges (τούς βασιλήιους δικαστάς), who were the interpreters of the laws of the land (ἐξηγηταί τῶν πατρίων θεσμῶν), whether such a union was permitted. Since exegesis was apparently a more dangerous occupation then than it is now, the judges replied, astutely but truthfully, that there was no law permitting it, but that there was a law according to which the king could do as he pleased (3.31).

Regarded as potential historical source material, the biblical texts may be said to lie somewhere between the inscriptions referred to and Herodotus. But whatever view one takes on this contentious issue, it can be claimed that Esther, the Diaspora tales in Daniel, and Ezra, in which texts the Persian loan word *dāt* occurs in both Hebrew and Aramaic, show familiarity with aspects of life under Persian rule. In this particular respect, at any rate, biblical usage corroborates or at least is not inconsistent with the conclusions reached on the basis of the nonbiblical literary evidence. Esther, purporting to describe events affecting Jewish communities during the reign of Xerxes (486–465), refers quite often to the royal laws (דתי המלך, 3:8), but in every case it is a matter of ad hoc decrees, not stipulations of law that could be part of a law code. Thus, there is a דת or edict governing

---

[12] By now this conclusion would command a broad consensus. See, e.g., Muhammad A. Dandamaev and Vladimir G. Lukonin, *The Culture and Social Institutions of Ancient Iran* (Cambridge: Cambridge University Press, 1989), 116–30; Briant, *Histoire de l'Empire Perse,* 526–28, 981–83; Richard N. Frye, *The History of Ancient Iran* (Munich: Beck, 1984), 119; Amelie Kuhrt, "Babylonia from Cyrus to Xerxes," *CAH*[2] 4:132.

the behavior of recalcitrant queens (Esth 1:13, 15, 19), recruitment for and the day-to-day operation of the harem (2:8, 12), access to the sovereign (4:11, 16), permission for Gentiles to kill Jews and for Jews to kill Gentiles (3:12–15; 4:3, 8), and permission to string up the corpses of the ten sons of Haman (9:14). The only exception occurs where Haman claims, falsely in the view of the author, that the Jewish דתים are incompatible with those of the king (דתי המלך, 3:8). In Daniel, as in Esther, דת designates one or another measure of a decidedly ad hoc nature, including a decree for the extermination of all the sages in the country (Dan 2:9, 13, 15) and for a thirty-day suspension of normal religious practices (6:9 [Eng. 6:8]). A more substantive and instructive instance is Darius's confirmation of the decree of Cyrus after it had turned up in the archives at Ecbatana (Ezra 6:1–12)—to which we shall return. The emphasis in these biblical texts on the immutability and irrevocability of such measures ("the laws of the Medes and the Persians that cannot be annulled," Esth 1:19; Dan 6:9, 13, 16 [Eng. 6:8, 12, 15]) reflects, not without a subversively sardonic note, a sense of the overwhelming, arbitrary power exercised by Persian rulers.

2. THE RELATION BETWEEN THE KING'S LAW AND PROVINCIAL LEGAL SYSTEMS

In the absence of a legal system imposed on the empire as a whole, a degree of legal autonomy in the provinces was inevitable, contingent on local systems remaining subordinate to and, where necessary, being brought into line with imperial *raison d'état* and the will of the sovereign. The remarkable variety of forms of political organization in the empire included satellite kingdoms with their own dynasts (Cilicia, Caria, Sidon); city-states, some with their own dependencies (e.g., Ashkelon under the control of Tyre); hyparchies (Bactria); tribal units (Kedarite Arabs); and temple communities (many examples in Mesopotamia, Egypt, and Asia Minor, and perhaps also Judah). Such a situation evidently ruled out one centralized legal system for all. In the matter of judicial control, the first concern of the central administration was the preservation of the *pax Persica* and the avoidance of insurrection. And since trouble could be expected to arise, and often did arise, from satrapal courts no less than from movements among the people, the authorization and enforcement of local laws could serve as one of several counterbalances to the ambitions of provincial governors.[13] The other major concern was fiscal, and in the

---

[13] In addition to representatives of the central administration in residence at satrapal courts, somewhat like Soviet commissars, we know of envoys who were sent on investigative missions, including Udjahorresne to Egypt, Histiaeus to Ionia (Herodotus 5.106–108), and Nehemiah to Judah (Neh 2:5–8)—the last two at their own request. The mission of Ezra is illustrative of the practice, even if historically

first place the prompt payment of taxes and tribute. In all instances of intervention on the part of the central administration, whether solicited or unsolicited, we may expect to find a fiscal issue playing a role. Apart from these basic concerns, the Achaemenid state was relatively noninterventionist compared with the Hellenistic kingdoms, perhaps in part due to its tribal past. One indication of this is linguistic: the language of the conquerors (Old Persian) was practically restricted to the ethnic ruling class; there are no private (nonroyal) inscriptions in the Old Persian cuneiform script. The same can be said of cultural influence: in most parts of the empire the archaeological record to date reveals negligible evidence for specifically Iranian culture.[14]

The phenomenon of imperial authorization documented by Peter Frei is one aspect of this tensive relationship between centralism and local autonomy, between coercive power projected from the center and provincial self-regulation. Understood as authorization for a local initiative solicited from the central administration, it was only one channel by which the latter projected and maintained its power throughout the empire, and not the most important one. Of the case histories from western Asia Minor presented by Frei, perhaps only one, the Xanthus trilingual inscription, fits the pattern. These case histories deal with special situations where some essential interest of the central government was perceived to be involved. Most are concerned with cultic initiatives, one or two deal with the settlement of intercity, territorial disputes, and others record grants of hospitality and citizenship (*proxenia*) or freedom from taxation or other civic burdens (*ateleia*), in favor of certain individuals. One of the more interesting of the case histories is the inscription discovered at Sardis in 1972 recording the erection of a statue to a local Zeus. To this was attached a prohibition addressed to the cult personnel associated with the statue against participating in the mysteries of Sabazios and other local deities. Since both the cult initiative and the prohibition originated with Droaphernes hyparch of Lydia, therefore with a high-ranking Persian in the imperial administration, it is not a case of imperial authorization in the terms defined by Frei. Together

---

suspect. There is also the official with the curious title "the King's Eye" (OP *spasaka* = ὀφθαλμὸς βασιλέως, Herodotus 1.114; Xenophon, *Cyr.* 8.6, 16), a kind of inspector sent to check on local officials, which may have suggested the role of the satan in the book of Job and the function of the *episkopos* in the Athenian League. On this last, see Jack Martin Balcer, "The Athenian Episkopos and the Achaemenid's 'King's Eye,'" *AJP* 98 (1977): 252–63.

[14] In agreement with the judgment of Briant, *Histoire de l'Empire Perse,* 7–8; and, for Judah, that of Ephraim Stern, "The Archeology of Persian Palestine," *CHJ* 1:88–114.

with the Gadatas inscription, however, it does illustrate the Persian tendency to regulate, one might almost say micromanage, local cult practice.[15] None of the cases from Asia Minor bears on the issue of local legal systems authorized by the central administration, much less provides evidence that all legal codes had to have explicit official approval as a matter of course.

While there is no question of reviewing Frei's case histories one by one, we might take a brief glance at the parade example of the trilingual Xanthus inscription which records the written approval by the satrap Pixodarus of a cultic initiative of the citizens of Xanthus.[16] Like the final redaction of the Egyptian laws and the imperial decrees in Ezra, the official text, somewhat more succinct than the Greek and Lydian versions, was in Aramaic. Leaving aside the possibility that this initiative in honor of Carian deities actually originated with Pixodarus, himself a Carian, and that therefore the one petitioning was also the one authorizing, we would assume that what necessitated approval were the conditions stipulated in the decree. These included tax-exempt status for the priest of the sanctuary and the withdrawal of city real estate vowed to the sanctuary from the local property tax base. If authorization was solicited by the Xanthians and their *perioikoi* (dependents), it would have been because they were aware that essential imperial interests were involved, in this case as in most financial interests, and that therefore it was a matter of prudence to forestall

---

[15] Interest in the operation of local cults seems, therefore, to be the one exception to the noninterventionist policy referred to earlier. The evidence has long been available, and much of it was brought together more than sixty years ago by Roland de Vaux, "The Decrees of Cyrus and Darius on the Rebuilding of the Temple," in *The Bible and the Ancient Near East* (Garden City, N.Y.: Doubleday, 1971), 63–96 (first published in *RB* 46 [1937]: 29–57). On the Sardis inscription, in addition to Frei, *Reichsidee*, 24–26, 90–96, see Louis Robert, "Une nouvelle inscription grecque de Sardes: Règlement de l'autorité perse relatif à un culte de Zeus," *CRAI* (1976), 303–31; M.-L. Chaumont, "Un nouveau gouverneur de Sardes à l'époque achéménide d'après une inscription récemment découverte," *Syria* 67 (1990): 579–608; Briant, *Histoire de l'Empire Perse*, 696–97. In the letter of Darius I to Gadatas, a Persian official in Ionia, the latter is threatened with punishment for levying a tax on the sacred gardeners of Apollo in Magnesia. In this text Darius refers to his "policy about deities" (τὴν ὑπὲρ θεῶν μου διάθεσιν; see R. Meiggs and D. Lewis, *A Selection of Greek Historical Inscriptions to the End of the Fifth Century B.C.E.* (Oxford: Clarendon, 1969), 20–22. It would be safe to assume that the decision of the citizens of Mylasa, decreeing punishment for the opponents of the satrap Mausollus, originated with or was instigated by the satrap himself; see Frei, *Reichsidee*, 27 n. 58, 99. In none of the other case histories from Asia Minor adduced by Frei is there a request for authorization.

[16] Frei, *Reichsidee*, 12–16, 32–34, 39–47.

future problems by getting official approval in writing. It seems exaggerated to conclude, as Frei does, that the satrap's written approval of this decree (דתה דך) was thereby taken up into the law of the empire.[17]

The importance of obtaining official clearance for matters in which the central authority had a fiscal interest is confirmed by inscriptions from the same region in which imperial taxes (βασιλικὰ τέλη) are explicitly excluded from the granting of an *ateleia* by provincial cities.[18] The steady flow of revenue into the imperial treasury could also be affected negatively by border disputes, which therefore called for intervention by the local satrap.[19] Other examples adduced by Frei from western Asia Minor are either too obscure or too incomplete to be of use.

The only non-Jewish case history presented by Frei that is of potential relevance to the issue of imperial authorization of pentateuchal law is the notice about the codification of Egyptian laws by command of Darius I around 518 B.C.E. The text is written on the verso of the Demotic Chronicle (papyrus 215 of the Bilbiotèque Nationale in Paris) from the Ptolemaic period. It records that Darius ordered the satrap of Mudriya (Egypt) to appoint a commission of priests, sages (scribes), and warriors in order to codify Egyptian laws in force up to the forty-fourth year of Pharaoh Amasis, that is, up to 526, about the time of the Persian conquest of the country. This stipulation falls into the category of imperial propaganda, since its intent was to emphasize Darius's respect for native Egyptian traditions. It would also have had the effect of repealing ordinances issued by Cambyses restricting the revenues of Egyptian temples,[20] and therefore serve as a *captatio benevolentiae* with the priesthood. The commission worked at it for sixteen years, and the result was written up in demotic Egyptian and "Assyrian," that is, Aramaic.[21] The authenticity and reliability

---

[17] Ibid., 14–15.

[18] See the inscriptions from Labrauna and Lagina in Caria; Frei, *Reichsidee*, 40–41, 99–10. Neither is a case of imperial authorization.

[19] E.g., the case history from Tralles in the Meander Valley (Frei, *Reichsidee*, 27 n. 58, 100); for the text, see Franciszek Sokolowsi, *Lois sacrées de l'Asie Mineure* (Travaux et mémoires 9; Paris: École française d'Athènes, 1955), 173–74. Frei (*Reichsidee*, 96–97) also lists an intervention by the satrap Struses in a border dispute between Miletus and Myus; cf. the solution by Artaphernes, satrap of Lydia, of a conflict among the Ionian cities involving a land survey (Herodotus 6.41–42). Taxation was probably an issue in both cases.

[20] This is stated explicitly in the Demotic Chronicle and is quite independent of the stories about Cambyses' sacrilegious disregard for Egyptian religion in the Greek historians, beginning with Herodotus (3.27–38).

[21] In addition to Frei, *Reichsidee*, 16–18, 47, see Wilhelm Spiegelberg, *Die sogenannte demotische Chronik des Pap. 215 der Bibliotèque Nationale zu Paris*

of the Chronicle is widely accepted and is supported by the reputation of Darius as the sixth great lawgiver of the Egyptians (Diodorus Siculus, *Hist.* 1.95.4–5).

A word of caution, however, is in order with regard to the claim that here at least we have a clear case of the compilation of traditional laws by imperial edict resulting in a fairly comprehensive code comparable to the major law collections in the Hebrew Bible. For it is possible that in this context it was more a case of patents, endowments, privileges and immunities rather than a law code in the normal sense of that term.[22] In view of the potential for internecine conflict arising out of conflicting claims in such matters, it would have been in the interests of the central government to see these issues settled. The length of time it took to settle them testifies to the tensions within Egyptian society that the pacification program of Darius sought to overcome. And, as suggested a moment ago, one of the principal objects of Darius's initiative would have been to win over the priesthood by restoring the revenues of the major temples, which Cambyses had drastically reduced. If this imperial initiative was in fact a special case, dictated by the potential for unrest following on measures adopted by Cambyses in Egypt and the Egyptian revolt at the beginning of the reign of Darius, the first of many during the two centuries of Persian rule, it suggests caution in taking it as illustrative of Persian imperial policy in general.

It is hardly coincidental that this initiative of Darius took place in the same year in which the Egyptian collaborator Udjahorresne was sent back to Egypt on a mission from Susa. The purpose of the mission was to supervise the work of restoration after the disturbances following on the death of Cambyses. Though in this matter the inscription is, understandably, vague, there were also disturbances at the beginning of the reign of Darius, for the Behistun inscription (II 7) lists Egypt among nine provinces in revolt at that time. The satrap Aryandes was confirmed in office and remained in office until 510, when he was executed, according to Herodotus (4.166), for over-ambitious minting of coinage. The mission of

---

(Leipzig: Hinrichs, 1914), esp. 30–32; N. J. Reich, "The Codification of the Egyptian Laws by Darius and the Origin of the 'Demotic Chronicle,'" *Mizraim* 1 (1933): 178–85; Georges Posener, *La première domination perse en Egypte* (Cairo: IFAO, 1936), 175–76; Briant, *Histoire de l'Empire Perse,* 488–500.

[22] A point made by John M. Cook, *The Persian Empire* (London: Dent, 1983), 71. Cook provides an interesting parallel to the codification of the Egyptian "laws." In 1908–1909, after the Russian occupation of Turkestan, the governor had a collection of Islamic laws put together from French codifications together with digests of case law from British India. These were written in Russian and published in the local language. See Cook, *Persian Empire,* 241 n. 13.

Udjahorresne was therefore almost certainly an important aspect of the pacification program in the early years of Darius's reign. It also prepared for the visit to Egypt of Darius, a visit that took place in 517.[23] In view of what the biblical sources tell us about the situation in the neighboring province of Judah, it is interesting to note that the goal of the mission was the restoration of the status quo ante, namely, the situation preceding the Persian conquest and the "very great turmoil" that, according to the inscription, accompanied it. The achievements of the mission reported by Udjahorresne are also of interest in view of information provided by Ezra-Nehemiah on the situation in Judah. Udjahorresne claims that, already during the reign of Cambyses, foreigners had been expelled from the state sanctuary at Sais, ritual impurities had been eliminated, legitimate cult personnel installed, traditional religious observances reinstated, and all this with the support of the Persian exchequer (lines 19–31). But the main purpose of the mission seems to have been the restoration of the "houses of life," centers of learning attached to temples (lines 50–52), and one of the principal activities of these centers of learning would have been the transcription and interpretation of the laws.[24]

In summary, the notice provided by the Demotic Chronicle does not oblige us to conclude that something of the sort also happened in the neighboring province of Judah or indeed anywhere else in the empire. On the other hand, Darius's action was part of a pacification program following on the crisis of 520–519, a crisis that was not confined to Egypt. The relevant biblical sources also attest that Judeans were affected by the events of that year and that there were expectations of the collapse of the Persian Empire and aspirations towards independence focusing on the person of Zerubbabel grandson of Jehoiachin, second-last king of independent Judah.[25] Judah was also of strategic importance on account of its proximity to Egypt, where revolt was endemic and which—in due course—proved open to penetration by Athenian land and sea forces. It is therefore at least plausible to

---

[23] See Frei, *Reichsidee,* 16–18, 47; Alan B. Lloyd, "The Inscription of Udjahorresnet: A Collaborator's Testament," *JEA* 68 (1982): 166–80; Joseph Blenkinsopp, "The Mission of Udjahorresnet and Those of Ezra and Nehemiah," *JBL* 106 (1987): 409–21; Briant, *Histoire de l'Empire Perse,* 67–71, 488–500.

[24] On this institution, see Alan H. Gardiner, "The House of Life," *JEA* 24 (1938): 157–79.

[25] Hag 2:20–23; Zech 6:9–15. Zerubbabel may have been sent to Judah with the idea of the eventual establishment of a client kingdom similar to several others within the Persian Empire. One possibility is that there were disturbances in Judah corresponding to prophetic rhetoric and that these disturbances led to the recall or execution of Zerubbabel and the end of any hope for a restoration of the kingdom.

suggest that the situation in Judah called for an intervention *of some kind* by the central administration at that time and that it may have taken a form analogous to what the Demotic Chronicle and the Udja-horresne inscription tell us happened in Egypt.

3. The Impact of Persian Imperial Policy on Jewish Civic and Religious Life

The fact remains that the only explicitly attested example of imperial interest in Jewish affairs apart from the biblical texts is the so-called Passover Papyrus from Elephantine written in 419 B.C.E. during the reign of Darius II.[26] In it a certain Hananiah informs his co-religionists in the settlement that Darius had sent an order concerning them to the satrap Arsames. The papyrus is lacunous, and its interpretation therefore remains uncertain in spite of an enormous volume of commentary. Hananiah, the bearer of the message, was certainly a Jew. If he was identical with the Hananiah mentioned in a letter written to the community leaders at Yeb by a certain Maʿuziah, his arrival in Egypt would have coincided with trouble between the Jewish garrison and the devotees of Khnum, the ram-headed god. But Hananiah is a common name, so this is no more than a possibility.[27] Alternatively, he may simply have been a secretary of Arsames who was tipping off the garrison about another regulation of concern to them that had arrived on the satrap's desk.[28] As for the content of the letter, while it is tolerably clear that it refers to the celebration of Passover even though this festival is not named in it, Hananiah was not quoting the decree verbatim and almost certainly not *in extenso*. The decree may therefore have dealt with religious observances in general, or it may have insisted that the garrison align its religious observances with Jerusalemite praxis. In any case, the decree was not stipulating a new observance, since we know that Passover was already being celebrated in the community, and the emphasis in the letter on the precise *timing* of the

---

[26] AP 21 in CAP, 60–65; more recently in *TAD* 1:54.

[27] For the reference to Hananiah, see AP 38, lines 7–8; CAP, 135–36. Porten (*Archives from Elephantine: The Life of an Ancient Jewish Military Colony* [Berkeley and Los Angeles: University of California Press, 1968], 128–31, 279–82) offers two options as to the identity of this Hananiah: first, that Hananiah is identical with Hanani, brother of Nehemiah (Neh 1:1; 7:2); and second, that he was a person commissioned by the Jewish authorities in Judah or Babylon to petition Darius II to allow the Elephantine garrison to celebrate Passover over the objections of the Khnum priesthood.

[28] A suggestion of Morton Smith, "Jewish Religious Life in the Persian Period," *CHJ* 1:230–33.

festival may have been the one point on which Hananiah's fellow-Jews needed a reminder.[29]

Relations with the civic and religious authorities in Judah are further illustrated by a letter written in 408 B.C.E. by Jedaniah, a leader of the garrison and probably a priest, to Bagavahya (Bagoas) governor of Judah requesting permission to rebuild the temple of Ya'u destroyed in a pogrom three years earlier.[30] Permission was received in a brief memorandum (זכרן) dispatched jointly by Bagavahya in Jerusalem and Daliyeh son of Sanballat of Samaria couched in language reminiscent of the edict of Darius in Ezra 7.[31] The Elephantine correspondence therefore suggests that we take the official documents cited in Ezra seriously as potential historical source material. And, incidentally, the correspondence between Yeb and Jerusalem adds plausibility to the view that Ezra's jurisdiction was not confined to Jews resident in the province of Judah (יהוד מדינתא), a point on which the firman cited in Ezra 7 is ambiguous (Ezra 7:14, 25).

Turning now to the biblical texts, some have found a similar instance of imperial interest in and supervision of local cults in the allusion to a royal disposition (מצות המלך) concerning Levitical liturgical musicians in Neh 11:22–23. Use of the term אמנה suggests that the decree dealt with their day-to-day obligations as temple personnel rather than their economic support. Since the Uzzi whom the same note mentions as overseer of the musicians appears to have been the great-grandson of Mattaniah, the precentor mentioned in the list immediately preceding (11:17), this note must have been written at least half a century later than the list in Neh

---

[29] A Bodleian Library papyrus and Berlin Papyrus 10679 refer to persons "making" Passover in Yeb in the early fifth century B.C.E.; see *TAD* 4:158, 174. The former is a letter asking a certain Hoshaiah when he will be celebrating Passover, which, as Morton Smith pointed out ("Jewish Religious Life," 230), seems to imply that in that period and in that place the timing was up to the individual household.

[30] AP 30 (CAP, 108–19) with the duplicate copy AP 31 (CAP, 119–22; *TAD* 1:68–75). The destruction of the temple is referred to at greater length in a petition addressed to the satrap Arsames ca. 410 B.C.E. (AP 27; CAP, 97–103).

[31] AP 32 (CAP, 122–24). Estimates of the historicity of the documents cited in Ezra should take account of the rather close parallels between the edicts permitting the rebuilding of the temples in Yeb and Jerusalem. Both are memoranda (זכרן, line 1; cf. דכרונה, Ezra 6:2) concerning the cult of the God of heaven (lines 3–4; cf. Ezra 6:9–10). In this type of official document the wording of the petition is routinely repeated in the response; e.g., the reference to "Waidrang that reprobate" in the Elephantine letter (line 6; cf. AP 30.6–7) and the return of the sacred vessels in Ezra-Nehemiah (Ezra 6:5; cf. 5:14–15). Finally, both documents stipulate that the temple is to be rebuilt "in its place" (באתרה, line 8; cf. על־אתרה, Ezra 6:7).

11:3–21, therefore close to the period usually assigned to the composition of Chronicles. In that case, as some commentators suspect, the king in question could be David and the מצוה could refer to a disposition of David with respect to the Jerusalem liturgy, as in 1 Chr 25 (cf. Neh 12:24, 47). On the other hand, the author of Chronicles never refers *tout court* to David as המלך, and even if the author had David in mind, this may be one of several instances of Chronicles backdating contemporaneous practice to the time of David. The balance of probability, supported by other well-known examples of Persian policy, therefore, favors a reference to a Persian king, perhaps Darius II, as in the "Passover papyrus," rather than to David as the originator of the decree.[32]

An even later note added to the above refers to a certain Pethahiah of the Zerah phratry who served as the royal adviser or counselor (ליד המלך, "at the king's hand") in matters concerning the people (Neh 11:24). The absence of the Zerah phratry from the lists in Ezra-Nehemiah would be consistent with the suggestion that this individual held a position at the Persian court charged with the task of advising the central administration on the king's Jewish subjects in general. If that is so, his function may have resembled that assigned to Ezra in chapter seven of the homonymous book.

This brings us to the decree of Artaxerxes[33] mandating Ezra's mission (Ezra 7:11–26). Its status as potential historical source material calls for discriminating judgment. Most scholars now admit that it has been extensively edited, perhaps even composed, by a Jewish scribe. Pointing in this direction is the reference to "Judah and Jerusalem," which is standard in Chronicles, the allusions to offerings freely made and people freely offering themselves (the verb התנדב, a favorite of the author of Chronicles), the order in which sacrificial animals are listed, "the wisdom of your God that is in your hand" (7:25) paralleling "the law of your God that is in your hand" (7:14) and reflecting a well-known Deuteronomic topos (cf. Deut 4:6), and the teaching function of judges and

---

[32] This is somewhat different from the conclusion reached in my *Ezra-Nehemiah: A Commentary* (OTL; Philadelphia: Westminster, 1988), 327, where I opted for a Davidic reference that the author of the following note (11:24) understood to refer to the Persian king. Understandably, some of the major recent commentators find it difficult to decide; e.g., David J. A. Clines, *Ezra, Nehemiah, Esther* (NCB; Grand Rapids, Mich.: Eerdmans, 1984), 218–19; and H. G. M. Williamson, *Ezra, Nehemiah* (WBC; Waco, Tex.: Word, 1985), 352–53. Wilhelm Rudolph (*Esra und Nehemia samt 3 Esra* [HAT 20; Tübingen: Mohr Siebeck, 1949], 187) is quite clear that the reference is to the Persian king.

[33] Either the first or the second ruler of that name, therefore the mission is to be dated either 458 or 398 B.C.E. For arguments in favor of the earlier date, see my *Ezra-Nehemiah*, 139–44.

magistrates (Ezra 7:25; cf. Deut 16:18; 2 Chr 19:4–11), to mention only
the more obvious examples. But redaction or even composition by a
Jewish scribe does not necessarily deprive the decree of historical value,
and its consistency with what we know of Persian imperial policy—in
particular the support of local cults and employment of native commissioners such as Udjahorresne and Histiaeus—suggests that it may be
unwise to dismiss it out of hand.[34]

In any case, we are concerned here only with Ezra's mission to
inquire about the law (v. 14), the command to appoint judges and magistrates to administer it and to instruct those who are unfamiliar with it,
and the graded punishments established for noncompliance (vv. 25–26).
We may begin by stating some negative conclusions. First, the phrase
דת אלהך די בידך (literally "the law of your God which is in your hand,"
7:14) refers not to a document Ezra brought with him from Babylon but
to Ezra's charge and therefore should be translated "the law with which
you are entrusted." It is not a new law; in fact, it is later made clear that
the law in question should be familiar to Ezra's co-religionists throughout
the Trans-Euphrates satrapy (7:25). Second, Ezra's mission is not a case of
imperial authorization in the sense defined by Frei since, as far as we
know and unlike Nehemiah's mission, it is not presented as responding
to a request from a Jewish individual or a Jewish community. More than
a century ago, however, Eduard Meyer suggested that the decree was written by a Jewish official with the precise purpose of submitting it for
approval to the Persian imperial authorities.[35] We might take this further
and suggest that it may have been a case of manipulating the authorities
in distant Susa in the interests of the rigorist party in the province, among
whom a certain Shecaniah and the חרדים ("tremblers") are mentioned
(Ezra 9:4; 10:2–3). These possibilities remain open, but it is also possible
that the decree was the expression of a direct imperial initiative occasioned by the critical situation in the western reaches of the empire,
including the revolt of Inaros in Egypt (460–454), which resulted in the
defeat and death of the satrap Achaemenes, and a formidable Athenian
fleet of two hundred vessels prowling the Aegean. Third, unlike the situation in Egypt under Darius I as described in the Demotic Chronicle, there
is no mention of the codification of laws. The laws already in existence
and deemed to be familiar must be taught, an activity that would

---

[34] The range of opinion on the historical status of the decree is reviewed in Frei,
Reichsidee, 51–61.

[35] Eduard Meyer, *Die Entstehung des Judenthums* (Halle: Max Niemeyer, 1896),
60–68, on which see Kurt Galling, *Studien zur Geschichte Israels im Persischen
Zeitalter* (Tübingen: Mohr Siebeck, 1964), 165–66.

presumably include interpretation (cf. Neh 8:7–8). A point of unclarity is the extent of Ezra's jurisdiction during the mission, whether limited to יהוד מדינתא (Ezra 7:14) or extending to the Jewish ethnos throughout the Trans-Euphrates satrapy (v. 25). Certainty is unattainable, but—as noted earlier—the request for permission to rebuild the Jewish temple at Yeb addressed to Jerusalem and the positive response of the latter (AP 30 and 32) suggest a broad range of influence for the civic and religious authorities in Jerusalem at that time and therefore support the wider range of Ezra's mandate.[36]

In Frei's discussion of Ezra's law as a case history of imperial authorization, a great deal hangs on the interpretation of the phrase "the law of your God and the law of the king" (7:26).[37] The issue here is whether the reference is to two distinct laws, that is, the Jewish law sanctioned by the God of Israel and Persian law expressing the will of the sovereign; or to Jewish law alone with a distinction between sacral or cultic law on the one hand and civil law on the other; or, finally, to Jewish law alone but now sanctioned by and subsumed under the supreme authority of the king and therefore the official law for Jews in the satrapy.[38] In view of the acknowledged fact that we do not have in front of us a transcript of the royal firman, we must introduce a further complication. The Jewish editor or redactor of the document, perhaps the author of Chronicles or someone belonging to the "Chronistic school," may have understood the reference to the law in a way rather different from the chancellery office in which—on the hypothesis of a genuine nucleus— it originated. In his account of Jehoshaphat's reign, the author of Chronicles records the establishment of a judicial system in which the chief priest was in charge of "the matter of YHWH" (דבר־יהוה) and a Judean prince was responsible for "the matter of the king" (דבר־המלך, 2 Chr 19:8–11), which sounds suspiciously similar to "the law of your God and the law of the king" in Ezra 7:26. Another parallel to the edict in the Chronicles passage is the remark that observance of the laws has the purpose of deflecting the divine anger (קצף, 2 Chr 19:10; Ezra 7:23). Elsewhere the author of Chronicles makes the same distinction between

---

[36] There are no grounds at all for supposing that the edict was imposing the Jewish law on the entire satrapy, Jews and Gentiles alike, as argued by Michael Heltzer, "The Right of Ezra to Demand Obedience to 'the Laws of the King' from Gentiles of the V Satrapy," *ZABR* 4 (1998): 192–96. "All the people in the Trans-Euphrates satrapy" is modified by the phrase immediately following, "all who are familiar with the laws of your God" (7:25).

[37] Frei, *Reichsidee,* 51–61.

[38] For bibliographical references, see ibid., 20 n. 34, 52–53.

spheres of law but without distinct jurisdictions (1 Chr 26:32).[39] But even
making all due allowance for such editorial elaboration, the fact that the
Jewish law is the only one mentioned in the decree (7:14, 21, 25) and that
the penalties for infraction of the laws, listed in descending order of sever-
ity, are characteristic of Persian rather than Jewish penal practice, suggests
the conclusion that the Jewish law that Ezra was authorized to enforce is
now invested with the absolute authority of the monarch and therefore is,
in effect, royal Persian law as far as Jews in the satrapy are concerned.

4. Ezra's Law and the Laws in the Pentateuch

If this conclusion is accepted, the question remains to be asked what
relation, if any, exists between Ezra's law and the Pentateuch, or at least
the legal content of the Pentateuch. The author of Ezra 7 clearly wishes
us to understand that "the law of your God" (דת אלהך, 7:14, 26; also in
the plural, 7:25) or "the law of the God of heaven" (דתא די־אלה שמיא,
7:12, 21) mentioned in the decree is identical with the law of Moses (7:6)
with which, according to the preface to the decree, Ezra as priest and
scribe is said to be professionally concerned (7:10).[40] In Jewish tradition
the mission of Ezra is understood in the sense that Ezra restored the law
of Moses, the written copy of which had either been burned in the sack of
Jerusalem (2 Esd 14:21–48) or had fallen into neglect and desuetude (*b.
Sukkah* 20a). If Moses had not preceded him, we are told, Ezra would have
been worthy to bring Torah into the world (*b. Sanh.* 21b). Wellhausen
stood this tradition on its head by arguing that the Pentateuch, or rather

---

[39] Similar distinctions are made in the Demotic Chronicle between the law of
Pharaoh, temple law, and the law of the people (i.e., civic law). See Spiegelberg,
Die sogenannte demotische Chronik, 30–32.

[40] The responsibility of the priest for torah, religious instruction, is well-attested in
Deuteronomy; see also Jer 18:18 and the parallel in Ezek 7:26 ("*torah* must not per-
ish from the priest"). Scribes, probably associated with priests, were responsible for
the drafting of laws; see, e.g., Jeremiah's denunciation of the false pen of the scribes
who have turned the law into a lie (Jer 8:8). Hans Heinrich Schaeder, *Esra der
Schreiber* (Tübingen: Mohr Siebeck, 1930), 39–59, who accepted the substantial
authenticity of the Artaxerxes edict, understood the reference to Ezra as ספר in Ezra
7:12, 21, by analogy with the Akkadian *šāpirum,* in the sense of a high official at the
Persian court, a kind of High Commissioner for Jewish affairs. While Rolf Rendtorff
("Esra und das 'Gesetz,'" *ZAW* 96 [1984]: 165–84) is chiefly concerned to deny that
Neh 8 deals with the same law as the one mentioned in Ezra 7, in the context of the
Persian period he makes too categoric a distinction between secular and religious
law. It is also difficult to see how "the law [דת] of your God" (Ezra 7:14, 26) could
exclude religious law, especially in view of the well-documented imperial concern
for cultic matters. The term דת clearly means תורה in Esth 3:8 and Dan 6:6.

the Hexateuch, was produced in Babylon, brought to Judah by Ezra in 458
B.C.E., and promulgated on the first day of the seventh month in 444 B.C.E.,[41]
and this view of the matter, or something like it, became, at least for a time,
part of the received wisdom.

A critical approach, however, cannot simply assume that either the Pentateuch with its narratives and laws or the legal content of the Pentateuch
alone was in place whole and entire either at the time of Ezra's putative
mission or at the time when the account was written. To resolve this issue
we would need a detailed study of allusions to and citations of pentateuchal
law in Ezra-Nehemiah and perhaps also 1 and 2 Chronicles. Such a study
cannot be undertaken here,[42] but some indications of the direction it would
take and some tentative conclusions may be stated. In these texts certain
actions are undertaken according to authoritative written prescription
(ככתוב, "as it is written"). Some of these reflect Deuteronomic laws, for
example, the setting up of an altar on settling in the land (Ezra 3:2; cf. Deut
27:6–7), the prohibition of marriage with native women (Ezra 9:11–12; Neh
10:31; 13:25; cf. Deut 7:3), and the exclusion from the community of certain
ethnic categories (Neh 13:1–2; cf. Deut 23:3–4). Others are more closely
related to the Priestly legislation, for example, the establishment of the daily
offering (תמיד, Ezra 3:3, 5; cf. Exod 29:38–42; Num 28:3–8), the method of
celebrating Passover (Ezra 6:19–22; cf. Exod 12:1–6, 19, 45; Lev 23:5–6; Num
9:3, 5), and the duties of priests and Levites (Ezra 6:18; cf. Exod 29; Lev 8).
Others again appear to be based on a combination of Priestly and non-
Priestly prescriptions.[43] Even stipulations widely understood to belong to a
late stage of redaction of the Pentateuch have their counterpart in Ezra-
Nehemiah and Chronicles, among them the tithe of tithes (Neh 10:38–40; cf.
Num 18:25–32) and the postponed Passover (2 Chr 30:2, 15; 35:12; cf. Num
9:6–14). It is therefore tolerably clear that the author of Ezra 7 was familiar
with what is now known as Deuteronomic and Priestly legislation, and the

---

[41] Julius Wellhausen, *Prolegomena to the History of Israel* (New York: Meridian
Books, 1957), 384–85, 405–7; trans. of *Prolegomena zur Geschichte Israels* (Berlin:
Reimer, 1878).

[42] Further developed in "Additional Note on Ezra's Law" in my *Ezra-Nehemiah*,
152–57. The references are listed and discussed in Judson R. Shaver, *Torah and the
Chronicler's History Work* (Atlanta: Scholars Press, 1989). As Sara Japhet points out
(*I and II Chronicles* [OTL; Louisville: Westminster/John Knox, 1993], 15), most of
the citations, paraphrases, and allusions have to do with the cult.

[43] This is claimed for the celebration of Sukkoth, which, according to Neh 8:18,
was carried out כמשפט ("according to [legal] custom"). See Thomas C. Römer and
Marc Z. Brettler, "Deuteronomy 34 and the Case for a Persian Hexateuch," *JBL* 119
(2000): 401–19, for whom the ספר תורת האלהים read throughout the festival (Neh
8:18) was the Hexateuch, which is so described in Josh 24:26.

Holiness Code too if it is thought to be a distinct compilation, though in
what form they were known to the author, and whether distinct or already
part of one compilation, cannot be determined.[44]

The situation becomes more complex and also more interesting when
we note in Ezra-Nehemiah injunctions and decisions justified by appeal to
legal authority but not derived from laws now in the Pentateuch. While
marital relations with the local population are forbidden following Deut
7:3–4 (Ezra 9:12; Neh 10:31; 13:23), we hear that the members of the *gôlâ*
community are to divorce wives originating outside the group and send
them packing together with their children. This coercive divorce measure is
to be implemented "according to the law" (Ezra 10:3), but it corresponds to
no law in the Pentateuch. The same holds for a number of dispositions concerning cultic matters. The great fast and confession of sin takes place on
the twenty-fourth day of the seventh month (Tishri) in Nehemiah (9:1),
which is two weeks later than the date set for Yom Kippur in the Pentateuch (Lev 16:29; 23:27–32; Num 29:7–11). Perhaps the date was not yet
fixed, as we have seen to be the case with Passover in the Jewish settlement in Elephantine. Some variations in the articles of Nehemiah's
covenant[45] vis-à-vis pentateuchal stipulations could be explained as cases
of *midrash halakah,* reflecting developments in legal theory and practice
that were certainly going on at that time. So, for example, the more passive
activity of buying on sabbaths and festivals (Neh 10:32a; cf. 13:15–22) is forbidden in addition to selling (cf. Amos 8:5), a step in the direction of the
thirty-nine forbidden activities in *m. Šabb.* 7:2. The wood offering (Neh
10:35; cf. 13:31) is necessitated by the fire on the altar (Lev 6:2, 5–6 [Eng. 6:9,
12–13]), but is the subject of explicit injunction only in the Mishnah.[46]

Other discrepancies could be due to the need to adjust laws to chang-
ing circumstances and exigencies. The temple tax is set at one third of a
shekel in Neh 10:33–34 and half a shekel in the Pentateuch (Exod
30:11–16; 38:25–26), and it continued at the same rate into the Roman
period (Josephus, *J.W.* 7.216–218; *Ant.* 18.312). Since taxation is known to

---

[44] On this subject it is almost a case of *tot capita quot sententiae.* Ulrich Kellermann ("Erwägungen zum Esragesetz," *ZAW* 80 [1968]: 373–85) may be taken to
represent the view that Ezra's law draws in the first place on Deuteronomic legislation, while Klaus Koch ("Ezra and the Origins of Judaism," *JSS* 19 [1974]: 173–97)
argued for primary influence from the Priestly law (P) and the Holiness Code (H).

[45] The arguments for locating the account of the covenant after ch. 13, and for
assigning it a later date, are discussed by Williamson, *Ezra, Nehemiah,* 325–31; and
Blenkinsopp, *Ezra-Nehemiah,* 310–13.

[46] See further David J. A. Clines, "Nehemiah 10 As an Example of Early Jewish
Biblical Exegesis," *JSOT* 21 (1981): 111–17; Michael Fishbane, *Biblical Interpretation in Ancient Israel* (Oxford: Clarendon, 1985), 129–34, 165–66, 213–16.

have an inexorable tendency to increase rather than decrease, this could suggest that the relevant pentateuchal laws are later than Nehemiah. On the other hand, the minimum age for Levites is thirty in some pentateuchal prescriptions (Num 4:3, 23, 30), twenty-five in others (Num 8:24), and twenty in Ezra 3:8 (also 1 Chr 23:24–27; 2 Chr 31:17). These variations might suggest that the age was progressively lowered to accomodate an increase in the range of Levitical responsibilities and that therefore the stage represented by Chronicles-Ezra-Nehemiah is later. But for both examples other explanations are possible.

In spite of these uncertainties, and the severe limitations of our source material, several scholars, perhaps the majority, have drawn the conclusion that Ezra's law corresponds to the legal content of the Pentateuch at a mature but not yet final stage of its evolution. This may be accepted as a plausible working hypothesis, but it would be misleading to think in terms of a direct and unilinear development of the legal traditions.[47] There may have been several different compilations accepted by different groups within Judean and diasporic Judaism evolving or devolving in different ways, a situation reflected in the legal practice of the Elephantine Jews or, much later, certain Jewish communities in the Greco-Roman period. The Ezra narrative suggests that compulsory divorce of foreign wives, not mandated by any law known to us, was an important plank in the rigorist party program, and one that its adherents claimed was to be implemented "according to the law" (Ezra 10:3). Nehemiah's covenant, which applied only to those who put their signature to it, also contained stipulations parallel to or over and above pentateuchal laws.[48] On the assumption of the basic authenticity of the Artaxerxes firman and the basic historicity of this part of the Ezra narrative, we would have to say that the law referred to may have meant different things to different parties: the king and his privy council, Ezra, and the compiler of the narrative. For the last named, it would have implied a combination of laws now designated Deuteronomic (D) and Priestly (P). As for Ezra, he would also presumably have been acquainted with these laws but would have used his mandate to put in place a less irenical and inclusive compilation than the pentateuchal laws, even if based on a certain interpretation of laws now in the Pentateuch,

---

[47] I therefore accept in principle the argument of Cornelis Houtman ("Ezra and the Law: Observations on the Supposed Relation between Ezra and the Pentateuch," *OtSt* 21 [1981]: 91–115) that the issue is too complex to allow for a simple identity between Ezra's law and pentateuchal legislation.

[48] Morton Smith, *Palestinian Parties and Politics That Shaped the Old Testament* (New York: Columbia University Press, 1971), 173–74, describes Nehemiah's sworn covenant as the first example of Jewish sectarianism.

had he been able to do so. By analogy with the codification of the Egypt-ian laws under Darius I, Artaxerxes I and his officials would have had in mind a compilation of traditional laws, with or without attached narrative, representing a compromise between different factions in Judean and dias-poric Judaism and a basis on which law and order could be maintained in Jewish communities west of the Euphrates.

That this is what actually happened when the Pentateuch finally emerged as a finished product is now being increasingly accepted. While there are hardly any detailed and concrete data in the Pentateuch pointing specifically to the Persian period,[49] several biblical scholars are now adopt-ing the "imperial authorization" explanation of the final compilation of the Pentateuch. The basis for the hypothesis is (1) the assumption that the Pen-tateuch in its final form is a product of the Persian period, and (2) the juxtaposition in the Pentateuch of mutually incompatible stipulations of law and mutually irreconcilable perspectives on law (especially D and P), which are taken to represent the same kind of compromise as the Demotic Chronicle attests was imposed on Egypt by Darius I.

Credit for being the first to apply the theory of *Reichsautorisation* to the Jewish law usually goes to Erhard Blum. He argues that the compre-hensive Deuteronomic work (his KD) and the Priestly work (his KP), with their contrasting prescriptions about such matters as the priesthood, festi-vals, tithes, and profane slaughter, were combined under pressure from the imperial authorities no later than Darius I.[50] Frank Crüsemann also sees pentateuchal law as a compromise between conflicting interests imposed by external pressure, but goes further in attempting to probe the divergent social forces at work in the province of Judah that produced this situation. He finds indications in the laws of a coalition between the temple priest-hood and independent landowners.[51] Several other scholars have taken a

---

[49] One exception are the linen trousers (מִכְנְסֵי־בַד, Exod 28:42; 39:28) worn by priests, since this article of clothing is characteristically Persian and unattested earlier.

[50] Erhard Blum, *Studien zur Komposition des Pentateuch* (BZAW 189; Berlin: de Gruyter, 1990), 333–60. Blum and Crüsemann may have reached this conclusion independently, as I myself did (see n. 54), but I am not in a position to decide the matter of priority.

[51] Frank Crüsemann, "Israel in der Perserzeit. Eine Skizze in Auseinandersetzung mit Max Weber," in *Max Webers Sicht des antiken Christentums. Interpretation und Kritik* (ed. W. Schluchter; Frankfurt: Suhrkamp, 1985), 205–32; idem, "Le Penta-teuque, Une Tora: Prolégomènes à l'Interprétation de sa Forme Finale," in *Le Pentateuque en Question* (ed. A. de Pury; Geneva: Labor et Fides, 1989), 345–54; idem, *The Torah: Theology and Social History of Old Testament Law* (trans. W. Mahnke; Minneapolis: Fortress, 1996), 339–45; trans. of *Die Torah: Theologie und Sozialgeschichte des alttestamentlichen Gesetzes* (Munich: Kaiser, 1992).

similar approach. Ernst Axel Knauf accepts the hypothesis in its broad lines, reading the Pentateuch as a monument to Persian policy with respect to minorities and religious affairs.[52] David M. Carr is aware of some of the problems but accepts the hypothesis as laid out by Blum.[53] My own view was (and, with modifications, still is) similar in the main lines and accepts that pressure from the center to consolidate the laws would have been most likely to occur as part of the reorganization and restoration carried out in successive stages by Darius I and Artaxerxes I, in both instances following on a period of political and military crisis.[54] In this connection we should mention Morton Smith's illuminating analysis of the social and religious tensions, alliances, and trade-offs within Jewish communities during the period in question. He did not refer to imperial authorization of the laws, but the role of the central government in the emergence of the Pentateuch as a compromise document between hard-liners and assimilationists is acknowledged.[55]

Before this hypothesis on the compilation of the Pentateuch becomes part of the received wisdom and achieves canonical status, some reservations should be registered. First, since there is no evidence that Jewish civil or religious authorities presented the laws for official approbation, this is not a case of imperial authorization as defined by Frei. The same is indeed true of the compilation of the Egyptian laws as described in the Demotic Chronicle. Second, we must be clear as to whether we are speaking of the Pentateuch whole and entire or the legal content of the Pentateuch. The legal compilations in the Pentateuch are inseparable from their narrative contexts and themselves contain a fair amount of narrative and historical reference, in the so-called motivation clauses, for example. Must we then suppose that the imperial authorities either mandated or authorized the juxtaposition of the larger narratives in which the legal compilations are embedded, and then checked them to make sure that they presented no threat to the *pax Persica?* Apart from the fact that there is no evidence that the Persian authorities monitored the religious literatures of the numerous peoples under their control, the idea seems inherently quite improbable.[56]

---

[52] Ernst Axel Knauf, *Die Umwelt des Alten Testaments* (Stuttgart: Katholisches Bibelwerk, 1994), 171–75.

[53] David M. Carr, *Reading the Fractures of Genesis* (Louisville: Westminster/John Knox, 1996), 327–30.

[54] Joseph Blenkinsopp, *The Pentateuch: An Introduction to the First Five Books of the Bible* (ABRL; New York: Doubleday, 1992), 239–43.

[55] Smith, *Palestinian Parties and Politics,* 119–25, 170–74.

[56] *Pace* Jean Louis Ska ("Un nouveau Wellhausen?" *Bib* 72 [1991]: 261–62), who points to several nationalistic texts in the Pentateuch dealing with the promise or

What it means is that we have no idea how the demand to produce a compromise legal document would have been implemented. Third, before the
hypothesis can be accepted in good academic conscience, we must ask
whether there are alternative and possibly better explanations for the
emergence of the Pentateuch, inclusive of its laws, as a compromise document. The existence of juxtaposed divergent and mutually incompatible
views in other biblical texts, the book of Isaiah, for instance,[57] invites us
in the first place to address the issue of editorial procedures in antiquity
and, more specifically, the practice of neutralizing by addition rather than
by deletion, before appealing to external factors. Imperial authorization of
the laws in the Pentateuch remains a *possible* hypothesis, but for the
moment no more than that.

---

conquest of the land, which he believes the Persians would have found unac-
ceptable. Maybe, if they had read them. For the same reason we may doubt that
the creation of a Pentateuch rather than a Hexateuch was due to the need to
exclude the account of the conquest of neighboring provinces and their incorpo-
ration into a "Greater Israel"; on which see, e.g., Crüsemann, "Le Pentateuque,
Une Tora," 359–60.

[57] E.g., on the destiny of foreign nations, a mission to the Gentiles, the contrasting profiles of the prophet in the narrative and the pronouncements.

"YOU SHALL APPOINT JUDGES": EZRA'S MISSION AND THE RESCRIPT OF ARTAXERXES[1]

Lisbeth S. Fried

University of Michigan

What was Ezra's mission? According to Ezra 7:11, Artaxerxes issued a decree that states in part:[2]

> And you, Ezra, according to the God-given wisdom you possess,[3] appoint magistrates and judges who would judge all the people who are in Beyond the River—all who know the law [דת] of your God and [all] who do not know, to inform them. All who would not execute the law [דתא] of your God and the law [דתא] of the king eagerly, let a judicial verdict [דינה] be executed on them: either for death, or flogging, confiscation of property, or imprisonment. (Ezra 7:25–26)[4]

---

[1] This paper has benefited from comments by Daniel Fleming, Bezalel Porten, Eugene Cruz-Uribe, and members of the Biblical Law group of the Society of Biblical Literature on an earlier draft. All errors are my own.

[2] I assume Artaxerxes II (404–358 B.C.E.); Ezra arrived in Yehud after Nehemiah's governorship. I consider the actual decree to be vv. 21–26 and the preceding verses to be the redactor's embellishment. For a discussion of these points, see my "The Rise to Power of the Judaean Priesthood" (Ph.D. diss., New York University, 2000), now in press as *The Priest and the Great King: Temple-Palace Relations in the Persian Empire* (Biblical and Judaic Studies from the University of California, San Diego; Winona Lake, Ind.: Eisenbrauns).

[3] Literally "the wisdom of your God that is in your hand." This translation is suggested by the NRSV.

[4] David Janzen ("The 'Mission' of Ezra and the Persian-Period Temple Community," *JBL* 119 [2000]: 619–43) argues that even vv. 21–26 are not authentic for several reasons. First, Janzen assumes the letter from Artaxerxes was initiated by Ezra, so he expects to see a quotation of the original request in the letter. I assume the letter was initiated by Artaxerxes. In any case, the response of Bagavahya and Daliyeh to the community at Yeb (*TAD* A4.9) does not quote the original request. Janzen argues, second, that if the mission were initiated by the king, he would not expect such detailed knowledge of the operation of the Judean cult as is present in v. 24. I agree. The list of temple officials was probably added by a redactor as

Most scholars assume Artaxerxes' command to Ezra ordered him to make the Mosaic Law code legally binding on Jews.[5] They differ on whether the command obligated only Jews in Yehud or if it included all the Jews in the entire satrapy of Beyond the River. Joseph Blenkinsopp assumes it refers to Jews in the entire satrapy.[6] H. G. M. Williamson agrees and cites as support "the fact of Achaemenid respect for the ancient laws of their peoples including religious law, and their willingness to see it put into effect as far as possible."[7] David Janzen thinks it possible that Ezra was

---

a gloss on the generic פלחי בית אלהא ("temple servants"). Janzen asserts, thirdly, that the particle די ("that") in v. 21, which introduces the command of Artaxerxes—"And from me (I, Artaxerxes the king) is placed an order to all the treasurers of Beyond-the-River *that* whatever Ezra (the priest, scribe of the law of the God of Heaven) shall ask of you, shall be done eagerly"—is nowhere used to introduce speech in any of the extrabiblical Persian-period official correspondence. He concludes the letter is not authentic. Yet, we see the same construction in *TAD* A6.13:4–5:

כעת ארשם כן אמר אנתם הנדרז עבדו לחתובסתי פקיד ורוהי

זי עד מנדת בניא זי ורוהי אספרן והדאבנו יהנפק

Now Arsames says thus: "You all, issue instruction to Ḥatubasti, official of Varuvahya, *that* he release the rent of the domains of Varuvahya in full and the accrued increment."

This construction is identical to that in v. 21 (I thank B. Porten for pointing this out to me). It is rare in biblical Hebrew, but does occur often in Persian-period texts (e.g., Esth 3:4; Job 36:24; 37:20; 1 Chr 21:18; cf. 2 Sam 24:18). It also occurs in Persian inscriptions. The Persian word *tya* ("that") introduces direct and indirect quotation (R. G. Kent, *Old Persian: Grammar, Texts, Lexicon* [AOSM 33; New Haven, Conn.: American Oriental Society, 1950], 93, 187: DB 1.32, 52; DNa 38–39; DNb 8, 10, 19). Janzen suggests, finally, that the reference to קצף (v. 23) appears "odd" since the word never appears in any extrabiblical Aramaic text. However, *xšap* is Persian from Sanskrit, *kṣap* ("night," Kent, *Old Persian,* 181), and the concept of a hostile "wrath" (*Aēšma*), the generic night-demon, is central to Zoroastrian thought (Yasna 29:2; 30:6; 48:12; cf. Mary Boyce, *The Early Period,* vol. 1 of *A History of Zoroastrianism* [Leiden: Brill, 1996], 87). For a too-often ignored discussion of the authenticity of the documents in the book of Ezra, see Bezalel Porten, "The Documents in the Book of Ezra and the Mission of Ezra" (Hebrew), *Shnaton* 3 (1978–1979): 174–96.

[5] E.g., Peter Frei, "Persian Imperial Authorization: A Summary," 5–40, in this volume (first published as "Die persische Reichsautorisation: Ein Überblick," *ZABR* 1 [1995]: 1–35). Frei states that Ezra "was ordered, among other things, to introduce a religiously based law book" ("Persian Imperial Authorization," 11). He cites as evidence Ezra 7:25–26.

[6] Joseph Blenkinsopp, *Ezra-Nehemiah: A Commentary* (OTL; Philadelphia: Westminster, 1988), 152–57.

[7] H. G. M. Williamson, *Ezra, Nehemiah* (WBC; Waco, Tex.: Word, 1985), 103–5.

sent to enforce Jewish law on all the Jews in the satrapy but that it is unlikely.[8] Lester Grabbe suggests the Achaemenids imposed it only on the province of Yehud. According to Grabbe, "it would not be surprising if local Jewish law was allowed to be enforced on the people of the Persian province Yehud."[9]

1. JUDGES AND MAGISTRATES

According to the plain meaning of the text, Ezra was to appoint judges and magistrates. That was his assignment. These judges were to judge all the people of the entire satrapy of Beyond the River (כל עמה די בעבר נהרה). They would adjudicate the cases of Jew and non-Jew alike (those who know the law and those who do not). There is no provision for separate judges for the separate ethnic groups. The same men would judge each person in the satrapy.

Contemporary documents from Egypt verify that under the Persians different ethnic groups appeared before the same judges. These judges were either royal appointees (judges of the king, *TAD* B5.1:3) or provincial appointees (judges of the province, *TAD* A5.2:4, 7).[10] In both the Elephantine archives and the Arsames letters, nearly every named judge was Persian. There were no Egyptian judges for the Egyptians, nor Jewish judges for the Jews.[11] As Bezalel Porten points out,

---

[8] Janzen ("'Mission' of Ezra," 620 n. 5) suggests that in his role as scribe, Ezra could have received a commission to enforce Jewish law upon the Jews in Beyond-the-River. Yet because there is no evidence for Persian kings sending people on missions to reform local legal practices, it is unlikely (pp. 637–43).

[9] Lester L. Grabbe, *Ezra-Nehemiah* (Old Testament Readings; New York: Routledge, 1998), 149–50. Grabbe concludes that the letter could be genuine but "in its present form is a piece of later Jewish propaganda" (p. 153).

[10] The distinction between royal and provincial judges refers to the mechanism of appointment. There is no mention of satrapal judges among the Egyptian archives. According to Herodotus (3.31), "royal judges are a picked body of men among the Persians, who hold office till death or till some injustice is detected in them." The judges for the satrapy are royal judges and appointed by the king; provincial judges are appointed by the governors. In Babylonia, beginning with Hammurabi's rule, judges for the major Babylonian cities and the areas around them were appointed by the king. They were called "judges of the king," and their seals titled them "servant of King NN." Judges for the smaller cities were appointed by the royally appointed provincial governors. See R. Harris, "On the Process of Secularization under Hammurapi," *JCS* 15 (1961): 117–20; J. N. Postgate, *Early Mesopotamia: Society and Economy at the Dawn of History* (London: Routledge, 1992), 277.

[11] Most situations that we would consider "legal" did not involve a judge. Sales and inheritances of goods, land, and offices were handled through contracts written

"Judges" appeared regularly in the contracts as one of the three parties before whom a complainant might bring a suit or register a complaint, the other two being lord and prefect (*TAD* B2.3:13, 24; B3.1:13, 19; B3.2:6; B3.12:28; B4.6:14; B7.1:13). In a case involving an inheritance they are called "judges of the king" [i.e., royal judges] (*TAD* B5.1:3) and in a petition seeking redress of grievances they are "judges of the province" (*TAD* A5.2:4, 7). When named, they were always Persian—Pisina (*TAD* A3.8:2), Bagadana (*TAD* A6.1:5–6), Damidata (*TAD* B2.2:6), Bagafarna and Nafaina (*TAD* A 5.2:6)—and once Babylonian—Mannuki.[12]

There were no Egyptian judges.[13] Moreover, the word translated "investigator" in a judicial context (*TAD* A4.2:3) is the Persian word *patifrasa,* meaning "investigator, examiner." The use of a Persian title for the office implies Persian officials and a Persian juridical process at both the satrapal and provincial levels. In addition to the judge and investigator, two other officials were involved in the Persian-period judicial system. The last two lines of the draft petition for reconstruction of the temple of YHW in Elephantine reads:

יתעבד מן דיניא תיפתיא גושכיא זי ממנין במדינת תשטרס
יתי[דע] למראן לקבל זנה זי אנחנה אמרן

If inquiry be made of the judges, police, and hearers who are appointed in the province of Tshetres, it would be [known] to our lord in accordance to this which we say. (*TAD* A4.5:9–10).

---

by Egyptian or Aramean scribes writing in Aramaic. See E. Seidl, *Agyptische Rechtsgeschichte der Saïten- und Perserzeit* (2d ed.; ÄF 20; Glückstadt: Augustin, 1968); Yochanan Muffs, *Studies in the Aramaic Legal Papyri from Elephantine* (Leiden: Brill, 1969).

[12] Bezalel Porten, *The Elephantine Papyri in English: Three Millennia of Cross-Cultural Continuity and Change* (Leiden: Brill, 1996), 136 n. 19.

[13] Those with Persian names were of Persian descent. Neither Egyptians, nor Arameans and Jews living in Egypt, tended to take Persian names. The Hermopolis letters (*TAD* A2.1–7) show that Arameans and Jews took Egyptian names, but not Persian ones. The more than fifty names cited there include Jewish, Aramean, and Egyptian names—but not Persian. Examination of all the Aramaic documents from Elephantine reveals only one Egyptian who gave his son a Persian name: Bagadata son of Psamshek (*TAD* B4.3:24; B4.4:20); one Aramean: Varyzata son of Bethelzabad (B3.9:11); and one Jew: Arvaratha son of Yehonatan (*TAD* B4.4:21), out of more than a thousand names. This strongly implies that those in Egypt with Persian names were Persian.

The Aramaic word for "police" is תִּיפְתָיֵא, from the Old Persian **tipati-*.[14] These men are listed in Dan 3:2 at the end of a list of officials that begins with the satrap. The Aramaic word for "hearers" is גֻּשְׁכִיָא, from the Old Persian **gaušaka*. These were known in classical sources as the "king's ears," that is, the intelligence officers.[15] The use of Persian loanwords suggests a completely Persian judicial system in the Egyptian satrapy, with provincial judges, police, and intelligence officers appointed by the Persian provincial governors.

Conditions would have been the same in the Persian satrapy of Beyond the River and the Persian province of Yehud. A completely Persian judicial system would have been installed in the satrapy Beyond the River with Persian judges and magistrates. Governors would have appointed the provincial officials, but the king, or his agent, would have appointed those at the satrapal level—the royal judges. This was Ezra's task: to appoint the royal judges for the satrapy Ebar Nahara.[16]

2. The Judicial System in Antiquity

2.1. Egypt

What law did these Persian judges enforce? The phrase "the law (דָּתָא) of your God and the law (דָּתָא) of the king" in Artaxerxes' Rescript (Ezra 7:26) parallels the phrase in the Demotic Chronicle 225: "the law [*hp*] of Pharaoh and of the temple."[17] According to the Chronicle, Darius ordered the satrap of Egypt to send to him in Susa "wise individuals from the ranks of warriors, priests, and scribes."[18] These men were to compile "the law (*hp*) of Pharaoh,

---

[14] Porten, *Elephantine Papyri,* 136 n. 20; idem, *Archives from Elephantine: The Life of an Ancient Jewish Military Colony* (Berkeley and Los Angeles: University of California Press, 1968), 50 n. 83.

[15] Porten, *Elephantine Papyri,* 136 n. 21; idem, *Archives,* 50 n. 84.

[16] We know that the king did not appoint the royal officers himself, but rather his agents did. After the conquest of Babylon and after Cyrus's triumphal entrance into the city, the Nabonidus Chronicle continues (III:20; A. Kirk Grayson, "Chronicle 7: The Nabonidus Chronicle," *Assyrian and Babylonian Chronicles* [Winona Lake, Ind.: Eisenbrauns, 2000], 110):

ᵐGubaru ˡᵘpāḫtašú ˡᵘpāḫ(at)ūtiᵐᵉˢ ina Bābiliₓⁱ ipteqid.

Gubaru, his governor, appointed the officials in Babylon.

[17] Wilhelm Spiegelberg, *Die sogenannte Demotische Chronik des Pap. 215 der Bibliothèque Nationale de Paris* (Leipzig: Hinrichs, 1914), col. C, line 11.

[18] See Donald Redford, "The So-Called 'Codification' of Egyptian Law under Darius I," in the present volume for a discussion of this tripart division of the elite into warriors, priests, and scribes, as well as a discussion of the tripartite division of law. The scribes were involved in recording and archiving court cases.

the temples, and the people" in force in the country at the time of the Persian conquest.[19] While often translated "law," the basic meaning of the word *hp* is "legal right" or "customary observance or act."[20] Bontty has shown that *hp* most often refers to tradition, right action, the norm.[21] These norms were to be written in both Aramaic and demotic, the Aramaic presumably for the satrapal chancellery, and the demotic presumably for the people of Egypt. According to this papyrus, Darius collected and codified the customs and traditions (*hpw*) that operated in Egypt prior to the Persian conquest.

What was the purpose in codifying Egyptian custom and tradition? Was it to assist in the governance of Egypt? To answer this question, it is necessary to understand the nature of law and the role of law codes in antiquity. This topic has received a great deal of research.[22] Martin Buss distinguishes two types of law: natural and positive.[23] Natural law "expresses an intrinsic morality based on the presence of inner connections between participants in reality," whereas positive law "expresses a lawgiver's free will, independent from others."[24] That is, natural law is grounded in a socially constructed inner morality, based on perceived reality. Positive law can be changed on a whim.

In Pharaonic Egypt, the source of positive law was Pharaoh.[25] Pharaonic law, or the *hp* of the pharaoh, refers to the pronouncements of the king. A comprehensive study of judicial cases dating from the Old to the New Kingdom shows that a reference to a specific ruling (*hp*) was a reference to a royal edict.[26] David Lorton cites several examples from texts from Deir el-Medina:

---

[19] Spiegelberg, *Demotische Chronik.*

[20] Eugene Cruz-Uribe, "Cambyses and the Temples in Egypt," unpublished manuscript, citing C. Nims, "The Term *hp*, 'Law,' 'Right,' in Demotic," *JNES* 7 (1948): 243–60. I thank Professor Cruz-Uribe for letting me see his manuscript. See also Redford, "So-Called 'Codification,'" in this volume.

[21] M. M. Bontty, "Conflict Management in Ancient Egypt: Law As a Social Phenomenon" (Ph.D. diss., University of California, Los Angeles, 1997).

[22] See recently, Bernard M. Levinson, ed., *Theory and Method in Biblical and Cuneiform Law: Revisions, Interpolation, and Development* (JSOTSup 181; Sheffield: Sheffield Academic Press, 1994), and references there.

[23] Martin Buss, "Legal Science and Legislation," in ibid., 88–90.

[24] Ibid., 88.

[25] This blanket statement should be modified depending on the degree of centralization in Egypt. See, for example, Aristide Théodorides, "La 'Coutume' et la 'Loi' dans l'Egypte Pharaonique," *Recueils de la Societé Jean Bodin* (1990): 39–47.

[26] David Lorton, "The Treatment of Criminals in Ancient Egypt through the New Kingdom," *JESHO* 20 (1977): 2–64; idem, "Legal and Social Institutions of Pharaonic Egypt," *CANE* 1:345–62, esp. 356.

1. "Now, 'give the goods to the burier', so says it, namely the law [*ḥp*] of Pharaoh." (P.Cairo 58092, recto, 10–11)
2. "Now, Pharaoh (Life! Prosperity! Health!), has said, 'Let each man do his desire with his goods.'" (P.Turin 2021, recto, 2, 11)
3. "Now, Pharaoh (l.p.h.) says, 'Give the *sfr* to each woman for her (own use).'" (P.Turin 2021, recto, 3, 4–5)[27]

These statements refer to royal pronouncements or decrees (*wḏ-nsw*). Yet such references were not the norm. Royal pronouncements, or the *ḥpw* of the pharaoh, were on an ad hoc basis; they would not have formed a law code.[28] The case of Peteesi is more typical of the judicial system. It deals with events from the reign of Psammetichus I through Cambyses.[29] Peteesi was a priest at the temple of Amun at Teuzoi (El-Hîbeh) under Darius I. According to Peteesi's petition, every wrong done his family (and there were many over the generations) necessitated a trip down river to plead the case to the district governor. The governor heard both sides and meted

---

[27] Lorton, "Treatment of Criminals," 63.

[28] See Redford, "So-Called 'Codification.'" *Pace* Lorton, "Treatment of Criminals," 63. Lorton suggests that Egypt had written law codes, but they haven't been discovered yet. According to Lorton: "Since these citations occur in statements to the court, it seems doubtful that they are verbatim quotations, but rather that they are references to the substance of the *ḥpw* in question. The fact that such references are made, however, greatly confirms the impression that all areas of law were treated by detailed written statutes of royal origin in ancient Egypt, and that the courts did not operate with a 'traditional,' unwritten law." In my opinion, these three examples (the only ones he brings) cannot show either that laws were written or that these royal pronouncements covered every aspect of law. Lorton also cites Diodorus Siculus (1.75) as evidence, but Diodorus wrote during the time of Julius Caesar. The only law code in Egypt I know stems from Ptolemaic times (cf. Schafik Allam, "Réflexions sur le 'code legal' d'Hermopolis dans l'Égypt ancienne," *ChrEg* 61 [1986]: 50–75; P. W. Pestman, "L'origine et extension d'un manuel de droit égyptien," *JESHO* 26 [1983]: 14–21; K.-T. Zauzich, "Weitere Fragmente eines juristischen Handbuches in demotischer Schrift," *EVO* 17 [1994]: 327–32. But cf. Redford, "So-Called 'Codification,'" for a discussion of these codes. See also N. Shupak, "A New Source for the Study of the Judiciary and Law of Ancient Egypt: 'The Tale of the Eloquent Peasant,'" *JNES* 51 [1992]: 1–18).

[29] F. L. Griffith, "The Petition of Peteesi," in vol. 3 of *Catalogue of the Demotic Papyri in the John Rylands Library, Manchester* (ed. F. L. Griffith; John Rylands Library 9; Manchester and London: John Rylands University Library of Manchester, 1909). The following remarks are true whether or not the petition is fictitious (see Günter Vittmann, "Eine misslungene Dokumentenfälschung: Die 'Stelen' des Peteese I (P. Ryl. 9, XXI–XXIII)," *EVO* 17 [1994]: 301–15; idem, *Der demotische Papyrus Rylands 9, Teil I and II* (Ägypten und Altes Testament 38; Wiesbaden: Harrassowitz, 1998).

out his decision. He cited no law, he referred to no royal pronouncement. The literary Tale of the Eloquent Peasant also illustrates the judicial system.[30] A peasant, wronged, took his case to the district head, who personally adjudicated it. No law is cited.

According to myth, Pharaoh was Legislator, the only source of positive law. In fact, the pharaoh delegated his power to a hierarchy of officials; district heads could compose edicts in the name of the king. Pharaoh—and his agents—bore the responsibility for every aspect of government. This included "the direction of the economy, the administration of justice, the maintenance of civil order, the defense of the realm, and the organization of the divine cult."[31] This was true in the Persian period as well.[32] In Pharaonic times, the vizier headed the official hierarchy; in Persian times, the satrap played the role of vizier, while the Great King in Susa played Pharaoh.[33] The hierarchical aspect of Egyptian law did not change with the advent of the Persians; Persian officials simply took it over.

Under the pharaohs, there was no professional judiciary. Pharaoh or his agents judged or appointed others to do so on an ad hoc basis; litigants argued their own cases. From the time of the emergence of the state, the authorities in a district (both religious and civil) met to decide cases.[34] In a few cases a single judge would decide. As there were no professional judges, there was no professional school. District officials judged according to previous legal decisions in their district, custom, and their own ideas of fairness and right (Ma'at). They also attended to the occasional edict from the king, if applicable. This is explicit in a text dated to the third year of Neb-kheperu-Re Antef, founder of the Seventeenth Dynasty. An official at the temple of Min at Koptos had committed a crime. The text of this royal decree was found inscribed on the temple door. It reads as follows:

> The king [Pharaoh Antef] commands the royal seal-bearer and first of the registry of Koptos Min-em-hat [the chief civil authority at Koptos], the king's son and commandant of Koptos Qi-nen [the chief military

---

[30] Shupak, "New Source."

[31] Alan B. Lloyd, cited in Lorton, "Legal and Social Institutions," 1:354.

[32] This aspect of Egyptian law under native and Persian pharaohs is discussed in Bernadette Menu, "Les juges égyptiens sous les dernières dynasties indigènes," in *Récherches sur l'histoire juridique, économique et sociale de l'ancienne Égypt* (2 vols.; Cairo: IFAO, 1998), 2:237.

[33] The role of satrap as vizier is detailed in ch. 4 ("Temple-Palace Relations in Egypt") of my dissertation, "The Rise to Power of the Judaean Priesthood" (= *The Priest and the Great King*).

[34] Schafik Allam, "Richter," *LÄ* 5:245–47.

authority at Koptos], the royal seal-bearer, stolist of Min and scribe of the temple Nerfer-hotep, the entire army of Koptos, and the lay priesthood of the temple in its entirety:

> Behold, this command is brought to you to inform you with regard to (the fact) that my majesty, life!, prosperity!, health!, has sent the scribe and god's seal-bearer of Amun si-Amun, and the elder of the portal Amun-user, to perform an audit in the temple of Min with regard to (the fact) that the lay priesthood of the temple of my father Min approached my majesty, l., p., h., saying, "An evil matter has reached the point of happening in this temple. An enemy has been taken (in) by ... Teti son of Min-hotep."

Let him be expelled from the temple of my father Min....[35]

The king commanded royal officials to hear the case. These were not professional judges but highly placed individuals in the king's court. The king dictated the punishment. This illustrates normal practice under the pharaohs. The district head—or his surrogate—conducted the investigations (here termed an "audit"). The district head—or his surrogate—would judge the case, determine the facts of the matter, and mete out the punishment. He based his decisions on his own understanding of what was appropriate in the matter before him. Laws were not cited.

2.2. MESOPOTAMIA

The Egyptian legal system differed little from that of the countries of the Fertile Crescent. Positive law in Mesopotamia resulted from the king's decree or from the decree of his agents, the royally appointed mayors, and provincial governors.[36] This was so, even though Mesopotamia had a tradition of local assemblies (*puḫru*) that Egypt did not have. Assemblies did not create law. A search among the Neo-Babylonian and Persian documents for the Akkadian terms *puḫru* ("assembly") and *paḫāru* ("to assemble") reveals this institution's purpose.[37] A *puḫru* was called for judicial decisions only: a sheep was stolen, or land needed to be reassigned.

---

[35] Lorton, "Treatment of Criminals," 19–20. Numerous onerous punishments are ordered by the king, but I do not detail them here.

[36] For early data on Babylon, see J. N. Postgate, *Early Mesopotamia: Society and Economy at the Dawn of History* (London: Routledge, 1992), 277; for later data, see ch. 2, "Temple-Palace Relations in Babylonia," of my dissertation, "The Rise to Power of the Judaean Priesthood" (= *The Priest and the Great King*).

[37] I am indebted to Martha Roth, Tim Collins, and Linda McLarnan of the Chicago Oriental Institute for their help in searching their database.

The parties to the transaction testified before judges, who gave their opinion. The scribe drew up the case; witnesses signed the document to certify that the matter had occurred and the decision rendered as described. The parties called to testify in the case did not sign the document as witnesses to the trial, although the same term is used (*mukinnu*). Members of the assembly (*puḥru*) who signed the tablet did not speak during the proceedings. They simply witnessed the trial and its outcome. There were often between twenty and thirty men signing as witnesses to a proceeding. These men formed the *puḥru*.[38]

The fact that there were no legislative assemblies means there was no occasion when an assembly met to discuss, for example, a new law, a new tax, or a new canal.[39] There is no hint of self-rule in any of these texts. The king, provincial governor, mayor, or temple-head made the decisions regarding these matters. The district leader called an assembly to hear the decision and to rubber-stamp its assent, but the assembly did not contribute to the decision-making process. There is no evidence of local participation in city governance in Mesopotamia prior to the Greek conquest.[40] In both Mesopotamia and Egypt, the source of positive law was the king or his surrogates, the local governors and mayors.

3. The Role of Law Codes

Darius collected and wrote down the norms (*ḥpw*) of Egypt practiced prior to the invasion of Cambyses. Perhaps he or his successors did the same in Yehud. Egypt had no tradition of written law codes, but in the countries of the Fertile Crescent, law collections were common.

---

[38] The only exceptions to this comes from literary texts (cf. Marc Van de Mieroop, *The Ancient Mesopotamian City* [Oxford: Clarendon, 1997], 118–41, with bibliography; idem, "The Government of an Ancient Mesopotamian City," in *Priests and Officials in the Ancient Near East* [ed. K. Watanabe; Heidelberg: Universitätsverlag C. Winter, 1999], 139–61; John Bloom, "Ancient Near Eastern Temple Assemblies" [doctoral diss., Annenberg Research Institute, 1992]; I thank Victor Hurowitz for pointing out this dissertation to me.)

[39] Van de Mieroop suggests that this may be an accident of scribal practices. He points out that Mesopotamian records are primarily concerned with the transfer of property, and no exchanges took place between government and citizenry (*Mesopotamian City*, 120). This cannot be the whole story. Decision-making powers belonged to the king. Whether or not citizens advised, the responsibility was the king's, or the king's surrogate. If citizens advised, this advice would not have been given publicly, but in private audience.

[40] *Pace* Janzen ("'Mission' of Ezra"), who cites an active role for local assemblies, but the data he provides all stem from the Hellenistic period.

They proclaimed the rulers' concern "to make justice prevail in the land, to abolish the wicked and the evil, to prevent the strong from oppressing the weak."[41] These law codes, inscribed on stelae set up in temples or in the marketplace or buried as foundation deposits in temple walls, demonstrated the ruler's concern to establish truth and justice. The Code of Hammurabi (ca. 1750) is an oft-cited example, but only one of many such codes.[42] These codes date as far back as the laws of Ur-Nammu (ca. 2100 B.C.E.)[43] and continue into the Neo-Babylonian period (ca. 700 B.C.E.).[44] Even while new codes were promulgated, old ones were copied and studied in the scribal schools as much as a thousand years later. Dozens of copies of some codes are still extant.[45]

The term *law code* to refer to these collections is a misnomer. The goal of modern law codes is to provide a complete and comprehensive list of all the laws and prescriptions that govern a legal jurisdiction. To this end, they are continually revised and updated. In this sense, the ancient law collections are not codes. They are notoriously incomplete.[46] Whole areas of law are missing; yet, they are not updated.[47] This is because custom was the actual law that governed. Cardascia states that "the lacunas—considerable—in the legislation prove that the juridical rules, necessary for all societal life, can only be found in custom."[48] Assyriologists who study these texts have noted this.[49] As Samuel Greengus points

---

[41] Code Hammurabi, quoted from Martha Roth, *Law Collections from Mesopotamia and Asia Minor* (Atlanta: Scholars Press, 1997), 76.

[42] Raymond Westbrook counts nine separately identifiable law codes that "have come down to us, in whole or in part" plus various fragments ("Biblical and Cuneiform Law Codes," *RB* 92 [1985]: 247–64).

[43] These may stem from the time of his son Shulgi (2094–2047). See Roth, *Law Collections,* 13–22, with discussion there.

[44] Ibid., 143–49, with discussion.

[45] Ibid., 74.

[46] Westbrook, "Biblical and Cuneiform Law Codes," 43; Jean Bottéro, "The 'Code' of Ḥammurabi," in *Mesopotamia: Writing, Reasoning, and the Gods* (ed. J. Bottéro; trans. Z. Bahrani and M. Van de Mieroop; Chicago: University of Chicago Press, 1992), 161.

[47] Hittite laws may be an exception. See Westbrook, "What Is the Covenant Code?" in *Theory and Method in Biblical and Cuneiform Law: Revision, Interpolation, and Development* (ed. B. M. Levinson; JSOTSup 181; Sheffield: Sheffield Academic Press, 1994), 15–26.

[48] G. Cardascia, "La Coutume dans les Droits Cunéiformes," *Receuils de la Société Jean Bolin* (1990), 62–63.

[49] E.g. Bottéro, "Code," 161; Westbrook, "What Is the Covenant Code?" 15–26; Samuel Greengus, "Some Issues Relating to the Comparability of Laws and the

out, there are no cases directly dealing with arson, treason, theft of live-stock, surety, barter, murder, manumission, or sale.[50] As Jean Bottéro suggests, these omissions are even more surprising when placed against the tens of thousands of court cases. Problems and conflicts arise that are never mentioned in the codes.[51] Yet, the codes are not updated to account for them.

Moreover, among thousands of court cases extant, none refers to any article from these codes, even when the case deals with a subject the codes cover.[52] Indicative is the fact that many cases are resolved entirely differently than the codes suggest, as if the codes did not exist.[53] One example is the case of the hungry *nadîtu*. This case is often cited as an example of the king's role in creating positive law.[54] The text in question is a letter (extant in four copies) sent from Samsuiluna (1749–1712) to the judges of Sippar.[55] (Samsuiluna took office immediately after Ham-murabi's death, and so soon after the erection of the Hammurabi's Code in Babylon.) The letter is a response to two problems the judges had put before the king. One problem concerns *nadîtu* women cloistered without dowry or support in the temple of Shamash in Sippar. They were forced

---

Coherence of the Legal Tradition," in *Theory and Method in Biblical and Cuneiform Law: Revisions, Interpolation, and Development* (ed. B. M. Levinson; JSOTSup 181; Sheffield: Sheffield Academic Press, 1994), 77–87.

[50] Greengus, "Some Issues," 78.

[51] Bottéro, "Code," 161.

[52] Ibid., 163; Roth (*Law Collections*, 5–7) notes two cases of reference to a stela. In a dispute concerning woven-textile workers, an Old Babylonian letter (A 3529 in the collections of the Oriental Institute) states, "the wages for a hired worker are recorded on the stela." A second letter also referred to a stela that publicized prices and wages (published by V. Scheil, *Mission en Susiane, Mélanges Épigraphiques* [Mémoires de la Mission Archéologique de Perse 28; Paris: LeRoux, 1939], 5 n. 3). As Westbrook points out, retrospective cancellation of debts, reorganization of the royal administration, or the fixing of prices and wages falls into the arena of royal edicts. These form an exception to the rule ("What Is the Covenant Code?" 24–25).

[53] Bottéro, "Code," 164.

[54] Sophie Lafont, "Ancient Near Eastern Laws: Continuity and Pluralism," in *Theory and Method in Biblical and Cuneiform Law: Revisions, Interpolation, and Development* (ed. B. M. Levinson; JSOTSup 181; Sheffield: Sheffield Academic Press, 1994), 99–100; R. Harris, "The *nadîtu* Laws of the Code of Hammurapi in Praxis," *Or* 30 (1961): 163–69; C. Janssen, "Samsu-Iluna and the Hungry *Nadîtums*," *Northern Akkad Project Reports* 5 (1991): 3–40; W. F. Leemans, "King Ḫammurapi As Judge," in *Symbolae iuridicae et historicae Martino David dedicatae* (ed. J. A. Ankum et al.; 2 vols.; Leiden: Brill, 1968), 2:107–29.

[55] Janssen, "Samsu-Iluna," 3–40.

to depend on the food supplies of the palace. Samsuiluna ordered that henceforth the cloister of Shamash would not admit women without adequate support: "If a *nadîtum* of Shamash is not taken care of, I ordered not to let her enter the Cloister" (lines 16, 17).[56] This contradicts number 180 of Hammurabi's Code.[57]

Lafont states that this text offers "exceptional testimony about the method whereby law was created."[58] Previous documents have shown the king acting as judge,[59] but "no text has hitherto described the concrete method whereby law was created."[60] According to Lafont, "the king rescinds the lenient rules of the Code. From now on, the support of a cloistered *nadîtum* is an exclusive duty of her family, the state refusing to care for them. Therefore, the rescript changes Hammurapian law."[61] This is also the view of Janssen, who states that "the letter bears testimony of the origin of new 'laws'."[62] In fact, the letter is no different with respect to the Code from the thousands of court cases referred to above. The letter does not refer to the Code and makes a decision as if the Code did not exist. Samsuiluna changed the criterion for admitting women to the cloister. This fact is irrelevant to the Code of Hammurabi. The Code itself remained unchanged. It continued to be copied as it was for a thousand more years. This letter shows that the king had the power to change long-standing procedure and custom. It also demonstrates the non-responsiveness of the law codes. The codes are separate from the life of the people.

Indeed, the notion of written law as binding on judges is a modern concept. It was not part of the understanding of the ancient Near East. As is often pointed out, there is no Akkadian word for "law," and such expressions as "to observe the law," "the validity of the law," or even "convicted according to law number x" never appear.[63] Benno Landsberger concluded that written law had very little influence on Babylon. F. R. Kraus concurs

---

[56] Ibid.

[57] CH no. 180: "If a father does not award a dowry to his daughter who is a cloistered *nadîtu* or a *sekretu*, after the father goes to his fate, she shall have a share of the property of the paternal estate comparable in value to that of one heir; as long as she lives she shall enjoy its use; her estate belongs only to her brothers" (Roth, *Law Collections,* 118).

[58] Lafont, "Ancient Near Eastern Laws," 97.

[59] Cf. Leemans, "King Ḫammurapi As Judge."

[60] Lafont, "Ancient Near Eastern Laws," 97.

[61] Ibid., 98.

[62] "Samsu-Iluna," 11.

[63] Benno Landsberger, "Die Babylonischen Termini für Gesetz und Recht," in *Symbolae ad Iura Orientis Antiqui* (ed. T. Folkers et al.; Leiden: Brill, 1939), 219–34.

that the Codex-Hammurabi is no lawbook but simply a series of legal decisions by Hammurabi himself in his primary role as Judge.[64] Bottéro also concludes that the articles of the Code are not *laws* but verdicts in particular cases.[65] Indeed, they are labeled "the just verdicts (*dînât mêšarim*) that Hammurabi, the experienced king, has imposed in order to establish firm discipline and good governance in his country."[66]

Hammurabi's Code contains 282 separate articles. As with all the codes, each article is structured in the form of a conditional proposition: they begin with a protasis introduced by the conjunction *šumma* ("if") and end with an apodosis describing a concrete situation in the imperfect tense. For example, article 209 states "If a man strikes a woman and thereby causes her to miscarry her fetus, he shall weigh and deliver 10 shekels of silver for her fetus."[67] This casuistic formula has caused scholars to label these articles as case law and to conclude that these laws record actual verdicts.[68]

The idea that the codes contain the actual verdicts of the king is questionable. It is now generally accepted that the codes constitute a scientific description of justice as a political ideal.[69] Their formulation, wording, and grouping are conspicuous and distinguish them from verdicts of actual cases. Normal judicial decisions are not phrased as conditional sentences. Rather, the codes are a work of literature in the true sense. They reflect a well-known cuneiform literary genre: the scientific treatise. Babylonian scholars studied and classified the world around them. The omen literature, for example, describes and categorizes the meanings of the livers of sacrificial animals; the medical literature describes, groups, and classifies diseases. All these "treatises" list groups of conditional sentences, with a protasis beginning with an "if" and an apodosis in the imperfect tense. For example, "if a man who is feverish has a burning abdomen, so that at the same time he feels neither pleasure nor dislike for food and drink, and also his body is yellow: this man has (will have) a venereal disease."[70] Or:

---

[64] F. R. Kraus, "Ein zentrales Problem des Altmesopotamischen Rechtes: Was ist der Codex Hammu-rabi?" *Genava* 8 (1960): 284.

[65] Bottéro, "Code," 47.

[66] Cited in ibid.

[67] Cited in Roth, *Law Collections,* 122.

[68] E.g., Greengus, "Legal and Social Institutions of Ancient Mesopotamia," *CANE* 1:472.

[69] Bottéro, "Code," 169–71; Kraus, "Ein zentrales Problem," 283–96; Westbrook, "Biblical and Cuneiform Law Codes"; Greengus, "Some Issues," 60.

[70] Quoted in Bottéro, "Code," 170.

If a woman gives birth, and the right ear (of the child) is (abnormally) small, the house of the man will be scattered.

If a woman gives birth, and the left ear (of the child) is (abnormally) small, the house of the man will expand.

If a woman gives birth, and both ears (of the child) are (abnormally) small, the house of the man will become poor.[71]

While representing the science of the time, these treatises are not scientific in our sense. They distill actual cases, but they also include the merely possible and the fantastic. For example, an omen text gives the predictions from two gallbladders (a rare but imaginable—and ominous— phenomenon). Yet it also discusses predictions to be derived from "three, five, and up to seven gallbladders"—impossible numbers.[72] These omina are not derived from empirical observation. This is also the case with the medical texts, where symptoms are listed such as births of five, six, seven, and eight children born to a woman at one time.[73] The goal of the scribe— the Babylonian scholar—was not to be empirical, not to record observable reality. His primary goal was to extrapolate in a truly scientific sense from the observable to the possible, and to the barely imaginable. In this way he predicts and controls the future by analogy to the past. This occurs in the law codes as well:

229. If a builder constructs a house for a man but does not make his work sound, and the house that he constructs collapses and causes the death of the householder, that builder shall be killed.

230. If it should cause the death of a son of the householder, they shall kill a son of that builder.

231. If it should cause the death of a slave of the householder, he shall give to the householder a slave of comparable value for the slave.

232. If it should cause the loss of property, he shall replace anything that is lost; moreover, because he did not make sound the house which he constructed and it collapsed, he shall construct (anew) the house which collapsed at his own expense.[74]

---

[71] E. Leighty, *The Omen Series Šumma Izbu* (TCS 4; Locust Valley, N.Y.: Augustin, 1970), 54 (3:5–7), cited in Westbrook, "Biblical and Cuneiform Law Codes," 252.

[72] Cited in Bottéro, "Code," 134.

[73] Ibid., p. 135.

[74] Roth, *Law Collections,* 125.

The law collections reflect this same genre of scientific literature, and their authors adhered to the same scientific principles. As with the omen texts, their goal in creating the law collections was not to record observed reality. It was to provide a framework in which to place the future. The author(s) of the code were no mere amanuenses, recording legal decisions as they occurred. Rather, they were scholars and scientists. Kraus finds confirmation of this in Hammurabi's self-designation as "the wise one (*emqum*), ... he who has mastered all wisdom" (iv 7).[75] This term is typical of the scribe, the scholar, not the king. It is by this term that Hammurabi distinguishes himself from almost all other kings, and this wisdom is the prerequisite for the emergence of the code.[76] The authors of the code belong to the scientific and scholarly community, not the judicial. The casuistic style does not imply a record of actual judgments, but a scientific treatise on justice.

Were these treatises created for academic purposes only? Like Bottéro,[77] Westbrook concludes that they had the additional practical purpose of instructing judges.[78] Just as the diviner would consult the omen series and the physician the medical lists, so the judge would consult the law collections. In support, Westbrook cites numerous examples of diviners who refer to omen texts. Regarding the use of law collections, Westbrook points to the fourteen tablets of Assyrian laws recovered from a gatehouse identified as the Gate of Shamash. It is presumably the gate where cases were tried.[79] Yet physicians and court diviners were part of the scribal profession. They studied, copied, and produced the texts they cited. This is not true of the judges. Judges were royal or gubernatorial appointees. There is no indication they could even read. They never cite the law codes. An Old Babylonian text from Sippar illustrates the behavior of judges:

> When my lord raised high the golden torch for Sippar instituting the *mišarum* for Shamash who loves him, and convened in Sippar Taribatum, the commander of the army, the judges of Babylon and the judges of Sippar, [at that time] they (re)viewed the cases of the citizens of Sippar, heard the tablets (read to them) dealing with purchases of

---

[75] Kraus, "Ein zentrales Problem," 290.

[76] Ibid. There had been law collections prior to that of Hammurabi's, but as far as is presently known, his was the first to employ the style of the conditional sentence common to other scientific literature. Cf. Roth, *Law Collections*.

[77] Bottéro, "Code," 177.

[78] Westbrook, "Biblical and Cuneiform Law Codes," 253–58.

[79] Ibid., 255. I don't know how the gate was identified as having this name, if it was named by modern scholars or by the ancients themselves.

fields, houses, and orchards (and) ordered broken those affected by the Edict.[80]

The court cases were read to the judges. To quote R. Harris:

> The Old Babylonian judge was … not necessarily a learned man—he might even be illiterate—but was one who knew what the community considered just and whose attitudes were respected by it and by the litigants. Thus, qualifications for the office of judge would be a position of respect in the community, and wealth, to remove the suspicion of personal interest.[81]

This is true not just of the Old Babylonian judge but is typical of judges throughout the ancient Near East and Egypt. While diviners and shamans consulted omen and medical treatises, this was not true of judges. There is no evidence judges were even aware of the so-called "law codes."

Judges in these societies were not guided by written codes but by their own socially constructed ideas of fairness and right. In Mesopotamia, this was termed *kittum* (pl. *kīnātu*). This word refers to "truth, justice, correct procedures, loyalty, fidelity, correctness, etc." (*CAD*). It is contrasted with *mišarum,* "equity" and "justice." Whereas *kittum* is intended to describe judges' decisions, *mišarum* was the king's obligation. It was his means to make the law function equitably.[82] These two terms were complementary and independent. It was the impersonal and immutable order tempered with equity and fairness.[83] The king exercised his authority through *mišarum.* Hammurabi embodied *mišarum,* but he received *kīnātu* from Shamash. As is written on his stela, "I, Hammurabi, just king, am he whom Shamash has granted the eternal truths [*kīnātu*]." Yet Shamash was not the source of *kīnātu*. The source for *kīnātu* lay not with the gods, but elsewhere. As Yaḫdun-Lim states in his dedication, "To Shamash, the king of the heavens and the earth, the judge of gods and men, whose allotted portion is *mišarum* and to whom *kīnātu* have been

---

[80] Jacob J. Finkelstein, "Some New *Misharum* Material and Its Implications," *Studies in Honor of Benno Landsberger* (ed. H. G. Guterbock and T. Jacobsen; AS 16; Chicago: University of Chicago Press, 1966), 233–46.

[81] Rivkah Harris, *Ancient Sippar,* 116–17; cited in Greengus, "Some Issues," 84.

[82] Shalom Paul, *Studies in the Book of the Covenant in the Light of Cuneiform and Biblical Law* (VTSup 18; Leiden: Brill, 1970), 5. See also, F. R. Kraus, *Ein Edikt des Königs Ammi-ṣaduka von Babylon* (Studia et Documenta ad Iura Orientis Antiqui Pertinentia 5; Leiden: Brill, 1958), 225–31; Jacob J. Finkelstein, "Ammiṣaduqa's Edict and the Babylonian 'Law Codes,'" *JCS* 15 (1961): 91–104.

[83] Paul, *Book of the Covenant,* 5.

granted as a gift."[84] Shamash received the *kīnātu* from yet a higher source. As Paul suggests, "the ultimate source of law was independent of the deities and belonged to a sphere of existence that surpassed both the human and the divine."[85] This sphere is natural law: a (socially constructed) concept of what is inherently, immutably right. In the figure atop Hammurabi's stela, the god is not shown giving Hammurabi a set of laws, but the rod and ring, symbols of justice and authority. The gods did not choose Hammurabi to promulgate laws. These have already been created and passed to him by Shamash from above. The gods chose him to execute the abstract concept of *kīnātu,* that is, natural law, which the laws exhibit. Hammurabi promoted *kīnātu* by his judgments and the judgments of the officials he appointed. The *dīnāt mīšarim* ("just decisions") on the stela serve as examples and instances of *kīnātu.* They represent the unwritten natural law—the divinely protected customs and traditions of generations. It was by the unwritten *kīnātu* that judges judged, not by what was written on stelae. Judges in Mesopotamia (under both Babylonians and Persians) functioned as they did in Egypt. They obeyed positive law—the edicts of kings and provincial governors. Besides that, they judged according to *kīnātu,* their socially constructed concepts of justice and fairness.

The purpose of Hammurabi's stela, therefore, was not to proclaim law, since it was not a law code in the modern sense. Rather, it was to demonstrate that the king had established justice in the land. To set up the concrete stela was to set up abstract justice. Hammurabi states:

> In order that the mighty not wrong the weak, to provide just ways for the waif and the widow, I have inscribed my precious pronouncements upon my stela and set it up before the statue of me, the king of justice, in the city of Babylon, the city which the gods Anu and Enlil have elevated, within the Esagil, the temple whose foundations are fixed as are heaven and earth, in order to render the judgments of the land, to give the verdicts of the land, and to provide just ways for the wronged....

> Let any wronged man who has a lawsuit come before me, the king of justice, and let him have my inscribed stela read aloud to him, thus may he hear my precious pronouncements and let my stela reveal the lawsuit for

---

[84] G. Dossin, "L'inscription de fondation de Iaḫdun-Lim, roi de Mari," *Syria* 32 (1955): 4, lines 1–6; cited in Paul, *Book of the Covenant,* 6. This translation is slightly different (and perhaps more literal) than the one in *ANET,* 556.

[85] Paul, *Book of the Covenant.* To my knowledge, only the Hebrew Bible presents laws as coming from the deity himself.

him; may he examine his case, may he calm his troubled heart, and may he praise me.[86]

The implication is not that a wronged man may see his case inscribed on the stela and so feel relieved about its outcome. The odds are not good that his particular case will be included. Rather, what he will see on the stela are instances of *justice itself*. He sees these and is reassured.

Darius's collection of the *hpw* of the Egyptians (and perhaps the תורות of the Jews) ought to be placed in the same context as other law collections of the ancient Near East. Laws were collected for scientific and antiquarian purposes. They were also collected and published as instances of justice—justice in the abstract. They were intended to reassure the populace that the new king was concerned to install justice in the land.[87]

Darius's concern for justice is portrayed in his own inscriptions. The Persian word *dāta* is similar to Akkadian *kīnātu* and to Egyptian *hp*. Specifically, it refers to order; *dāta* requires that everything be in its rightful place, that everything be as it is intended to be. In a study of the known instances of the term, Pierre Briant concludes that *dāta* "designates that which has been fixed, that which corresponds to order.... The words *dāta*, *arta* (justice and truth), and *drauga* (its antonym, the lie) refer to a dynastic and religious ethic rather than to a legal reality. Justice is first and foremost fidelity to the rule of Ahura Mazda and to the power of the king."[88] Pierre Lecoq finds a "transparent secularization" in the term *dāta*.[89] That is, the law of the king and the law of Ahura Mazda have merged; the will of the king is the will of the god.[90] This is visible in Darius's Behistun inscription:

> Thus says Darius the King: These are the countries which came unto me; by the favor of Ahura Mazda they were my subjects; they bore tribute to me; what was said unto them by me either by night or by day, that was done.

> Thus says Darius the King: Within these countries, the man who was excellent, him I rewarded well; he who was evil, him I punished well;

---

[86] Quoted in Roth, *Law Collections,* 133–34.

[87] *Pace* Redford, in this volume.

[88] Pierre Briant, "Social and Legal Institutions in Achaemenid Iran," *CANE* 1:517–28, esp. 523.

[89] "Läicisation transparaît": Pierre Lecoq, *Les inscriptions de la Perse achéménide* (Paris: Gallimard, 1997), 167.

[90] This is also the finding of Rolf Rendtorff in a study of the term's biblical occurrences ("Esra und das 'Gesetz,'" *ZAW* 96 [1984]: 165–84).

by the favor of Ahura Mazda these countries showed respect toward my law [*dāta*]; as was said to them by me, thus was it done. (DB 1.17–24)[91]

In Inscription E from Susa:

Thus says Darius the King: Much which was ill-done, that I made good. Provinces were in commotion; one man was smiting the other. The following I brought about by the favor of Ahura Mazda, that the one does not smite the other at all, each one is in his place. My law [*dāta*]—of that they feel fear, so that the stronger does not smite nor destroy the weak. (DSe 30–41)[92]

In Inscription A from Naqsh-i-Rustam, Darius's tomb:

A great god is Ahura Mazda, who created this earth, who created yonder sky, who created man, who created happiness for man, who made Darius king, one king of many, one lord of many.

I am Darius the Great King, King of Kings, King of countries containing all kinds of men, King in this great earth far and wide, son of Hystaspes, an Achaemenian, a Persian, son of a Persian, an Aryan, having Aryan lineage.

Thus says Darius the King: By the favor of Ahura Mazda these are the countries which I seized outside of Persia; I ruled over them; they bore tribute to me; what was said to them by me, that they did; my law [*dāta*]—that held them firm [then follows a list of countries seized]. (DNa 1–30)[93]

The word of the king—or his delegates—constitutes the law of the king. It also constitutes the law of the god Ahura Mazda. By his favor to Darius, Ahura Mazda grants the king obedience from the subject peoples. Darius asserts that by making him king, Ahura Mazda made Darius's word law among them. This is evident also in the inscriptions of the later kings. Inscription H of Xerxes from Persepolis reads in part:

And among these countries (where I was king) there was (a place) where previously false gods were worshipped. Afterwards, by the favor of Ahura Mazda, I destroyed that sanctuary of the demons, and I made proclamation,

---

[91] Kent, *Old Persian,* 119.

[92] Ibid., 142.

[93] Ibid., 138.

"The demons shall not be worshipped!" Where previously the demons were worshipped, there I worshipped Ahura Mazda and Arta reverently.[94]

And there was other (business) that had been done ill; that I made good. That which I did, all I did by the favor of Ahura Mazda. Ahura Mazda bore me aid, until I completed the work.

You who (will be) hereafter, if you will think, "Happy may I be when living, and when dead may I be blessed," have respect for that law [*dāta*] which Ahura Mazda has established; worship Ahura Mazda and Arta reverently. The man who has respect for that law [*dāta*] which Ahura Mazda has established, and worships Ahura Mazda and Arta reverently, he both becomes happy while living, and becomes blessed when dead. (XPh 35–56)[95]

According to this inscription, Ahura Mazda has established law, *dāta*. This *dāta* is prima facie the word of the king. It is also order, equity, fairness, and justice. Artaxerxes' Rescript demands that judges judge according to the *dāta* of the king, that is, the word of the king. In addition to this positive law, judges were commanded to base their decisions on "the דתא of your (Ezra's) God."[96] This does not imply that the Persian judges were now suddenly to base their decisions on a local law code. This notion was foreign to judicial concepts of the ancient Near East. Rather, I suggest "the law of the god" is natural law, the divinely protected but socially derived concepts of fairness and justice (*dāta*/דתא, *arta, hp, kīnātu*). To appoint judges who judge according to this law is to appoint them to judge according to the immutable and impersonal order of the cosmos. It is to judge according to "truth, justice, order, correct procedures, loyalty, fidelity, correctness, etc."

---

[94] Heleen Sancisi-Weerdenburg ("Yaunā en Persai: Grieken en Perzen in een ander perspectief" [Ph.D. diss., Leiden, 1980]) "has presented strong arguments that this inscription is not historical" (Amelie Kuhrt and Susan Sherwin-White, "Xerxes' Destructions of Babylonian Temples," *The Greek Sources: Proceedings of the Groningen 1984 Achaemenid History Workshop* [ed. H. Sancisi-Weerdenburg and A. Kuhrt; AH 2; Leiden: Nederlands Institute voor het Nabije Oosten, 1987], 69–78).

[95] Kent, *Old Persian,* 151–52.

[96] To Artaxerxes, Ezra's God was אלה שמיא, "the God of Heaven" (Ezra 7:12, 21, 23), and likely a local manifestation of Ahura Mazda (cf. Thomas M. Bolin, "The Temple of יהו at Elephantine and Persian Religious Policy," in *The Triumph of Elohim: From Yahwisms to Judaisms* [ed. D. Edelman; Grand Rapids, Mich.: Eerdmans, 1995], 127–42; also ch. 5, "Temple-Palace Relations in Yehud," of my dissertation, "The Rise to Power of the Judaean Priesthood" (= *The Priest and the Great King*). Rendtorff ("Ezra und das 'Gesetz'") suggests that the law of the king was the law of the god (and vice versa) no matter who the god was.

The Persians may have authorized the Jews to collect and transcribe the customs and traditions of Yehud, as they did in Egypt. Yet it was not intended that this collection be binding on the decisions of the Persian judges Ezra appointed. They were no more binding on them than was Hammurabi's Code on the judges of Babylon, or the laws of the Demotic Chronicle on the Persian judges in Egypt.[97] As was true everywhere, the judges Ezra appointed would have judged according to their own socially constructed notions of fairness and justice.

This was Ezra's mission: Ezra, the Persian official, was to appoint royal judges for the satrapy and for each of its provinces. (This command, as stated in Ezra 7:25–26, suggests an interesting facet of Persian administration. It was not the satraps or the governors who appointed the royal judges in their jurisdiction, but a separate official. These Persian judges—appointed independently of the satrap and governors—could then serve as additional "eyes and ears" of the king.)[98] Ezra had no other administrative authority. He was not governor.[99] The judges he appointed were not bound to obey him. Their obligation was to the governor, the satrap, and the king.

4. Mosaic Laws in Yehud

If law codes were not intended to influence the decisions of judges, how and why were such Mosaic laws as the Sabbath and the laws against intermarriage enforced? If the judges were Persian, as they were in Egypt, how would they even know about the Sabbatical laws? How could Persian

---

[97] *Pace* Jon L. Berquist, *Judaism in Persia's Shadow: A Social and Historical Approach* (Minneapolis: Fortress, 1995), 55. Berquist offers no evidence for his statement that laws once codified took on imperial force and helped to standardize administration.

[98] That judges would be chosen directly by the king (or his agent) rather than by the satrap is reminiscent of Xenophon's remark on the installation of local garrison commanders. These were to be chosen directly by the king as well, not by the satrap. According to Xenophon: "When [Cyrus the Great] arrived in Babylon, he decided to send out satraps to govern the nations he had subdued. But the commanders of the garrisons in the citadels and the colonels in command of the guards throughout the country he wished to be responsible to no one but himself. This provision he made with the purpose that if any of the satraps, on the strength of the wealth or the men at their command, should break out into open insolence or attempt to refuse obedience, they might at once find their opposition in their province" (*Cyr.* 8.6.1). The garrison commanders were appointed directly by the king (or his agent) so that they would serve as "eyes and ears" of the king within the satrapy. It appears that the same function is attested here for the royal judges. See also n. 16 above.

[99] *Pace* Berquist, *Judaism,* 55.

judges enforce these laws if they judged according to Persian social norms? To answer these questions, I must turn to the role of Nehemiah.

Artaxerxes' Rescript applies Persian sanctions to infractions of "the law of your God and the law of the king":

> And you, Ezra, according to the God-given wisdom you possess, appoint magistrates and judges who would judge all the people who are in Beyond the River—all who know the law [דת] of your God and [all] who do not know, to inform them. All who would not execute the law [דתא] of your God and the law [דתא] of the king eagerly, let a judicial verdict be executed on them: either for death, or flogging, confiscation of property, or imprisonment.

The term שרשו, translated "flogging," is most likely from the Persian *sraošyā* and denotes "beating, flogging, caning, or other types of corporal punishment."[100] Although flogging and imprisonment may have been used in Judah, they are characteristic of Persian penal practice.[101] By this command, Artaxerxes orders Ezra to appoint judges for Ebar Nahara's Persian penal system, a system no different from that throughout the Achaemenid Empire.

The phrase "the law of the king" in the edict refers to the edicts of the great king, but it also refers to delegated power. The law of the king includes the edicts of satraps, provincial governors, and mayors. These local rulers were the source of positive law in their districts; their commands were the "law of the king." If the governors were Jewish, as they seem to have been in Yehud,[102] they could impose Jewish customs upon the people in their province.

In Judah in 445, the Persian provincial governor was the Jew Nehemiah. According to Neh 13:23–25, Nehemiah enacted an edict against intermarriage:

---

[100] F. Rundgren, "Zur Bedeutung von ŠRŠW—Esra vii 26," *VT* 7 (1957): 400–4; *pace* Williamson (*Ezra, Nehemiah,* 97), who interprets the שרשו as "uproot," from the Hebrew שרש with the RSV.

[101] Blenkinsopp (*Ezra-Nehemiah,* 152) implies that flogging was not used in Judah prior to the Persian period. Yet, provisions are made for it in Deut 25:2–3. Do these verses express only Persian-period customs? According to the book of Jeremiah, the priest Pashhur, a leading temple official, struck the prophet Jeremiah and placed him in the stocks (Jer 20:2). Later, officials beat Jeremiah and put him in prison. Did these beatings actually occur? Were they official acts or renegade? I suspect they occurred and were part of normal jurisprudence.

[102] For a discussion of the governors of Yehud, see ch. 5 ("Temple-Palace Relations in Yehud") in my dissertation (= *The Priest and the Great King*).

And in those days, I saw Jews who married Ashdodite, Ammonite, and Moabite women. Half their children spoke Ashdodite. None of them knew how to speak Judean, but only the language of the various peoples.

I entered into a dispute [אריב] with them, cursed them, beat some of them, pulled out the hair of their beards [ואמרטם], and I made them swear by God [saying], "You shall not give your daughters to their sons, nor take their daughters for your sons or for yourselves."[103]

The root ריב used here can denote physical fighting, such as in Exod 21:18: וכי־יריבן אנשים והכה־איש את־רעהו באבן או באגרף ולא ימות ונפל למשכב ("when men struggle [יריבן] and one strikes the other with a stone or fist...") It can also refer to a legal dispute, such as in Isa 3:13: נצב לריב יהוה ועמד לדין עמים ("YHWH stands forth to argue [לריב] his case; he stands to judge peoples"). As in Isaiah, the situation described in Nehemiah refers to a judicial preceding, not a physical struggle. The term might reasonably be translated "prosecute." According to Heltzer:

> In general, we know that in the whole Eastern Mediterranean in ancient time, cutting or plucking of the hair and beard by force was considered to be an act of disgrace and humiliation of free persons and that, to the contrary, special styles of beards and hair coiffures were esteemed as a sign of honor. Taking this into account, it is difficult to imagine that the aristocrats of Judah stood in line, and the governor Nehemiah in person was beating them and plucking their beards.[104]

---

[103] Philip R. Davies ("Minimalists and Maximalists," *BAR* 26.2 [2000]: 72) describes the society reflected in the books of Ezra and Nehemiah as "xenophobic." This passage depicts the society as not being xenophobic enough for Nehemiah's taste. The large amount of intermarriage against which both Nehemiah and Ezra fulminate argues against a xenophobic society. It also argues against the notion of a "culture of resistance" suggested by Daniel Smith (-Christopher) in "The Politics of Ezra: Sociological Indicators of Postexilic Judaean Society," in *Second Temple Studies 1. Persian Period* (ed. P. R. Davies; JSOTSup 117; Sheffield: Sheffield Academic Press, 1991), 73–97; and against "the attempt [by the *gôlâ* community] at inward consolidation of a threatened minority" (idem., "The Mixed Marriage Crisis in Ezra 9–10 and Nehemiah 13: A Study of the Sociology of Post-Exilic Judaean Community," in *Second Temple Studies 2: Temple and Community in the Persian Period* [ed. T. C. Eskenazi and K. H. Richards; JSOTSup 175; Sheffield: Sheffield Academic Press, 1994], 243–65).

[104] Michael Heltzer, "The Flogging and Plucking of Beards in the Achaemenid Empire and the Chronology of Nehemiah," *AMI* 28 (1995–1996), 305–7. I thank Pierre Briant for calling this article to my attention.

Rather than an impetuous act, plucking hair from the head and beard was an official punishment in the Achaemenid Empire. According to a cuneiform text from the Murašû archive (CBS 5213), two men agree by contract to do groundbreaking on the land of Rimūt-Maš. The text then states:

> If they have not completed the groundbreaking by the first day of the fifth month, they shall be beaten one hundred times with a *niṭpu,* their beards and hair (of the head) shall be plucked out, and Rêbat, son of Bēl-Irība, servant of Rimūt-Ninurta, shall keep them in the workhouse.[105]

The text is dated to the fifth year of Darius II, 420 B.C.E. Here we see the punishments of flogging and imprisonment, as well as that of plucking the head and beard.

In this judicial proceeding, Nehemiah accused (לריב) some men of marrying foreign women, judged them guilty, and ordered their punishment—all according to Persian law.[106] The men submitted because they had no choice (one possible sanction for disobedience was death). Nehemiah, as Persian governor, had the right and ability to create law and its interpretation and to execute sanctions for its disobedience.[107] The prohibition against intermarriage may have been part of Mosaic law, and the Persians may have been involved in codifying it. Yet no law code could give Nehemiah the right to prohibit intermarriage. His right lay in his office of governor.[108]

Nehemiah also enforced the Sabbath laws (Neh 13:15–22). He did this without appeal to a law book, law code, or law collection. He simply commands. Again, his authority stems not from a law code but from his status as governor. This is evident from the following passage:

> In those days I saw in Judah people pressing wine on the Sabbath, bringing heaps [of grain] and loading [them] on donkeys (and even wine,

---

[105] Quoted from Heltzer, "Flogging and Plucking of Beards," 306.

[106] *Pace* Blenkinsopp (*Ezra-Nehmiah,* 364), who considers the incident an example of Nehemiah's "impulsive and even intemperate nature"; and also Williamson (*Ezra, Nehemiah,* 398) who states: "Nehemiah's violent outburst may have been a spontaneous reaction to his discovery; ... the fact that he beat but 'some of the men' is not suggestive of any kind of judicial procedure."

[107] In this sense, here is the "imperial authorization" of which Frei speaks. I argue, however, that Nehemiah, as governor, was its source in Yehud.

[108] For a discussion of just why Nehemiah, the Persian governor, enforced Mosaic intermarriage and Sabbatical laws, see my "The Political Struggle in Fifth Century Judah," forthcoming in *Transeu* 24 (2002).

grapes, figs, and every kind of burden) and bringing [them] to Jerusalem on the Sabbath. I warned [them] against selling food then.

Even the Tyrians who settled there[109] were bringing fish and every type of merchandise and were selling them on the Sabbath to the Jews in[110] Jerusalem.

I prosecuted [ואריבה] the nobles of Judah, and I said to them, "What is this evil thing you are doing to desecrate the Sabbath? Is this not what your fathers did so that our God brought upon us all this evil and upon this city? And you add wrath upon Israel by profaning the Sabbath?

And it was just as the shadows fell on the gates of Jerusalem before the Sabbath that *I commanded* the doors be closed. *I commanded* they should not be opened until after the Sabbath. *I set some of my men to guard the gates* and not to let anyone bring burdens into the city on the Sabbath. (Neh 13:15–19)

Nehemiah established the Sabbatical law and enforced it by means of the men under his command—soldiers from the garrison. Nehemiah was the source of positive law in his district; as he commanded, so it was done. His commands may have coincided with a Mosaic law code, but the law code was not the source of his authority. As elsewhere throughout the Achaemenid Empire, Nehemiah's authority stemmed from his status as governor and from the soldiers under his command.

5. CONCLUSIONS

If Ezra 7:25–26 was part of a genuine commission from the Persian king, Artaxerxes, to a person named Ezra, and I believe it was, then Ezra's assignment was to appoint judges and magistrates. These would have been Persian and would have judged first according to the *dāta* of the king and his representatives (the satrap or governor), and second according to the *dāta* of the god. The former term refers to positive law, created by edict. The latter term refers to "natural" law. Judges would not have judged according to a law code—the law collections were not *codes* in the modern sense. Rather, they would have made their decisions according to their socially constructed concepts of right, fairness, and justice. These would necessarily be Persian concepts—not Jewish! In 445, however, the governor of Yehud was Nehemiah the Jew. He outlawed

---

[109] The Hebrew has בה ("in it"), referring to either Judah or Jerusalem.

[110] Deleting the *wāw*.

business on the Sabbath and prohibited intermarriage between Judaeans and non-Judeans. His authority stemmed not from a law collection but from his office as governor. The judges Ezra appointed were bound by Nehemiah's edicts.

Artaxerxes' Rescript puts the behavior of the local leadership (ראשי האבות, זקנים) and the local assembly (קהל) in perspective. The sanctions listed in the edict (i.e., the ability to confiscate land and property, to threaten with death, flogging, and imprisonment) were not given to a קהל or to the local leadership. Artaxerxes assigned these powers to Persian officials—to the royal judges and magistrates Ezra appointed. He did not authorize local leaders or local assemblies to formulate law or to enforce it. As was true throughout the Persian Empire, local leaders and assemblies met only to hear the law imposed upon them by satrap or governor.[111] Persian judges and officials (שׂרים) executed that law. There was no self-rule in Judah, as there was none in any province in the empire.

The שׂרים who informed Ezra of the marriage of Jews to the peoples of the lands (Ezra 9:1), who had the power to order the confiscation of property (10:7–8), and who had the power to impose sanctions for failure to divorce (10:14, 16) would not have been local leaders or local "heads of father's houses." Those with power in the Persian Empire were royally appointed Persian judges and magistrates. In the case of early fourth century Yehud, they were appointed by Ezra, the royal agent.

---

[111] Several scholars (e.g., Blenkinsopp, *Ezra-Nehemiah,* 174–76; Williamson, *Ezra, Nehemiah,* 127, 280) place Neh 8 (reading the law) between Ezra 8 (Ezra arrives in Judah) and 9 (the people realize they aren't following the law). Scholars make this change because they realize the law against intermarriage was not formulated by the people in a popular assembly but was part of an edict officially imposed upon them.

THE LAW OF MOSES IN THE EZRA TRADITION: MORE VIRTUAL THAN REAL?

Lester L. Grabbe
University of Hull, England

When you read the books of Ezra, Nehemiah, Esther, and Daniel, you could be forgiven for thinking that at the time of the Persian Empire, the Jews had really taken over the joint. You can hardly turn around without stepping on a Jewish minister, governor, advisor, favorite of the emperor, and even the odd queen. Yehud seems to have been the most esteemed province in the entire Persian Empire, on which was lavished constant attention, a stream of favorable decrees, and great quantities of precious metal. This is hardly surprising, since it is the nature of these texts to promote the cause of Judaism. What is truly surprising is how many scholars have not only embraced this propaganda of the text but have even greatly extended it. The text stops short of making one of the Persian kings Jewish, but never fear! A scholarly theory shall soon fill this gap. Don't be at all surprised if in the near future Cyrus is discovered to be a Benjaminite; Darius, a worshiper of YHWH; and Xerxes, circumcised on the eighth day.

One of these Judeans whose cause and persona was allegedly furthered by a decree from the "king of kings" himself was Ezra. Was the "law in Ezra's hand" really promulgated by the authority of the Persian Empire? In order to answer this question, I shall attempt to do several things: (1) look at what the Ezra tradition says about the "law of Moses" or "the book of the law" (by Ezra tradition, I mean primarily 1 Esdras and Hebrew Ezra 7–10 with Neh 8); (2) examine "the law of Moses" and "the book of the law" elsewhere in Jewish literature likely to be from the Persian period; and (3) ask about law in general under the Persian Empire.

1. "The Book of the Law" in the Biblical Tradition

This section will concentrate on the worldview of the Ezra tradition within the wider biblical tradition. What does it actually say? How does it understand the law, the book of the law, and the like? The concern will not initially be with whether this picture is correct or not. Questions of historicity—my ultimate aim—will be dealt with later.

1.1. The "Artaxerxes Firman" (Ezra 7)

The main passage usually appealed to is the supposed decree of Artaxerxes in Ezra 7:12–26, partly because it is assumed to be an actual Persian royal decree and thus a primary source. The main elements of the document are the following:

- Ezra is a priest (7:12).
- Ezra is a scribe of the law (דתא) of the God of heaven (7:12).
- The king gives the order that all who are willing from the people of Israel, the priests, and Levites may go up to Jerusalem (7:13).
- Ezra is commissioned to "investigate" (לבקרא) Judah and Jerusalem by the law of God that is in his hand (7:14).
- Ezra is to use the money given to him by the king and others to buy animals and other goods to offer on the altar in Jerusalem (7:15–17).
- Ezra is to deliver the vessels given for the house of God in Jerusalem (7:19).
- Any other needs of the temple are to come from the royal treasury, with the treasurers of Ebar Nahara supplying Ezra what he requests, up to one hundred talents of silver (7:20–22).
- There is to be no tax on any priest, Levite, singer, and other servant of the temple (7:24).
- Ezra is to appoint judges and magistrates to judge all the people in the province of Ebar Nahara who know the laws of God and teach them to those who do not (7:25).
- Anyone not obeying "the law of your God and the law of the king" is to be put to death (7:26).

It is difficult to be certain whether a genuine royal decree lies behind Ezra 7 for the simple reason that we have no such decrees. Apart from one alleged letter quoted in Greek by Thucydides (1.128–129)—whose genuineness some doubt—and the Gadatas inscription (also in Greek and disputed), along with the Behistun inscription, which is a special case, we have no Persian royal decrees preserved for us. And, of course, none of these is in Aramaic, the normal administrative language of the Persian Empire (apart from the fragments of an Aramaic translation of the Behistun inscription). To assert the genuineness of Ezra 7 assumes that we have enough information to make a reasonable judgment, but in fact we do not. In the end, all we can do is ask whether there is evidence against genuineness and decide whether we are willing to accept genuineness when there are no clear contrary indications. Such a position may be legitimate, but it is not the same as having positive evidence; we simply do not have enough information to make a positive judgment. For example, with Greek documents we have a good number of examples with which to compare any questionable document. Although a good forgery might not show any clear deviation from the genuine examples, at least we have sufficient data on which to make a comparison. This does not pertain with the alleged decree in Ezra 7.

What should be noted here is that this alleged Persian decree has a number of features of post-Achaemenid Aramaic.[1] The most notable are the pronouns רי, דנה (instead of זי and זנה/א) and the noun דהב (instead of זהב). Although we find a very few instances of -*d*- instead of -*z*- for Proto-Semitic *-*d*- in Achaemenid period documents, these are not usually in official documents of the Persian administration.[2] There is no question that if an official Persian decree lies behind this passage, it has been "updated" by Jewish scribes after the Persian period.

There is, however, updating and updating: to change -*z*- to -*d*- seems to be a fairly common process by copyists. Much less likely is the change of the pronominal endings on nouns from the Achaemenid כם- and הם- to the later כון- and הון-. This document has a mixture of the earlier (7:16, 17, 18, 24) and the later forms (7:17, 21). One might wonder whether over the centuries of copying, the earlier forms were gradually replaced more and more by the later as copyists made sporadic but unconscious assimilation to the later speech forms. This does not seem to be the case, however. The earlier and later forms are scattered in roughly equal measure through the document and sometimes appear in clusters (cf. two later forms in v. 17 and two earlier ones in v. 24). The pattern is not what one might expect of random scribal assimilations over a lengthy period of copying, but rather the consequence of additions made to an earlier document.

The content indicates that several passages are later additions or revisions. All the genuine Persian-period documents refer to "Jews" and "Judah" (יהוד, יהודיא/יהודין), yet 7:13 speaks of the "people of Israel"; similarly, 7:15 refers to the "God of Israel." In 7:17 are two examples of the ending הון-, which is a later form. In 7:21–22, not only is the promise of

---

[1] For a preliminary outline, see Lester L. Grabbe, "The Authenticity of the Persian 'Documents' in Ezra," read to the Aramaic Section of the Society of Biblical Literature annual meeting, San Francisco, November 1992. See the summary of some of the main points of this article in *Ezra-Nehemiah* (Old Testament Readings; New York: Routledge, 1998), 128–32, 139–40. The most recent study of Achaemenid Aramaic is M. L. Folmer, *The Aramaic Language in the Achaemenid Period: A Study in Linguistic Variation* (OLA 68; Leuven: Peeters, 1995).

[2] The usage of -*d*- instead of -*z*- is complex and cannot be quickly summarized (see especially Folmer, *Aramaic Language,* 49–63). My purpose here is not to discuss every possible exception but to make a general point that is clearly valid when the data are looked at as a whole.

one hundred talents of silver—one third of the entire revenue for Ebar Nahara for a year (cf. Herodotus 3.91)—incredible, but the late form כֹּן- also occurs. The reference to not imposing any tax on temple officials in 7:24 is suspect, as will be discussed below, but at least the Achaemenid forms כֹּ- and הֹ- are present. In 7:25, it is unlikely that Ezra would be allowed to impose his own choice of judges and magistrates and also the laws of his God on all of Ebar Nahara, especially considering that this region had a powerful satrap who seems to be ignored.[3]

Thus what we do find in the alleged decree of Artaxerxes in Ezra 7:12–26 are a number of features that are almost certainly post-Achaemenid. Some of these are grammatical; others look much more directly like Jewish propaganda. If there really was a Persian edict relating to Ezra, some portions of the present text represent additions or revisions from the Greek period. Unfortunately, although some parts look distinctly inauthentic, it is difficult to make a positive judgment about what might have constituted an original document. The most we can say is that a genuine Persian degree might *possibly* lie behind the present text, but to try to reconstruct this decree is very problematic.

1.2. The Reading of the Law (Neh 8–10)

Although Neh 8 occurs in the Hebrew book of Nehemiah, it has been widely accepted as a part of the Ezra tradition. For example, the core of it is found in the Greek 1 Esdras (9:37–55), which has nothing of the Nehemiah tradition in it. The main points of this chapter for our purposes are the following:

- The people (Israelites settled in their towns) assemble in Jerusalem in the seventh month (8:1).
- Ezra, at their request, reads from the book of the torah of Moses (8:1–3).
- The Levites explain the torah (8:7–8).

---

[3] The duties of the satrap were in theory curtailed under Darius, with the fiscal functions relegated to another official; however, this does not appear to have continued. See the discussion in Muhammad A. Dandamaev and Vladimir G. Lukonin, *The Culture and Social Institutions of Ancient Iran* (Cambridge: Cambridge University Press, 1989), 96–116. Although the power and office of the satrap varied from place to place, time to time, and even individual to individual, they were usually members of the royal family with a great deal of independence and power, including military command and troops. Prima facie, it seems odd that Ezra would be allowed to interfere in the legal and judicial system of the satrapy without some reference to the satrap.

- Ezra and the Levites tell the people that the day is holy and to rejoice, not mourn (8:9–12).
- On the second day of the reading, they find the instructions to dwell in booths in the festival of the seventh month; they search out appropriate vegetation and build booths (8:13–17).
- This had not been done since the days of Joshua son of Nun (8:17).
- The scroll of God's torah is read every day, with a celebration of eight days total (8:18).

There is no doubt that this is a very interesting and curious chapter, though it is too often taken at face value.[4] The assembly of the people in the seventh month seems no accident, and they know of the book of Moses' torah because they ask for it to be read to them. Yet when Ezra proclaims the day a holy day, it comes almost as a surprise. What was clearly unknown to them was the custom of building booths, which they did not learn until the second day of the reading. Although the festival is nowhere referred to as the Festival of Booths, it is described in no uncertain terms as that very festival that occurs in the month of Tishri. The details correspond to those in Lev 23 as opposed to those in Deut 16: although the Festival of Booths of Neh 8:13–18 is referred to in Deut 16:13–15, the requirement to build booths and live in them for the eight days is not found there but in Lev 23:39–43; also with regard to Neh 8:18, it is Lev 23:36, 39 that mentions celebrations on the first and eighth days, whereas Deut 16:13–15 mentions only seven days.

A second reading takes place in Neh 9–10, but this is not usually identified as part of the Ezra tradition:

- The reading evidently takes place shortly after the end of the Feast of Booths (9:1).
- The occasion is one of mourning and separating from the "foreigners" (9:2).
- The law seems to be read by Levites, with Ezra nowhere mentioned (9:3–4).
- A long recital of Israel's history is given, covering events known from the present Pentateuch and the Deuteronomistic History (9:6–37).
- A pledge is made and signed by officials, Levites, heads of the people, temple personnel, and others, with Nehemiah's name at the head of the list (10:1–30).

---

[4] For example, Michael Fishbane, *Biblical Interpretation in Ancient Israel* (Oxford: Clarendon, 1985; repr. with addenda, 1989), 107–13.

- The main concern seems to be marriage with "the peoples of the land" (10:29–30; cf. 9:1–2).
- A number of other observances are mentioned, most found in the present form of the Pentateuch and most relating to the temple and its support (10:31–40).
- The one exception is the requirement to bring wood for the altar (10:35), which is not found in the present biblical text.

Even though the events of Neh 9–10 seem to follow directly on Neh 8 in the present text of Ezra-Nehemiah, there are some significant differences between the two episodes. Ezra is entirely absent in Neh 9–10, and the Levites associated with the reading of the law have different names than those listed in Neh 8. This helps confirm the common analysis that Neh 8 is a part of the Ezra tradition and different from Neh 9–10. In both cases, the book read is that of the torah of Moses (Neh 8:1; 9:3, 14, 29). Thus, we have a tradition that strongly associates the reading and promulgation of the torah of Moses with Ezra, and *a separate tradition* that associates the reading and promulgation of the same law with Nehemiah, the Levites, and the people as a whole, without any mention of Ezra.

When we ask about the content of the law in Neh 9–10, it seems clear that a considerable portion of our present Pentateuch is referred to in one way or the other: creation (9:6), Abraham (9:7–8), the oppression in Egypt and the exodus (9:9–11), the wilderness sojourn and the giving of the law (9:12–21), and the conquest of the Transjordanian kingdoms (9:22). Then there are some items from the Deuteronomistic History, including the conquest of Canaan (9:23–25), though the emphasis here is on a general denunciation of disobedience without much reference to events (9:26–37).

1.3. Ezra's Law in Ezra 8–10

Certain aspects of Ezra's law seem to be presupposed by the section of the Ezra tradition in Ezra 8–10. Can we tell anything about the character of Ezra's law from the text? The main references to marriages with "foreigners" in the Pentateuch are in Deut 7. Ezra 9:1–2 has a good deal of affinity with Deut 7:1–3 (cf. also v. 6) and 20:17–18, and Ezra 9:12 looks similar to Deut 7:3; however, Ezra 9:11 looks more like Lev 18:24–30.

When we put Ezra 8–10 and Neh 8 together, as part of the common Ezra tradition, it emerges without doubt that the book of the law presupposed included both Deuteronomic and P traditions. It is difficult to go beyond that with any certainty, but the existence of the Pentateuch in much its present form would be quite consistent with this narrative. On the other hand, there is no reason to date the Ezra tradition to the alleged time of the events described (whether 458 or 398 B.C.E.). The narrative itself could be as late as the Greek period in its present form, so that the law presupposed by it was not that extant in the fifth century B.C.E. but at a much later time.

1.4. OTHER REFERENCES TO THE BOOK OF THE LAW IN THE HEBREW BIBLE

The "torah of Moses," "the book of the torah," "the torah of God," and similar designations occur in many passages in the Old Testament. With the meaning of "teaching," *torah* occurs in a variety of contexts, but our concern is with the word where it implies something written down. A survey of usage soon makes it apparent that a written torah is referred to primarily in two collections of writings: (1) Deuteronomy and the Deuteronomic passages of the Deuteronomistic History, and (2) the books of Chronicles.

Apart from "book of the covenant" in Exod 24:7, the passages in the Pentateuch are all in Deuteronomy or in passages of the Deuteronomistic History that show the Dtr hand. The king is to write a copy of the law (17:18). The plagues that will befall Israel for disobedience are written in the book (28:58, 61; 29:19–20, 26), as are the commandments and statutes (30:10). Moses writes all the words in the book and places it in the ark of the covenant (31:24, 26). Outside the Pentateuch, Joshua has quite a number of references to the "book of the torah" or the "torah of Moses" (1:8; 8:31–32, 34; 23:6). Joshua himself recorded the words of the covenant in the "book of the torah of God" (24:26). In 1 Samuel 10:25 Samuel writes the *mišpaṭ* of the monarchy in a book. David instructs Solomon to keep what is written in "the torah of Moses" (1 Kings 2:3). All the rest relate in some way to Deuteronomy: 2 Kgs 14:6 quotes Deut 24:16; the other passages are all in the context of Josiah's reform (2 Kgs 22:8, 11, 16; 23:2, 21, 24–25), usually seen as involving the book of Deuteronomy or some portions of it.

Although the books of Chronicles naturally have a number of references to a book in connection with Josiah's reform (2 Chr 34:14–16, 18, 19, 21, 24, 30, 31; 35:12), the other passages speaking about the book of the law are more dispersed. A great deal having to do with the cult, priests, and temple is said to be done according to the (book of the) torah of YHWH/ Moses (1 Chr 16:40; 2 Chr 17:9; 23:18; 30:16; 31:3–4). Other passages refer more generally to keeping it (1 Chr 22:12; 2 Chr 25:4; 33:8). Apart from the references in Ezra and Nehemiah already discussed, the torah of Moses is referred to in Malachi (3:22 [Eng. 4:4]) and Daniel (9:11, 13).

1.5. BEN SIRA

The book of Ben Sira contains extremely important data about the development of the biblical text as Scripture. The "praise of the fathers" in Sir 44–50 gives a good indication of what books were considered authoritative by Ben Sira. It becomes clear that his "Scriptures" included the Pentateuch, by and large in its present form, because of the content referred to in 44:1–45:26.[5] He also speaks of the "book of the covenant of God Most High, the law that Moses commanded to us" (Sir 24:23).

Ben Sira's grandson, who translated the book into Greek, refers more explicitly to the books considered authoritative in a prologue to his translation. He refers to "the law, the prophets, and the other books" (Prolog. 1–2, 8–10, 24–25). When this is put together with Sir 44–50, we have the picture of a collection that contains most or all the contents of the Torah and the Prophets in our present Hebrew canon; however, the third division, the Writings, has only some of the contents. Allowing time for the Torah of Moses as a collection to become widely authoritative among the various Jewish communities would point to the Pentateuch's completion by the end of the Persian period.

1.6. Hecateus of Abdera

Although Hecateus is not strictly part of the biblical tradition, he is a major source who is best considered here rather than elsewhere. Writing about 300 B.C.E., Hecateus is an important witness to Jewish beliefs and history at this time. It seems likely that his information came from Jewish informants rather than a personal visit to Palestine.[6] The question of what Hecateus wrote is complicated by the fact that the material quoted in his name in Josephus has been widely disputed.[7] However, the most recent discussion of the question confirms the view that the quotations in Josephus

---

[5] For more detailed arguments to support this conclusion, see Lester L. Grabbe, "Jewish Historiography and Scripture in the Hellenistic Period," in *Did Moses Speak Attic? Jewish Historiography and Scripture in the Hellenistic Period* (ed. L. L. Grabbe; JSOTSup 317; European Seminar in Historical Methodology 3; Sheffield: Sheffield Academic Press, 2000), 129–55; cf. also idem, *Judaic Religion in the Second Temple Period: Belief and Practice from the Exile to Yavneh* (London: Routledge, 2001), 152–57.

[6] For a discussion, see Eric Gruen, *Heritage and Hellenism: The Reinvention of Jewish Tradition* (Hellenistic Culture and Society 30; Berkeley and Los Angeles: University of California, 1998), 49–55; also Lester L. Grabbe, *The Persian and Greek Periods,* vol. 1 of *Judaism from Cyrus to Hadrian* (Philadelphia: Fortress, 1992), 173; idem, *Judaic Religion,* 37–39.

[7] See especially the discussion in Menachem Stern, *Greek and Latin Authors on Jews and Judaism* (3 vols.; Jerusalem: Israel Academy of Arts and Sciences, 1974–1984), 1:20–46.

are the product of a later Jewish writer or writers.[8] This means that our main source is Diodorus of Sicily, who in turn drew on Hecateus (40.3.1–7). According to Hecateus, Moses was the founder of the Jewish temple, priesthood, and state. His successors are the high priests who have authority, since the Jews have never had a king (*sic*). For our present purposes, his most interesting statement is the following: "And at the end of their laws there is even appended the statement: 'These are the words that Moses heard from God and declares unto the Jews'" (Diodorus 40.3.6, translation from the LCL).

Nothing is said about a "book of the law," and the laws could exist in a nonwritten form. On the other hand, this statement is fully compatible with a written "book of Moses" by Hecateus's time. As seen above, Ben Sira's acceptance of the Pentateuch a century later is unlikely to have been possible if the "book of the torah of Moses" was not complete by the time of Hecateus.

1.7. SUMMARY OF THE BOOK OF THE LAW IN THE BIBLE

A number of points arise from this quick survey of the "book of the law" in the biblical tradition, including some inferences about history.

1. There is more than one tradition of the reading of the law. The one most often remembered is that in Neh 8, in which Ezra does the reading; this is reinforced by the alleged decree of Artaxerxes authorizing the promulgation of that law. All too often, that particular tradition is the only one noticed, yet there are other traditions. Nehemiah 9–10 has the law read by Levites, with no mention of Ezra. There is no reason to give priority to the Ezra tradition.

2. Some passages, particularly in the Ezra tradition, can be explained by knowledge of Deuteronomy alone. Yet other passages, such as Neh 9–10 and the reference to the Festival of Tabernacles in Neh 8, suggest a knowledge of P as well or, more likely, the complete Pentateuch in much of its present form.

3. It is clear that by the writing of Ben Sira about 200 B.C.E., the Pentateuch and the Prophets were more or less in the same shape as the present Hebrew canon. This is demonstrated not only from the Prologue contributed by Ben Sira's grandson about 130 B.C.E. but from the contents described in Sir 44–49. The collection of the Twelve Minor Prophets was already accepted as a unit by Ben Sira's time (Sir 49:10).

---

[8] Bezalel Bar-Kochva, *Pseudo-Hecataeus, On the Jews: Legitimizing the Jewish Diaspora* (Hellenistic Culture and Society 21; Berkeley and Los Angeles: University of California Press, 1996), esp. 122–81.

4. Furthermore, judging from Hecateus of Abdera and Ben Sira, the Pentateuch was already extant in much its present form by the end of the Persian period. This does not tell us anything about the law in Ezra, however, though the Ezra tradition seems to presuppose the book of the law with both D and P. On the other hand, the Hebrew Ezra-Nehemiah, as well as the original version (in Hebrew?) of the Greek 1 Esdras, may be post-Persian in their present forms. Thus, whether the Pentateuch was already extant by the mid- or late-fifth century B.C.E. is still a matter for debate.

2. Law under the Persian Empire

There is still a lot not known about the administration and the place of law under Achaemenid rule. This makes it hard to assert a negative (e.g., that the Persians did not do certain things). Nevertheless, this does not absolve us of the historian's responsibility to make the best judgment we can from the extant data. It is often asserted that the Persians were interested in establishing the rule of law in their empire. The classic statement of this position is given by Olmstead.[9] He points out that Darius I was remembered as a lawgiver. However, the evidence is too thin to assert that Darius I or any of the other Persian kings had a systematic policy of legal reform throughout the empire. Some of the inscriptions and documents should be considered here.

2.1. Passover Decree from Elephantine[10]

The interpretation of this important document is made more difficult by its fragmentary nature. Since only the lefthand side is preserved, the exact width of the column can only be guessed at, making reconstruction of the original text highly arbitrary. The following portion of the text is preserved (quoted here with a minimum of restoration):

Recto
Je]daniah and his colleagues the Jewish ga[rrison,] your brother Hanan[i]ah.
May God/the gods [seek after] the welfare of my brothers [
And now, this year, year 5 of King Darius, it has been sent from the king to Arsa[mes
] ... Now, you thus count four[
ob]serve and from the 15th day until the 21st day of [

---

[9] A. T. Olmstead, *History of the Persian Empire* (Chicago: University of Chicago Press, 1948), 119–34.

[10] *TAD* A4.1 = AP 21.

] be pure and take heed. [Do] n[ot do] work [
] Do not drink [...] not [eat] anything of leaven

Verso
] at sunset until the 21st day of Nisa[n
b]ring into your chambers and seal up during [these] days. [
Address
To] my brothers Jedaniah and his colleagues the Jewish garrison, your
brother Hananiah s[on

A variety of plausible reconstructions of the lacunae have been made.
The word "Passover" does not occur in the extant text,[11] though the subject seems unmistakable because of the content. There are several points
to notice about the text. It is not an official Persian decree but a letter from
someone called Hananiah to fellow Jews; however, the king and the satrap
Arsames (Aramaic Aršam) are invoked, suggesting that the letter might be
based on a official directive of some sort. Whatever might have come from
the king or satrap, the celebration of the Passover was not a new idea: the
word appears a couple of times in the ostraca from Elephantine in a way
that suggests the festival was a part of the people's lives.

What was the background of the Passover papyrus, then? In light of
the intriguing gaps in the text, one might come up with a number of plausible scenarios. One of the most likely is that the letter reflects a permit
from the Persian court to continue celebrating the Passover, possibly in the
light of local opposition. The local Khnum priest may well have opposed
the sacrifice of lambs.[12] Keep in mind that this was a few years before the
destruction of the Jewish temple, and friction between the two temple
communities seems to have built up over a period of time. If so, the decree
might not have permitted the use of lambs, since only leaven is mentioned
in the portion of the text preserved, but we cannot be sure. What seems
quite unlikely is that the government was primarily trying to tell the
Jews how to celebrate one of their festivals or that it was establishing

---

[11] The word פסח does not occur anywhere in the extant Elephantine papyri. The
word occurs twice in the ostraca, however, in its Aramaic form of פסחא: *TAD*
D7.6:9–10 (= *RÉS* 1793); *TAD* D7.24:5 (= Sachau 77.2). In both cases, the observance is mentioned in passing in letters, indicating that it was a part of their normal
lives. (My thanks to Professor Blenkinsopp, who made available to me his copy of
this *TAD* volume.)

[12] Whether the exodus story was a part of the Passover celebration at this time
or, if so, whether the Egyptians knew it and objected to it is a matter of speculation, though some commentators have argued this point. On the subject, cf. Gruen,
Heritage and Hellenism, 60–63.

the Jewish religion in some way. Like the other examples of Persian decrees known to us, this was probably a response to a request from the Jews themselves, not a unilateral act on the part of the Persian king.

2.2. Correspondence about the Elephantine YHW Temple

One of the most direct pieces of evidence about how subject peoples appealed to the Persian administration and how the latter responded in turn is found among the letters written by the Jewish community at Elephantine:

> Memorandum of what Bagohi and Delaiah said
> to me, saying: Memorandum: You may say in Egypt (ERASURE: bef)
> before Arsames about the Altar-house of the God of (ERASURE: Heav)
> Heaven which in Elephantine the fortress built
> was formerly before Cambyses (and)
> which the wicked Vidranga demolished
> in year 14 of King Darius:
> to (re)build it on its site as it was formerly
> and they shall offer the meal-offering and the incense upon
> that altar just as formerly
> was done.[13]

It is useful to compare this official authorization to rebuild the temple and reestablish its cult with the original request:

> Now your servant Jedaniah and his colleagues say thus: In the month of Tammuz, year 14 of King Darius, when Arsames had departed and gone to the king, the priests of Khnum the god who are in Elephantine the fortress, in agreement with Vidranga who was Chief here, (said), saying, "Let them remove from there the Temple of YHW the God which is in Elephantine the fortress." ... Moreover, before this—at the time that this evil was done to us—we sent a letter (to) our lord, and to Jehohanan the High Priest and his colleagues the priests who are in Jerusalem, and to Ostanes the brother of Anani and the nobles of the Jews. They did not send us a single letter.... Now, your servants Jedaniah and his colleagues and the Jews, all (of them) citizens of Elephantine, say thus: If it please our lord, take thought of that Temple to (re)build (it) since they do not let us (re)build it. Regard your obligees and your friends who are here in Egypt. Let a letter be sent from you to them about the temple of YHW the God to (re)build it in Elephantine the fortress just as it was formerly built. And they will offer the meal-offering and the incense, and the holocaust on the

---

[13] *TAD* A4.9 = AP 32.

altar of YHW the God in your name and we shall pray for you at all times—we and our wives and our children and the Jews, all (of them) who are here. If they do thus until the Temple be (re)built, you will have a merit before YHW the God of Heaven more than a person who offers him holocaust and sacrifices (whose) worth is as the worth of silver.... Moreover, we sent in our name all these words in one letter to Delaiah and Shelemiah sons of Sanballat governor of Samaria.[14]

A further document to compare is an offer of payment for the expenses if the temple is allowed to be rebuilt:[15]

Your servants—
  1 named Jedaniah son of Gem[ariah],
  [1] named Mauzi son of Nathan,
  1 named Shemaiah son of Haggai,
  1 named Hosea son of Jathom,
  1 named Hosea son of Nattun: all (told) 5 persons, Syenians who are heredi[tary-property-hold]ers in Elephantine the fortress—say thus:
  If our lord [...] and our Temple of YHW the God be rebuilt in Ele-phantine the fortress as it was former[ly bu]ilt—and sheep, ox, and goat are [n]ot made there as burnt-offering but [*they offer there*] (only) incense (and) meal-offering—and should our lord mak[e] a statement [*about this, then*] we shall give to the house of our lord si[lver ... and] a thousa[nd] ardabs of barley.

What these letters make clear is that the original request asked to renew the animal sacrifices. This seems to have been a problem, since in the later document the offer is made that animals would not be sacrificed, and it is this version that is endorsed by the satrap. This confirms that the Persians responded to the requests and complaints of the local peoples, including those relating to cultic practice, rather than initiating such decrees themselves.

2.3. Udjahorresne Inscription

Udjahorresne was an important Egyptian court official and commander of the royal navy under both the Saite and the Persian regimes.

---

[14] Two copies of the same letter have been preserved (*TAD* A4.8 and A4.9 = AP 30–31), one more fragmentary than the other, but most of the text can be reconstructed as a result of the overlap. Although I have used the translation in *TAD,* for ease of reading I have not indicated in any special way the insertions between lines or other corrections.

[15] *TAD* A4.10 = AP 33.

At his death he followed wide convention by leaving behind a statue inscribed with a personal testament, including a brief biography. The relevant parts read as follows:[16]

> The Great Chief of all foreign lands, *Cambyses* came to Egypt, and the foreign peoples of every foreign land were with him. When he had conquered this land in its entirety, they established themselves in it, and he was Great Ruler of Egypt and Great Chief of all foreign lands. His majesty assigned to me the office of chief physician. He made me live at his side as companion and administrator of the palace....
>
> I made a petition to the majesty of the King of Upper and Lower Egypt, *Cambyses,* about all the foreigners who dwelled in the temple of Neith, in order to have them expelled from it, so as to let the temple of Neith be in all its splendor, as it had been before. His majesty commanded to expel all the foreigners [who] dwelled in the temple of Neith, to demolish all their houses and all their unclean things that were in this temple....
>
> The prince, count, royal seal-bearer, sole companion, prophet of those by whom one lives, the chief physician, Udjahorresne, born of Atemirdis, he says: The majesty of the King of Upper and Lower Egypt, *Darius,* ever-living, commanded me to return to Egypt—when his majesty was in Elam and was Great Chief of all foreign lands and Great Ruler of Egypt—in order to restore the establishment of the House of Life—, after it had decayed. The foreigners carried me from country to country. They delivered me to Egypt as commanded by the Lord of the Two Lands. I did as his majesty had commanded me. I furnished them with all their staffs consisting of the wellborn, no lowborn among them. I placed them in the charge of every learned man [in order to teach them] all their crafts. His majesty had commmanded to give them every good thing, in order that they might carry out all their crafts. I supplied them with everything useful to them, with all their equipment that was on record, as they had been before. His majesty did this because he knew the worth of this guild in making live all that are sick, in making endure forever the names of all the gods, their temples, their offerings, and the conduct of their festivals.

Several points are to be noted about this inscription. First, Udjahorresne was a high official and important to the king, which explains why he had direct contact with the king. Secondly, the king was willing to accommodate a personal request about one temple in Egypt; the inference from this

---

[16] The translation is from *AEL* 3:36–41. For the Egyptian text and a discussion, see G. Posener, *La première domination perse en Egypte: Recueil d'inscriptions hiéroglyphiques* (Bibliothèque d'Etude de l'Institute Francpapais d'Archéologie Orientale, 11; Cairo: IFAO, 1936), 1–26, 164–75. See also Joseph Blenkinsopp, "The Mission of Udjahorresnet and Those of Ezra and Nehemiah," *JBL* 106 (1987): 409–21.

is that other temples were not given such special privileges or attention. Thirdly, although the king could have unilaterally initiated the decision to send Udjahorresne to take charge of the "house of life," this seems unlikely. Even if the inscription does not say so explicitly, the most likely interpretation is that Udjahorresne himself suggested the idea to the king or that the king was responding to a request from the Egyptian side.

2.4. The Susa Statue of Darius[17]

This statue of Darius I, with an inscription in the languages of Old Persian, Elamite, Babylonian, and Egyptian, was discovered in Susa. Because of the hieroglyphic inscription, some have thought that it was originally made in Egypt; if so, it was later moved to Persia itself. The Egyptian inscription reads as follows:

> May the good god and sovereign of both lands (i.e. Upper and Lower Egypt) Darius live forever. The King of Upper and Lower Egypt, the sovereign of the creation of matter (i.e. possessing magical force) ... the lord who has taken possession of the double crown (i.e., the crown of both parts of Egypt), great through his supremacy in the hearts of all people and imposing in face to him who sees him, the offspring of Aten ... Chosen (from among others) by Aten, the sovereign of On (i.e. Heliopolis) in order (to become) the sovereign of all that is surrounded by the solar disk (i.e. of the entire earth). He (i.e. Aten) found out that this is his son, his protector ... (the goddess) Neith gave him her bow, which was in her hand, so that (he might) cast down all his opponents.... His might is like unto (the might of the god of war) Mont ... the giant, the king of kings ... [the son] of the god Vishtaspa, an Achaemenid, who has begun to shine as the king of Upper and Lower Egypt on the throne of Horus of the living like unto the Sun, who goes before the gods eternally.... The image (i.e. statue) was made for the sovereign of both lands and was created by his majesty out of a desire to erect a monument to him so that they might remember his person along with his father Aten . . . forever. He (the god of the Sun) created a payment for him (the king) with life, with every kind of prosperity, with every aspect of good health, and with every joy—as to the Sun.[18]

---

[17] For information on this statue, see M. Kervran et al., "Une statue de Darius découverte à Suse," *Journal asiatique* 260 (1972): 235–66. See also the special section in the *Cahiers de la délégation archéologique française en Iran* 4 (1974), esp. the articles by F. Vallat, "Les textes cunéiformes de la statue de Darius," 161–70; "L'inscription trilingue de Xerxès à la porte de Darius," 171–80.

[18] English translation taken from Dandamaev and Lukonin, *Culture and Social Institutions,* 355.

This inscription shows Darius's desire to appear in the image of the traditional kings of Egypt. It, along with the Udjahorresne inscription, shows him as concerned about the prosperity of the Egyptian temples. However, this is not the same as exempting the temples from taxes or granting all of them special privileges carte blanche. Compare the Egyptian tradition about Cambyses that made him the destroyer of temples and the Egyptian sacred, even to the point of killing the Apis bull—negative propaganda that distorted the Persian role. The truth is in between: the Persian conqueror did not suppress traditional Egyptian worship, but he did take away many of the traditional privileges of the temples and bring them under the tax regime. He did occasionally grant special privileges (e.g., the temple of Neith, at the request of Udjahorresne), but these were exceptions. Darius continued what Cambyses had begun.

2.5. XANTHUS TRILINGUAL[19]

This inscription in Aramaic, Greek, and Lycian is an authorization of a cult at Xanthus in Lycia. It seems to be dated to the first year of a king Artaxerxes; this is probably Artaxerxes IV (contrary to the original publication), or about 337 B.C.E.[20] It is particularly relevant because it shows how the Persian government dealt with the establishment of a local cult. The Aramaic version is likely to be the official Persian decree:[21]

> In the month Siwan, year 1 of King Artaxerxes, in the fortress Arnna, Pixodarus son of Katommno, the satrap who is in Karka and Termmila has said: The landowners of Arnna have instituted a cult to worship the Lord god of *kbydšy* and [. . .]. And they made Simias son of Koddorasi priest. And there is a fief which the landowners gave to the Lord God. Year after year the sum of a mina and a half will be given by the region. The aforesaid priest will sacrifice a sheep every new moon to the Lord God and to . . . and an ox every year. And the aforesaid domain which has been free is his (i.e., the god's). This edict (hereby) inscribed is the one that conveys the title to the property. And if someone takes away from the Lord

---

[19] See the intitial publication of the text, with discussion and commentary, in H. Metzger et al., eds., *Fouilles de Xanthos 6: La stéle trilingue du Létôon* (Paris: Klincksieck, 1979).

[20] Cf. T. R. Bryce, "Political Unity in Lycia during the 'Dynastic' Period," *JNES* 42 (1983): 31–42, esp. 40.

[21] The following translation is essentially that of Javier Teixidor, "The Aramaic Text in the Trilingual Stele from Xanthus," *JNES* 37 (1978): 181–85. He reads the text slightly differently from Dupont-Sommer (in Metzger et al., *Fouilles*) in one or two places.

God (of Caunus) or from the priest what has been solemnly promised (to them), he will take it away from the Lord God of Xanthus; and from the gods Leto, Artemis, Hšatrapati, and the other (gods) he will take (it) away; therefore, these gods will seek him out.

The Lycian and Greek versions differ in small but interesting ways from the Aramaic, being slightly more expansive at several points. The Lycian is probably the version representing the request by the townspeople to establish the cult, but the Greek differs little from it. It also adds details about the local situation that the satrap did not feel necessary to include in the official version. Note also that the land for the cult came from the city or region, and the city also provides the financial support of the priest and offerings. There is nothing here about the Persian government giving land, money, or other imperial support to the cult. The satrap is the one to whom the request goes, not the king, and the satrap has issued the authorization.

2.6. GADATAS INSCRIPTION

This Greek inscription has been long known and is often cited. It reads as follows:

> The King of Kings Dareios son of Hystaspes to Gadatas, his slave, thus speaks: I find that as to my injunctions you are not completely obedient. Because you are cultivating my land, transplanting from (the province) beyond the Euphrates fruit trees to the western Asian regions, I praise your purpose and in consequence there will be laid up in store for you great favor in the Royal House. But because my religious dispositions are being nullified by you, I shall give you, unless you make a change, proof of a wronged (King's) anger. For the gardeners sacred to Apollo have been made to pay tribute to you; and land which is profane they have dug up at your command. You are ignorant of my ancestors' attitude to the god, who told the Persians all of the truth and [...].[22]

---

[22] For the English translation, see Charles W. Fornara, *Archaic Times to the End of the Peloponnesian War* (2d ed.; Translated Documents of Greece and Rome 1; Cambridge: Cambridge University Press, 1983), 37, no. 35. The Greek text is conveniently available in Russell Meiggs and David Lewis, eds., *A Selection of Greek Historical Inscriptions to the End of the Fifth Century B.C.* (Oxford: Clarendon, 1969), 20–22, no. 12. Two recent studies addressing the question of authenticity are O. Hansen, "The Purported Letter of Darius to Gadates," *Rheinisches Museum* 129 (1986): 95–96 (against its authenticity), and Joseph Wiesehöfer, "Zur Frage der Echtheit des Dareios-Briefes an Gadatas," *Rheinisches Museum* 130 (1987): 396–98 (in favor of it). Other studies include the translation and study by W. Brandstein and

Although not recognized by everyone, the Gadatas inscription is problematic to use as a source. Apart from questions of interpretation, there is the important problem of whether it is authentic or not. Its authenticity has often been taken for granted without discussion, yet a number of important studies have condemned it as a forgery. Peter Frei, for example, ignores it, leaving the inference that he regarded it as inauthentic or at least too problematic to use.[23] Yet it must be said that it has also been strongly defended, on the grounds that it shows evidence of being translated from Aramaic.

It will not be possible to try to settle the question here, but some points should be made. The present inscription appears to date from the second century C.E., centuries after the Achaemenid era. Some have suggested that it is a copy of the original, preserved by the local people because it gave evidence of certain ancient claims. This may well be true, but that does not prove its genuineness, since it could be an ancient forgery; alternatively, it could be a genuine decree that has been altered in certain ways to favor the present possessors of the land.[24]

If for the sake of argument the inscription is accepted as authentic, it would show the emperor's intervention in a local cult. However, the context is a very specific issue about this particular sacred site—the importance of this shrine because of the divine message of the god Apollo to a previous Persian emperor. The Gadatas inscription cannot be used as evidence that the Persians had a policy of supporting financially all local temples and cults.

2.7. PERSEPOLIS TABLETS

The Persepolis Treasury Tablets and Persepolis Fortification Tablets are an important addition to our knowledge of Persian times, especially in the administrative and economic areas. A large number of texts in Elamite were found in the 1930s and have only been partially

---

M. Mayrhofer (*Handbuch des Altpersischen* [Wiesbaden: Harrassowitz, 1964] 91–98), which assumes its genuineness, and the article of M. van den Hout, "Studies in Early Greek Letter-Writing," *Mnemosyne* 2 (1949): 19–41, 138–53, esp. 144–52 (against its authenticity).

[23] Peter Frei and Klaus Koch, *Reichsidee und Reichsorganisation im Perserreich* (2d ed.; OBO 55; Fribourg: Universitätsverlag, 1996), 24–26, 90–107.

[24] On this question, see the discussion above about the alleged Persian documents in Ezra. On the forgery in some Jewish sources, see Lester L. Grabbe, "Reconstructing History from the Book of Ezra," *Second Temple Studies 1: Persian Period* (ed. P. R. Davies; JSOTSup 117; Sheffield: JSOT Press, 1991), 98–107.

published.[25] They mainly record the distribution of rations from government stores to various individuals, though they also contain the receipt of taxes and the like. One of the more interesting features is the payment of rations and support to various priests and cult attendants. One might come to the conclusion that it was general Persian policy to support religion, temples, and the like in its empire. This was not the case, however.

The alleged support of cults is often exaggerated in modern literature because of the propaganda of the Persian kings themselves.[26] It is true that the Persians continued what was already general policy in the Near Eastern empires: to tolerate local cults as long as they did not threaten insubordination.[27] Yet little evidence exists that cults generally received state support, as sometimes alleged, which is hardly surprising, since temples usually had their own incomes.[28] On the contrary, temples were regulated and taxed, both in goods and services.[29] Overall Persian policy was rather to reduce the income of temples.[30] They also granted special favors (not necessarily permanent) to certain specific cults for political reasons.[31]

---

[25] George G. Cameron, *Persepolis Treasury Tablets* (Chicago: University of Chicago Press, 1948); Richard T. Hallock, *Persepolis Fortification Tablets* (Chicago: University of Chicago Press, 1969). A summary of the contents of these tablets is given in idem, "The Evidence of the Persepolis Tablets," *CHI* 2:588–609.

[26] Amelie Kuhrt, "The Cyrus Cylinder and Achaemenid Imperial Policy," *JSOT* 25 (1983): 83–97.

[27] Dandamaev and Lukonin, *Culture and Social Institutions,* 356–60.

[28] Some documents of the Persepolis Treasury and Fortification Texts mention the issuance of rations for cultic purposes, though the exact significance of this is unclear. See Hallock, *Persepolis Fortification Tablets,* texts 3159, 6663. It may be that these are only for certain official state cults; cf. Cameron, *Persepolis Treasury Tablets,* 5–9, and texts 10–11.

[29] Christopher Tuplin, "The Administration of the Achaemenid Empire," in *Coinage and Administration in the Athenian and Persian Empires: The Ninth Oxford Symposium on Coinage and Monetary History* (ed. I. Carradice; BAR International Series 343; Oxford: B.A.R., 1987), 109–66, esp. 149–53; Dandamaev and Lukonin, *Culture and Social Institutions,* 362–66; Simon Hornblower, *Mausolus* (Oxford: Clarendon, 1982), 161–63; Posener, *La première domination perse en Egypte,* 164–76.

[30] Dandamaev and Lukonin, *Culture and Social Institutions,* 362–66; Tuplin, "Administration of the Achaemenid Empire," 149–53.

[31] For example, the cults of certain temples in Egypt, according to the Demotic Chronicle: Wilhelm Spiegelberg, *Die sogenannte demotische Chronik des Pap. 215*

3. Conclusions

In order to evaluate the question of Ezra's law and its relationship to the context of Persian rule, one must keep in mind several points.

1. There is no evidence that it was Persian policy to fund and support religious cults and temples in general. On the contrary, they usually taxed temples. Only in exceptional cases were temples or temple personnel treated in a privileged way, such as by being exempted from tax. This provision apparently included the various cults to the central deities, as known from the Persepolis Fortress and Treasury texts, but outside the central Persian homeland, including Babylonia, Egypt, and Asia Minor, temples normally had to pay taxes. There is no reason to think that the Jerusalem temple and priesthood would have had decrees favoring them by tax exemptions under normal circumstances.

2. It has been suggested that Judah's position on the border with Egypt would have made it of particular concern to the Persian authorities.[32] This is possible, and some of the arguments are plausible in themselves. Yet it is curious that there is no direct evidence. No Persian document refers to Yehud in this regard, even though there are a variety of sources that mention Egypt and relate to the question of military stategy and activity in this region. What is even more curious is that none of the biblical traditions suggests such a role. Ezra goes to Yehud to bring the law. When he gets there, his only other concern is mixed marriages. Neither of these suggests anything about Persian military strategy or even Persian administration. As for Nehemiah, he asks to go to Judah, not to build up the defenses in a border area, but because Jerusalem is in a bad state. True, he builds up the walls, but these seem more to keep outsiders from influencing the Jews than to protect the borders. In any case, it was Nehemiah who instigated the trip, not the king. If the Persians were concerned about the strategic position of Jerusalem, they were remarkably laid back about the matter, apparently doing nothing until the Jews themselves approached them about going there. The fact is that apart from the highly partisan and exaggerated passages in Jewish literature, there is no evidence for any unusual treatment of Judah, the Jewish people, or Jerusalem.

3. The evidence of the inscriptions surveyed is that the Persian bureaucracy would respond to particular petitions from its subjects,

---

der Bibliotheque Nationale zu Paris (Leipzig: Hinrichs, 1914), 32–33. For examples from Mesopotamia, see Tuplin, "Administration of the Achaemenid Empire," 150.

[32] E.g., Kenneth G. Hoglund, *Achaemenid Imperial Administration in Syria-Palestine and the Missions of Ezra and Nehemiah* (SBLDS 125; Atlanta: Scholars Press, 1992).

especially if granting the request did not inconvenience or contravene its own operations. Thus, Udjahorresne's request to the king to grant certain privileges to the temple at Neith were accepted, no doubt as a reward for the Egyptian's help in establishing Persian rule over the country. In this case, a high official was able to approach the king himself. Rather more modest was the request to rebuild the Elephantine temple, which went to the local governor. It was approved, but not the request to offer animal sacrifices as before. A request to set up a local cult in Xanthus was approved, but the cost and the annual support of the priest came from the town, not the Persian government. This also illustrates another point often overlooked: most authorizations came from the satrap or governor, not from the king. The exceptions were those individuals who were already close to the throne because of their high position. (In this context, the assumption of the alleged involvement of the emperor with Ezra seems ill-supported.)

4. The suggestion that the Pentateuch was put into shape in the Persian period is confirmed by the data examined in this article. Ben Sira is clear that the Pentateuch in the same or a similar form to that known today was widely accepted as authoritative by 200 B.C.E. When we look at 1 and 2 Chronicles (probably completed in the early Greek period) and Hecateus of Abdera and consider also the time it would take after completion to become widely accepted as sacred literature, it seems clear that the Pentateuch was complete in much of its present form by the end of the Persian period. However, this did not immediately mark off Judaism as a "religion of the book." The Pentateuch was hardly available to a wider public for some time. Initially, it was in the hands of the priests and scribes (though these scribes, like Ben Sira, may have had a close connection with the priesthood or even have been priests themselves[33]). The cult could operate quite well without a written law. As argued elsewhere, the emphasis in Judah itself was on worship in the temple, and the shift to other forms of worship was only gradual and primarily under influence from the Diaspora.[34] The question is how this law was propagated.

5. The Ezra tradition makes Ezra the lawgiver par excellence, though it refers to the law that he brought as the "book of the torah of Moses," not the "torah of Ezra." Its attempt to push Ezra forward, however, founders on the many exaggerations and absurdities in the tradition. The

---

[33] Cf. Lester L. Grabbe, *Priests, Prophets, Diviners, Sages: A Socio-historical Study of Religious Specialists in Ancient Israel* (Valley Forge, Pa.: Trinity Press International, 1995), 65, 170, 198–99, 219–20.

[34] See Grabbe, *Judaic Religion,* esp. 334.

idea that Ezra was granted a slush fund amounting to one third of the entire tribute from the satrapy of Ebar Nahara is exceeded in its absurdity only by the frequency with which it has been accepted by modern scholars without question. Similarly, the idea that Ezra brought a new law or new customs to Jerusalem does not seem likely in light of the textual emphasis on the temple, cult, and priesthood as fully functional long before his time. There were no doubt new things in the law associated with him, or at least some things that differed from current priestly practice, but most of it was a codification of long-established tradition and practice. Some aspects of the law in the Pentateuch seem idealizations rather than current reality (e.g., the Jubilee year in Lev 25), but overall it is unlikely to have come as much of a shock. The reaction of the people to the reading of the law in Neh 8 probably owes more to literary imagination than to historical reality.

What is clear is that other traditions speak of the reading and promulgation of the law with no mention of Ezra (e.g., Neh 9–10). The association of Ezra with the law of Moses is only one point of view; it is not a universal one. There is certainly no need to give preference to the Ezra tradition. The question then becomes how to explain Ezra 7. Ezra 7 in its present form is not the product of the Achaemenid age. It could be an outright invention, though the presence of earlier forms in parts of it suggests that it would have to be based on a forgery of the Persian period. On the other hand, there could have been an actual decree from Artaxerxes lying behind Ezra 7, though this decree has been worked over by Jewish scribes of a later age to produce the present text, which in no way came from Artaxerxes.

6. If there was a real decree, however, it was most likely not one giving great power and authority to Ezra but rather a permission to teach the "law in his hand." This would fit the other decrees surveyed here. A request by Ezra or a Jewish group or even the Jews of Judah to promulgate a newly created "book of the torah of Moses" would probably have met with a favorable response from the Persian government, though the idea that this would have come to the king's direct attention and that he would be concerned to issue such a decree in his own name is unlikely. It is easy to accept the idea of permission to teach, without all the gross exaggerations about gifts of great wealth or divine intervention to make the Persian king show favoritism to the Jews.

. But however much we accept Ezra's existence, he was not the sole possessor of this new Pentateuch, assuming that he had the whole Pentateuch. If he were the only one to make known the law, it is hardly likely that so many traditions would have ignored or forgotten him. He was only one of many who accepted the new book. Others also saw it as their duty to teach and extend knowledge of this creation. Whatever Ezra's role—or lack of it—the result was that by the end of the Persian period "Moses' law" was in existence. Within another century, and perhaps sooner, it was widely known among the Jews and also widely accepted as authoritative and sacred.[35]

---

[35] My thanks to Professor Philip Davies, with whom I discussed some of these ideas, and to Professor Mary Douglas, whose article, "The Priests and the Foreign Wives: A Speculation," helped to clarify my thinking. Neither, of course, bears any responsibility for the fervid interpretations in the present article.

AN ACHAEMENID IMPERIAL
AUTHORIZATION OF TORAH IN YEHUD?

Gary N. Knoppers
Pennsylvania State University

The nature and extent of the legal relations between local communities and the central administration constitute some of the most interesting, difficult, and important issues in the study of the Achaemenid Empire. The recent work of Frei and Koch commendably explores a number of salient issues concerning the nature of the Achaemenid Empire—its leadership, diplomatic relations, executive hierarchy, system of communications, and relationships to the periphery.[1] Frei's provocative thesis, in particular, draws upon primary texts from a number of different centuries and from a variety of ancient Mediterranean sites to argue for a consistent and highly structured Persian legal policy toward the tremendous range of local communities within its domain.[2] His work has already stimulated and influenced a variety of other studies, including some that deal with the formation of the Pentateuch.[3] In what follows, I would like to concentrate on

---

[1] Peter Frei and Klaus Koch, *Reichsidee und Reichsorganisation im Perserreich* (OBO 55; Fribourg: Universitätsverlag, 1984); Peter Frei, "Die persische Reichsautorisation: Ein Überblick," *ZABR* 1 (1995): 1–35. I wish to thank James W. Watts for making available to me his translation of this article, "Persian Imperial Authorization: An Overview" (published on pp. 5–40 in this volume). Unless otherwise noted, all quotations of the work of Frei and Koch are taken from the second edition of their *Reichsidee und Reichsorganisation im Perserreich* (2d ed.; OBO 55; Fribourg: Universitätsverlag, 1996).

[2] Peter Frei, "Zentralgewalt und Lokalautonomie im Achämenidenreich," *Reichsidee,* 8–131. Cited hereafter as Frei, *Reichsidee.*

[3] E. Blum, *Studien zur Komposition des Pentateuch* (BZAW 189; Berlin: de Gruyter, 1990), 346–60; J. Blenkinsopp, *The Pentateuch: An Introduction to the First Five Books of the Bible* (ABRL; Garden City, N.Y.: Doubleday, 1992), 239–43; R. Albertz, *From the Exile to the Maccabees,* vol. 2 of *A History of Religion in the Old Testament Period* (OTL; Louisville: Westminster/John Knox, 1994), 467–68; J. L. Berquist, *Judaism in Persia's Shadow* (Minneapolis: Fortress, 1995), 138–39; F. Crüsemann, *The Torah: Theology and Social History of Old Testament Law*

a few significant aspects of the Persian imperial authorization hypothesis and its treatment of certain texts written in Yehud, namely, Ezra and Nehemiah. Since another late Persian-period text, Chronicles, relates to these matters, I would like to add it to the larger discussion.

My interest in relating these texts to the proposed theory is addressed to a few specific issues. This paper will not revisit the question of whether either the central government or a regional authority occasionally intervened within the local affairs of a community. One of the contributions of Frei's study has been to provide examples of such interventions. Hence if, as the Passover papyrus from Elephantine seems to indicate, a Persian authority gave his assent to the imposition of some regulations about the celebration of the Passover in a local community, that would not appear to contradict what generally is known about the general procedures employed by the Persian government.[4] If, as the text of Nehemiah indicates, there was someone who functioned as a *liaison* between the Jewish community and the Persian authorities concerning local matters, that should not occasion great surprise.[5] Such assignments

---

(trans. W. Mahnke; Minneapolis: Fortress, 1996), 334–39; J. W. Watts, *Reading Law: The Rhetorical Shaping of the Pentateuch* (Biblical Seminar 59; Sheffield: Sheffield Academic Press, 1999), 137–43. J. Wiesehöfer ("'Reichsgesetz' oder 'Einzelfallgerechtigkeit'?" *ZABR* 1 [1995]: 36–46) and U. Rüterswörden ("Die persische Reichsautorisation der Thora: Fact or Fiction?" *ZABR* 1 [1995]: 47–61) provide critical assessments of Frei's work.

[4] The letter, which contains instructions from Hananiah son of Jedaniah, whose identity is in question (Frei takes him to be one of the community leaders of the Jewish garrison at Elephantine), makes reference (line 3) to a decree of Darius (II) issued in his fifth year (419/418 B.C.E) to Arsames. The letter is fragmentary, but lines 5–10 seem to contain detailed ritual instructions about observing the Passover and Unleavened Bread (CAP, xvi, 60–65; P. Grelot, *Documents araméens d'Égypt* [LAPO 5; Paris: Cerf, 1972], 378–83; *TAD* A4.1, pp. 54–55). The question arises, of course, whether the Persian king is actually the lawgiver of the Passover stipulations, in the sense of authorizing statutes formulated by a representative or a Jewish body. Frei contends for the affirmative, disputing the claim that a Persian king would not trouble himself with such details and adopt Jewish regulations (*Reichsidee,* 48–49). For reservations, see H. G. M. Williamson, review of Peter Frei and Klaus Koch, *Reichsidee und Reichsorganisation im Perserreich, VT* 35 (1985): 379–80; L. L Grabbe, *The Persian and Greek Periods,* vol. 1 of *Judaism from Cyrus to Hadrian* (Philadelphia: Fortress, 1992), 53–55. For a different interpretation of the letter and its context, see B. Porten, *Archives From Elephantine: The Life of an Ancient Jewish Military Colony* (Berkeley and Los Angeles: University of California Press, 1968), 128–33, 311–14; idem, "The Jews in Egypt," *CHJ* 1:372–400; Rüterswörden, "Reichsautorisation," 10–11.

[5] Neh 11:24, cited by Frei in support of his hypothesis (*Reichsidee,* 21–22), mentions that "Pethahiah son of Meshezabel of the sons of Zerah son of Judah was at

would enhance the lines of communications among the center, the satrapies, and the periphery in the vast Achaemenid Empire.[6] Certainly the administrative bureaucracies within the Neo-Assyrian and Neo-Babylonian empires, which preceded the very large bureaucracy established during the Persian realm, also had to have subordinates in and contacts with far-flung communities within the territories they controlled.

But there are larger and more important ramifications of the Frei hypothesis that merit close scrutiny. One question is whether the Persian crown, or regional authorities acting on its behalf, encouraged the collection, if not writing and codification, of local law codes and authorized such works.[7] According to Frei, laws that were established by a local authority were not only approved and accepted by the central authority but also adopted as its own.[8] The royal Achaemenid authorization of local statutes elevated the status of such ordinances to the level of imperial law.[9] "The local norms are thereby established and protected within the framework of the entire state association, that is, the empire, as higher-ranking norms binding on all."[10] In this view, local regulations could be guaranteed through

---

the king's hand in all matters concerning the people." LXX[B] Neh 11:24 is, however, briefer, καὶ Παθαια υἱὸς Βασηζα πρὸς χεῖρα τοῦ βασιλέως εἰς πᾶν ῥῆμα τῷ λαῷ ("and Pathiah son of Baseza was at the king's hand for every matter of the people"). The list in 1 Chr 9, often regarded as a parallel to the list in Neh 11, reads in v. 6: "from the sons of Zerah: Jeuel and their kinsmen—690" (מִן־בְּנֵי־זֶרַח יְעוּאֵל וַאֲחֵיהֶם שֵׁשׁ־מֵאוֹת וְתִשְׁעִים). The lineage is completely different, apart from the reference to Zerah. The relationship between these two lists is much more complicated than some scholars have imagined. For the view that the lists in Neh 11 and 1 Chr 9 should not be regarded as close parallels, see my "Sources, Revisions, and Editions: The Lists of Jerusalem's Residents in MT and LXX Nehemiah 11 and 1 Chronicles 9," *Textus* 20 (2000): 141–68.

[6] Whether such a person was stationed at the Persian court (Frei, *Reichsidee,* 21–22, 98), at the satrapal seat, or functioned locally is unclear.

[7] Frei groups this consideration together with the Achaemenid authorization of an individual statute. Nevertheless, it seems to me that a distinction can be made between the two. Imposing a certain norm on a local community is different from authorizing (or imposing) an entire law code for such a community. The latter involves significantly more labor, communication, and coordination between the periphery and the center. The role of the regional authority (the larger province or the satrapy) would also have to come into play.

[8] Frei, *Reichsidee,* 14–15. See also the comments of K. Hoglund, *Achaemenid Imperial Administration in Syria-Palestine and the Missions of Ezra and Nehemiah* (SBLDS 125; Atlanta: Scholars Press, 1992), 207–47.

[9] Frei, *Reichsidee,* 28–29.

[10] Frei, "Persian Imperial Authorization," 7; idem, *Reichsidee,* 15.

imperial authority as long as those local regulations did not contradict imperial regulations and interests. This is, of course, a much stronger claim than simply asserting that the Persian crown permitted in a general way the introduction of a local lawbook. Because local law codes became imperial law, they were safeguarded as such. Moreover, Frei argues that the imperial authorization of local law occurs only in the Achaemenid Empire.[11] In this respect, the Achaemenid kingdom is said to be unique, differing from all empires that preceded it and from the empire of Alexander the Great that succeeded it. The Persian realm can be regarded as "the first supranational empire of the Mediterranean cultural sphere that deserves this name not just because of its size, but because it manifested to some degree an imperial way of thinking."[12]

Also meriting careful scrutiny is Frei's assertion of a close working relationship between local power-holders and their Persian overlords, a much more coordinated, constitutional, and constant relationship between the center and the periphery than most have been willing to recognize.[13] In the view of many scholars, no single, consistent, uniform infrastructure is discernible from the available documents dealing with relations between Achaemenid rulers and the provinces they controlled.[14] In writing about the administrative structures found within the Persian Empire, some have posited, in fact, a loose relationship between the periphery and the center, between local communities and the Persian crown. Aside from basic issues of taxes, tribute, political loyalty, and military cooperation, significant local autonomy has been assumed.[15]

This new theory, while affirming some measure of regional self-determination, contends for a much closer and highly structured relationship between local authorities, satraps, and the Persian king. This close legal association between the center and the periphery is also said to be remarkably invariable, extending from the late sixth century into the

---

[11] Frei, *Reichsidee,* 110–13.

[12] Frei, "Persian Imperial Authorization," 40.

[13] Frei, *Reichsidee,* 110.

[14] E.g., J. M. Cook, *The Persian Empire* (New York: Barnes & Noble, 1983), 167–82; C. Tuplin, "The Administration of the Achaemenid Empire," in *Coinage and Administration in the Athenian and Persian Empires: The Ninth Oxford Symposium on Coinage and Monetary History* (ed. I. Carradice; BAR International Series 343; Oxford: B.A.R., 1987), 109–66.

[15] E.g., M. A. Dandamaev, *A Political History of the Achaemenid Empire* (Leiden: Brill, 1989), 145–46; idem, "Achaemenid Imperial Policies and Provincial Governments," *Iranica Antiqua* 34 (1999): 269–82; Wiesehöfer, "Reichsgesetz," 45. We will return to this issue later (section 3).

mid-fourth century B.C.E.[16] In Frei's view, imperial authorization entailed a coordinated and multilevel international process. Following consultation and perhaps some adjudication, the central authority would issue in writing a standard proposed by subordinates somewhere in the empire.[17] In this way, an act of high-level legislation would be transferred to the domain of local law. Much like the king's own advisers, subordinates within a given area could apply to the king or to the regional satrap and ask him for an authorization fixed in writing. This would be a first step in the process toward the implementation of an imperial authorization.[18]

To sustain his hypothesis, Frei has to demonstrate a great degree of interest and formal intrusion into the internal affairs of provinces and local communities on the part of the central authorities. This is a point Frei seems to acknowledge. "Obviously, the term [imperial authorization] does not rule out the possibility that this institution can (also) serve to help the higher authority control the lower."[19] Or, again: "due to the initiative of members of a subordinate community, an important intervention in the structure of that community was undertaken by means of imperial authorization."[20] Indeed, local office-holders could appeal to the crown on the basis of the legal security afforded them by an imperial authorization. Precisely because local law could become state law, local officials could cite such a centrally ratified ordinance as legal warrant to impose their will upon the central authorities.[21]

I. Did Yhwh's Law Become the King's Law?

In applying the imperial-authorization hypothesis to the situation in Yehud, Frei points to the mission of Ezra as a prime example of how local officials were entrusted by their overlords to enact legislation that had been

---

[16] Frei, *Reichsidee,* 12–18, 39–47.

[17] In an alternative form of the hypothesis, the imperial chancellory demands that a given local community assemble and codify a corpus of traditional law that the Persian government could authorize either directly or through regional representatives (Blum, *Studien,* 358; Blenkinsopp, *Pentateuch,* 240; Berquist, *Judaism,* 138). In this view, the codification of law constitutes a local community's response to a central governmental directive.

[18] Frei, "Persian Imperial Authorization," 33.

[19] Ibid., 7.

[20] Frei, "Persian Imperial Authorization," 12.

[21] Frei cites the maneuvers of Pixodarus in the trilingual Letoon inscription as an example (*Reichsidee,* 107–9). For the inscription, see H. Metzger et al., eds., *Fouilles de Xanthos 6: La stèle trilingue du Létôon* (Paris: Klincksieck, 1979). For a different interpretation of this work, see Rüterswörden, "Reichsautorisation," 55–59.

certified by the Persian crown.[22] Frei cites the reference to "the law of your
God and the law of the king" (דתא די־אלהך ודתא די מלכא) in the rescript
attributed to Artaxerxes (Ezra 7:26) as evidence for the Persian authorization of a local law code (understood to be the Torah) in Yehud.[23] Ezra was
purportedly ordered to introduce a religiously based lawbook. For Frei "[i]t
is self-evident that the introduction of a lawbook by a commissioner
empowered for that purpose was not possible unless the central government approved of its contents."[24] The question naturally arises as to the
form that this approval took. In Frei's thesis, this was not a case in which
the Persian authorities permitted in some general way the introduction of
a local legal code. Rather, the emperor provided state authorization so that
this lawbook became legally binding. He confirmed these statutes as his
own.[25] Since the book mentions Ezra's commission in the province of
"Beyond the River" (7:25), some construe his law to be juridically binding
on all Jews within this particular satrapy.[26]

---

[22] Frei, *Reichsidee,* 51–61.

[23] This is not the place to revisit the controverted debate whether Ezra's lawbook was the completed Pentateuch or some earlier collection of legal material.
Most scholars incline toward the latter view; see the recent detailed study of
J. Shaver, *Torah and the Chronicler's History Work: An Inquiry into the Chronicler's References to Laws, Festivals, and Cultic Institutions in Relationship to
Pentateuchal Legislation* (BJS 196; Atlanta: Scholars Press, 1989), although I do not
agree with all of his analysis and conclusions. R. Rendtorff argues in favor of a distinction between דת, a judicial statute, and תורה, a collection of laws ("Esra und
das 'Gesetz,'" *ZAW* 96 [1984]: 165–84; idem, "Noch einmal: Esra und das Gesetz,"
ZAW 111 [1999]: 89–91). Similarly, M. A. Dandamaev and V. Lukonin think that the
דת (cf. Persian *dāta;* Neo-Assyrian *dātu*) of the king refers to a legal order established by an Achaemenid monarch and does not denote a single, uniform law
code (*The Culture and Social Institutions of Ancient Iran* [Cambridge: Cambridge
University Press, 1989], 116–17). The evidence pertaining to דת in the relevant
portions of the Hebrew and Aramaic Scriptures is, however, not entirely consistent. See Crüsemann, *Torah,* 338–39; *HALOT* 234b, 1856b; and J. Blenkinsopp,
"Was the Pentateuch the Civil and Religious Constitution of the Jewish Ethnos in
the Persian Period?" (pp. 41–62 in this volume).

[24] Frei, "Persian Imperial Authorization," 11; idem, *Reichsidee,* 28–29. L. L.
Grabbe takes a different view (*Persian and Greek Periods,* 94–98), expressing profound doubts about whether the Persian king would send a religious leader to
consolidate a border community (to Egypt). See also his essay in this volume.

[25] Frei, *Reichsidee,* 20–21, 60–61. This particular interpretation is, of course, not
new. See, for example, W. Rudolph, *Esra und Nehemia* (HAT 20; Tübingen: Mohr
Siebeck, 1949), 79.

[26] Frei does not seem to speak directly to this issue (*Reichsidee,* 51–61), but see
H. G .M. Williamson, *Ezra, Nehemiah* (WBC 16; Waco, Tex.: Word, 1985), 104–5;

Certainly there are some grounds for seeing the weight of Persian authority behind the lawbook brought back by Ezra. The nature and extent of Ezra's own authority are very much matters of debate, but his lawbook enjoys a privileged status.[27] Ezra is neither a governor nor a high priest, yet the consequences of transgression against "the law of your God and the law of the king" are severe.[28] Whoever does not comply with the

---

J. Blenkinsopp, *Ezra-Nehemiah: A Commentary* (OTL; Philadelphia: Westminster, 1988), 151–52; Blum, *Studien,* 350–51. Here and elsewhere, one is inevitably frustrated by the limitations of our sources. While Ezra is described as a scribe and priest with backing from his Persian superiors, the text makes no mention of a governor of Yehud in his time. Nor does the text clarify the nature of and extent of Ezra's own authority. Is one to suppose that Yehud did not have a governor in the time of Ezra? Or did the authors of Ezra-Nehemiah, in their drive to uphold Ezra's stature and his strictures against intermarriage, not see fit to mention any other major political or religious authority in Yehud?

[27] The identity of Ezra and the nature and extent of his mission are still very much matters of debate. See K. Galling, *Studien zur Geschichte Israels im persischen Zeitalter* (Tübingen: Mohr Siebeck, 1964), 170; L. L. Grabbe, "What Was Ezra's Mission?" *Second Temple Studies 2: Temple and Community in the Persian Period* (ed. T. C. Eskenazi and K. H. Richards; JSOTSup 175; Sheffield: JSOT Press, 1994), 286–99. Three examples will suffice. In the view of Williamson, Ezra was sent with Persian authority to investigate the condition of the Jerusalem temple cult (*Ezra, Nehemiah,* 102–7). In contrast, R. North contends that Ezra had no civil authority and "no mission other than to exercise his religious calling freely in accord with his conscience and his special talents" ("Civil Authority in Ezra," *Studi in onore di Edoardo Volterra* [Milan: Giuffré, 1971], 6:404). H. Niehr views both Ezra and Nehemiah as fictitious and dates their book to the Hellenistic age ("Religio-Historical Aspects of the 'Early Post-Exilic' Period," in *The Crisis of Israelite Religion: Transformation of Religious Tradition in Exilic and Post-Exilic Times* [ed. B. Becking and M. C. A. Korpel; OTS 42; Leiden: Brill, 1999], 243).

[28] To be sure, the author provides Ezra (7:1–5) with an impressive pedigree, tracing his ancestry through Seraiah (2 Kgs 25:18, 21; Jer 52:24, 27; 1 Chr 5:40 [Eng. 6:14]), Zadok (2 Sam 8:17; 1 Chr 5:34 [Eng. 6:8]; 18:16), Phinehas (Exod 6:25; Num 25:1–13; Josh 24:33; Judg 20:28; 1 Chr 5:30 [Eng. 6:4]), and Eleazar (Num 20:28; Josh 14:1; 1 Chr 5:29 [Eng. 6:3]) back to Aaron, who is proclaimed to be a "chief priest" (הכהן הראש; cf. 1 Esd 8:2: πρώτου ἱερέως ["first priest"]). The ascending genealogy links Ezra to some illustrious figures in his nation's sacerdotal past. Nevertheless, Ezra is himself called a "scribe" and a "priest" but not a "high priest" or a "chief priest" (*pace* K. Koch, "Ezra and the Origins of Judaism," *JSS* 19 [1974]: 190–93; P. R. Ackroyd, "The Chronicler As Exegete," *JSOT* 2 [1977]: 18–19; F. M. Cross, *From Epic to Canon: History and Literature in Ancient Israel* [Baltimore: Johns Hopkins University Press, 1998], 162). Within the administrative hierarchies of the Persian Empire, the office of scribe was not a high office but that of a civil servant (Dandamaev and Lukonin, *Culture and Social Institutions,* 89–116).

ordinance(s) is subject (7:26) to death, bodily punishment,[29] confiscation of property, and imprisonment (not necessarily in that order!). But the very juxtaposition of royal law and divine law also gives rise to some questions. What is the relationship, if any, between the two? Were imperial law and local law conceived as distinct, complementary, related, or identical? Are we dealing with two laws, one a local Judean law and the other an imperial royal or civil law? Did the latter perhaps legitimate the Judean law but remain formally distinct from it? Frei thinks in terms of identity. The *wāw* ("and") expresses the identity of the two laws; hence he understands the expression "the law of your God and the law of the king" to mean "the law of your God, namely, the law of the king."[30] Ezra's lawbook is simultaneously the law of Ezra's God and the law of the Persian king.[31] "One is subject to it in the same way that one is subject to royal law, and the corresponding sanctions are therefore also listed (Ezra 7:26). The validity of local norms thereby withstands every challenge, and legal security within the imperium is strengthened."[32]

But are "the law of your God and the law of the king" to be equated? Ezra is simply called "a scribe in the law of the God of heaven" (Ezra 7:12, 21), who is commissioned by the king and his seven counsellors "to conduct an inquiry [לבקרא] concerning Judah and Jerusalem according to the law of your God in your possession" (Ezra 7:14).[33] According to the edict ascribed to Artaxerxes, Ezra has authority to appoint magistrates and judges to judge the people, defined as "all those who are acquainted with the laws of your God"

---

[29] On this rendering of Kethib שרשו/Qere שרשי (cf. 1 Esd 8:24 τιμωρίᾳ, "physical punishment"), see F. Rundgren, "Zur Bedeutung von *ŠRŠW*—Esra VII 26," *VT* 7 (1957): 400–4; Z. Falk, "Ezra VII 26," *VT* 9 (1959): 88–89; F. C. Fensham, *The Books of Ezra and Nehemiah* (NICOT; Grand Rapids, Mich.: Eerdmans, 1982), 108; Blenkinsopp, *Ezra-Nehemiah*, 152.

[30] He cites שפטין ודינין in Ezra 7:25 as a proximate example. For other possible examples, see E. Vogt, *Lexicon linguae Aramaicae Veteris Testament* (Rome: Pontifical Biblical Institute, 1971), 53–54; R. J. Williams, *Hebrew Syntax* (2d ed.; Toronto: University of Toronto Press, 1976), §434. The comparative evidence from other postexilic texts does not support, however, reading the *wāw* as explicative here (see below).

[31] Frei, *Reichsidee*, 60–61; Rendtorff, "Ezra und das 'Gesetz,'" 172 (with some redefinition); Blum, *Studien*, 348; Crüsemann, *Torah*, 336–37.

[32] Frei, "Persian Imperial Authorization," 38; idem, *Reichsidee*, 28–29.

[33] The NJPS translates the infinitive of בקר, as "to regulate," but the normal designation of this Aramaic verb in the *paʿel* is "to investigate" or "to examine" (Ezra 4:15, 19; 6:1; *DNWSI* 187; *HALOT* 1837b–38a). The difference in meaning is not inconsequential to grasping the force of Ezra's assignment.

(כל־יָדְעֵי דָתֵי אֱלָהָךְ, Ezra 7:25).[34] Ezra has the power to instruct any among this group who do not acknowledge the laws of his deity. The references are oblique, but the text seems to suggest a distinction between sacral and royal decrees, even though loyalty to both will be enforced in the Judean community.[35]

2. THE LAW OF THE KING AND THE LAW OF GOD IN CHRONICLES

Two texts in Chronicles bear on the interpretation of this issue. While the author of this work is not likely to be the same as the author of Ezra, there is some important terminological overlap between the passages in Chronicles and the passage in Ezra.[36] Both involve the appointment of judges or officials, and both make a similar distinction to the one made in Ezra between "the law of your God and the law of the king." One of the texts in Chronicles deals with the judicial reforms attributed to King Jehoshaphat, while the other deals with King David's administration over outlying areas within his realm. This material dealing with David and Jehoshaphat is unique to Chronicles; it has no parallel in Samuel-Kings. My supposition is that the Chronicler, living in the late Persian or early

---

[34] Whether Ezra himself has the power to function either as a chief magistrate/judge or merely as one of those magistrates/judges is unclear.

[35] So also Fensham, *Ezra and Nehemiah,* 107; J. Blenkinsopp, "The Mission of Udjahorresnet and Those of Ezra and Nehemiah," *JBL* 106 (1987): 409–21; Williamson, *Ezra, Nehemiah,* 104–5.

[36] On the distinction between the authorship of Chronicles and that of Ezra-Nehemiah, see S. Japhet, "The Supposed Common Authorship of Chronicles and Ezra-Nehemiah Investigated Anew," *VT* 18 (1968): 330–71; idem, "The Relationship between Chronicles and Ezra-Nehemiah," *Congress Volume: Leuven, 1989* (ed. J. A. Emerton; VTSup 43; Leiden: Brill, 1991), 298–313; H. G. M. Williamson, *Israel in the Books of Chronicles* (New York: Cambridge University Press, 1977), 5–70; I. Kalimi, "Die Abfassungszeit der Chronik—Forschungsstand und Perspectiven," *ZAW* 105 (1993): 223–33; S. Talmon, "Esra und Nehemia: Historiographie oder Theologie?" in *Ernten, was man sät: Festschrift für Klaus Koch zu seinem 65. Geburtstag* (ed. D. W. Daniels et al.; Neukirchen-Vluyn: Neukirchener Verlag, 1993), 329–56. Some of the arguments for disunity have been challenged by J. Blenkinsopp, *Ezra-Nehemiah;* D. Talshir, "A Reinvestigation of the Linguistic Relationship between Chronicles and Ezra-Nehemiah," *VT* 38 (1988): 165–93; K.-F. Pohlmann, "Zur Frage von Korrespondenzen und Divergenzen zwischen den Chronikbüchern und dem Esra/Nehemia-Buch," *Congress Volume: Leuven, 1989* (ed. J. A. Emerton; VTSup 43; Leiden: Brill, 1991), 314–30. In my judgment, more than one author is responsible for Chronicles and Ezra-Nehemiah, but I would not deny that some connections exist between them.

Hellenistic period, constructed the past in categories familiar to him in his own time.[37]

According to the Chronicler's highly stylized account of Jehoshaphat's reign, this monarch appears as an energetic leader who exhibits a keen interest in establishing legal reforms within both the center and the periphery of his state.[38] Early in his reign, Jehoshaphat initiates a campaign to send his officers (שָׂרָיו), priests, and Levites into the towns of Judah to teach "the scroll of the torah of YHWH" (2 Chr 17:7–9). In a later phase of his career Jehoshaphat personally travels among his people from Beer-sheba to the hill country of Ephraim, "restoring them to the God of their fathers" (2 Chr 19:4b).[39] This restoration functions as a prelude to the revamping of the nation's judiciary. Having earlier assigned troops and prefects to all the fortified towns (2 Chr 17:2), Jehoshaphat stations שֹׁפְטִים ("judges") within each of these towns (2 Chr 19:5). The new reform transforms the administration of justice within his kingdom. The two-tiered judiciary the king establishes—consisting of courts operating within towns throughout his realm and a high court in the capital of Jerusalem—draws on certain characteristics of earlier Israelite judicial sytems depicted in Exodus (18:13–27) and Deuteronomy (1:9–18; 16:18–20; 17:8–13), but it also manifests its own distinctive traits.

The court the king establishes in Jerusalem is staffed by Levites, priests, and ancestral heads (2 Chr 19:8), who address cases referred to them by their kinsmen in the towns (2 Chr 19:10). The Chronicler may also construe their duty as adjudicating disputes within the city of Jerusalem, but this is

---

[37] Assuming that Jehoshaphat's reforms reflect ninth-century B.C.E. legal realities, many scholars have thought that the characteristics of these reforms historically precede the judicial ordinances of Deuteronomy. But the Chronicler's presentation of Jehoshaphat's judicial reforms is best understood as combining elements found separately in Exodus and Deuteronomy. The author does not simply duplicate this older legal material; he selects, combines, supplements, and hence transforms earlier forensic theory and precedent. The judiciary posited during Jehoshaphat's tenure resonates with certain features of both Moses' judicial reform and the Deuteronomic reforms, yet it ultimately manifests the author's own distinctive perspective (G. N. Knoppers, "Jehoshaphat's Judiciary and the Scroll of YHWH's Torah," *JBL* 113 [1994]: 59–80).

[38] G. N. Knoppers, "Reform and Regression: The Chronicler's Presentation of Jehoshaphat," *Bib* 72 (1991): 500–24; K. Strübind, *Tradition als Interpretation in der Chronik: König Josaphat als Paradigma chronistischer Hermeneutik und Theologie* (BZAW 201; Berlin: de Gruyter, 1991).

[39] The geographic scope of this second campaign is extensive, including sections of the northern kingdom over which he held sway (2 Chr 17:1–2).

textually uncertain.[40] In any event, the high-court judges do not function in isolation. They are aided by Levitical officials, presumably in secretarial matters and in implementation (2 Chr 19:11).[41] The judicial system Jehoshaphat creates reflects substantial royal involvement in the organization of justice but paradoxically no direct royal involvement in adjudicating legal disputes. The courts are related to one another, but self-standing. There is neither a clear role for the king himself in the national justice system he inaugurates nor any indication that the king needs to authorize any of the decisions made by the courts. There is no direct mechanism by which participants in the courts may petition or appeal judicial verdicts to the king.

To be sure, the judicial officials in the Jerusalem court are subject to higher authorities: to Amariah, the chief priest, in every matter of YHWH (כל דבר־יהוה), and to Zebadiah, the commander of the house of Judah, in every matter of the king (כל דבר־המלך, 2 Chr 19:11).[42] The text does not define precisely what a matter of the king is, as opposed to a matter of YHWH.[43] Presumably, the former might include royal decrees, taxes, tax exemptions, and certain issues of civil and criminal law, while the latter might include cultic obligations, directives about religious practices, endowments, dispositions with respect to the sanctuary, sacerdotal personnel, and

---

[40] 2 Chr 19:8. The MT reads ולריב וישבו ירושלם, while the LXX has καὶ κρίνειν τοὺς κατοικοῦντας ἐν Ἰερουσαλήμ. On the basis of the LXX, some scholars posit an original, ולריבי ישבי ירושלם ("and for the cases concerning Jerusalem's residents"). A third option (RSV) is to repoint the MT as ישבו ("they sat" [at Jerusalem]). Along with W. Rudolph (*Chronikbücher* [HAT 21; Tübingen: Mohr Siebeck, 1955], 256), I think that the LXX lemma makes the most sense.

[41] M. Weinfeld, "Judge and Officer in Ancient Israel and in the Ancient Near East," *Israel Oriental Studies* 7 (1977): 65–88.

[42] The title "commander" (נגיד) is used for a variety of different positions in Chronicles. In fact, this title appears twice as often in Chronicles as in any other biblical book (Knoppers, "Jehoshaphat's Judiciary," 75-76). It is interesting to observe that even though this נגיד is responsible for royal matters, he is formally connected to "the house of Judah."

[43] The distinction is, however, widely recognized to be a postexilic one (Rudolph, *Esra und Nehemia*, 74–77; R. R. Wilson, "Israel's Judicial System in the Preexilic Period," *JQR* 74 [1983]: 229–48; Blenkinsopp, *Ezra-Nehemiah*, 150–51; Frei, *Reichsidee*, 56–58). Whether such matters were always so clearly distinguished in preexilic times is in doubt. See Exod 22:27; Judg 7:18, 20; 1 Sam 25:26; 2 Sam 15:21; 1 Kgs 21:10, 13; Isa 8:21; Zeph 1:5; Prov 24:21 (I thank my colleague B. Halpern for these references). The recently published seventh-century inscription from Ekron includes a dedication *lbʾl wlpdy* "to Baal and to Padi" (S. Gitin and M. Cogan, "A New Type of Dedicatory Inscription from Ekron," *IEJ* 49 [1999]: 193–202).

temple operations.[44] In any case, this Persian-period text promotes obedience to both royal statutes ("every matter of the king") and sacral statutes ("every matter of YHWH") yet clearly distinguishes between them. If the distinction were to be collapsed, there would be no effective difference between the cultic domain and the royal domain and no reason to subject the former to the commander of the house of Judah and the latter to the chief priest. Quite the contrary, Jehoshaphat's distinction between issues pertaining to the king and issues pertaining to YHWH suggests that the author, living in a postexilic context, made some sort of differentiation between sacral and royal statutes. Two different kinds of officials are responsible for two different kinds of law.

The classification pertaining to matters of YHWH and matters of the king also appears within the description of David's reign. As with Ezra and Jehoshaphat, the context deals with administrative and legal issues. Chronicles asserts, in fact, great Davidic attention to a variety of civil, administrative, and sacral appointments. To prepare for the transition to his divinely chosen successor, an aging but still lucid King David establishes a national administration to serve Solomon (1 Chr 23:1–27:34).[45] Part of this planning involves the appointment of administrators for remote areas within his state (1 Chr 26:29–32). For both this work and for the supervision of the treasuries the king draws from the ranks of his Levitical civil service.[46] The Izharites, Chenaniah and his sons, are made responsible for

------

[44] See further the comments about the Egyptian term *hp* in association with temples by D. B. Redford, "The So-Called 'Codification' of Egyptian Law under Darius I" (pp. 135–59 in this volume).

[45] The authorship of 1 Chr 23–27 is debated. I view a substantial part of this material as an integral part of the Chronicler's work. See S. Japhet, *The Ideology of the Book of Chronicles and Its Place in Biblical Thought* (BEATAJ 9; Frankfurt am Main: Lang, 1989); J. W. Wright, "The Legacy of David in Chronicles: The Narrative Function of 1 Chronicles 23–27," *JBL* 110 (1991): 229–42; idem, "From Center to Periphery: 1 Chronicles 23–27 and the Interpretation of Chronicles in the Nineteenth Century," in *Priests, Prophets, and Scribes: Essays on the Formation and Heritage of Second Temple Judaism in Honour of Joseph Blenkinsopp* (ed. E. C. Ulrich et al.; JSOTSup 149; Sheffield: JSOT Press, 1992), 20–42; W. M. Schniedewind, *The Word of God in Transition: From Prophet to Exegete in the Second Temple Period* (JSOTSup 197; Sheffield: JSOT Press, 1995), 165-70.

[46] In Chronicles the Levites serve a variety of functions. Their duties encompass more than simply cultic affairs. See further, J. W. Wright, "Guarding the Gates: 1 Chronicles 26.1-19 and the Roles of Gatekeepers in Chronicles," *JSOT* 48 (1990): 69–81; G. N. Knoppers, "*Hierodules,* Priests, or Janitors? The Levites in Chronicles and the History of the Israelite Priesthood," *JBL* 118 (1999): 49–72; idem, "Treasures Won and Lost: Royal (Mis)appropriations in Kings and Chronicles," in *The*

the outlying work (למלאכה החיצונה) in Israel as officials (שטרים) and judgës (שפטים, 1 Chr 26:29).[47] This work in external affairs pertains to the governance of remote regions outside of Jerusalem.[48] From the Hebronites, Hashabiah and his kinsmen are put in charge of the supervision of Israel in the land westward of the Jordan[49] for every matter of Yhwh and for the service of the king (לכל מלאכת יהוה ולעבדת המלך, 1 Chr 26:30).[50] Other Hebronites, men of substance, are appointed to be in charge of the Reubenites, the Gadites, and the half-tribe of Manassites, for every matter of God and for (every) matter of the king (לכל־דבר האלהים ולכל] דבר המלך, 1 Chr 26:31-32).[51]

The significance of some details in this presentation are not altogether transparent.[52] In any case, it seems evident that the Chronicler's David employs his civil servants to supervise both cultic affairs and royal affairs on his behalf. If one wants to argue the contrary position, that the author made no distinction between affairs of state and affairs of religion, one has to maintain that "the service of the king" is one and the same as the "matters of Yhwh." Certainly David is cast as a pious monarch, who has the

---

Chronicler As Author: Studies in Text and Texture (ed. M. P. Graham and S. L. McKenzie; JSOTSup 263; Sheffield: Sheffield Academic Press, 1999), 181–208.

[47] The lxx reads τοῦ γραμματεύειν καὶ διακρίνειν (= לסופרים ושופטים: "scribes and judges"). In the earlier Levitical census mandated by David (1 Chr 23:3–5), "6,000 were officials [שטרים] and judges" (שפטים). Judges also appear alongside the ancestral heads and other leaders in Solomon's first national assembly (2 Chr 1:2).

[48] In Nehemiah certain Levites are assigned "the outside work for the house of God" (המלאכה החיצנה לבית האלהים, Neh 11:16).

[49] The expression מעבר לירדן מערבה (literally, "from beyond the Jordan to the west") is quite unusual; cf. מ/בעבר לירדן ימה, "(from) beyond the Jordan to the sea" (Josh 5:1; 22:7).

[50] See n. 5 above.

[51] The lxx* reads "for every command [πρόσταγμα] of Yhwh and for [every] matter [λόγον = דבר] of the king." The term πρόσταγμα may reflect a different *Vorlage* from that of the mt (= חק in 1 Chr 16:17; 22:13; 29:19; 2 Chr 33:8; 34:31; מצוה in 2 Chr 29:15, 25; 30:6, 12; 31:21), but this is not certain (λόγον = דבר; 2 Chr 19:11).

[52] Noticing the occurrence of Jazer (cf. 1 Chr 26:31) in the Levitical town lists, some scholars (e.g., Y. Aharoni, *The Land of the Bible* [rev. ed. by Anson Rainey; Philadelphia: Westminster, 1979], 302) tie this material to the Levitical town lists (Josh 21:1–42; 1 Chr 6:39–66). The sites in these lists were purportedly administered by Levites, because they were part of the government's land holdings. But if our passage is to be cited as historical evidence for a central administrative strategy, that strategy may not be keyed to the Levitical towns at all. The references in vv. 30 ("Israel beyond the Jordan") and 32 ("the Reubenites, the Gadites, and the half-tribe of Manassites") are geographical and tribal in nature.

authority to delegate oversight in both areas. Chronicles depicts Israel's revered king as making all sorts of Levitical and priestly appointments, but the book does distinguish between spheres of sacerdotal and political responsibility. For this reason, the Chronicler's King Uzziah finds himself in great trouble after he displays great arrogance by entering the temple and burning incense upon the incense altar (2 Chr 26:16–17).[53] Confronted and admonished by the priests, Uzziah becomes angry only to be struck by leprosy. He spends the rest of his days as a leper cut off from the temple (2 Chr 26:18–21).[54]

The distinction between the matters of YHWH and matters of the king maintained by the Chronicler may be compared with distinctions observed by other late writers, for example, the differentiation between the office of governor and the office of high priest in the dyarchic leadership of Zerubbabel the governor of Judah (פחת יהודה) and Jeshua the high priest (הכהן הגדול).[55] One also thinks of the careful distinction made in the program of Ezekiel between the office of "prince" (נשיא) and the positions held by the priests.[56] The restrictions imposed on the "prince" with reference to the sanctuary and the priests who minister there are quite remarkable.

Whereas the authors of Haggai, Chronicles, Ezra, and Ezekiel apply the political/cultic distinction to the polity of their people, other writers, such as the authors of Ezra-Nehemiah, apply such a broad distinction to differentiate between Judean laws and imperial laws.[57] The authors of Esther distinguish between the laws of a particular group and those of a larger royal authority. In speaking to King Ahasuerus, Haman casts this distinction in a negative sense by declaring that "there is a certain people,

---

[53] The text repeatedly uses מעל to refer to Uzziah's actions, one of the Chronicler's choice terms for profound infidelity and disobedience (R. Mosis, *Untersuchungen zur Theologie des chronistischen Geschichtswerkes* [Freiburg: Herder, 1973], 29–33; J. Milgrom, *Cult and Conscience: The Asham and the Priestly Doctrine of Repentance* [SJLA 18; Leiden: Brill, 1976], 16–35). See also W. M. Schniedewind, "King and Priest in the Book of Chronicles and the Duality of Qumran Messianism," *JJS* 45 (1994): 71–78 and the references cited there.

[54] The detail about his leprosy and quarantine is also found in 2 Kgs 15:5, but the rest of the Chronicler's story is unparalleled in Kings.

[55] Hag 1:1, 12, 14; 2:2, 4, 21–23; Zech 4:6; 6:11; Ezra 2:2; 3:6–13 [cf. 1 Esd 5:53–65]; 5:1–2; Neh 7:7.

[56] Ezek 37:24–28; 44:1–3; 45:1–25; 46:1–10, 12, 16–18; 48:21–22.

[57] Obviously, this represents a narrowing of the application of indigenous law to certain cultic, juridical, and social practices. Older biblical legislation contained, of course, a significant amount of material (e.g., Deut 17:14–20) of a clear political nature.

scattered and dispersed among the peoples throughout all the provinces of your realm, whose laws differ [וְדָתֵיהֶם שֹׁנוֹת] from those of every other people and who do not observe the king's laws" (וְאֶת־דָּתֵי הַמֶּלֶךְ אֵינָם עֹשִׂים, 3:8). The authors of Daniel also differentiate between imperial royal decrees or laws (2:13, 15; 6:9, 13, 16 [Eng. 6:8, 12, 15]) and the laws of Daniel's deity (6:6 [Eng. 6:5]). In short, whether applied internally to Judah or more broadly to the Achaemenid realm, the distinction between sacral and royal orders is important, because it provides insight into how certain Persian and Hellenistic writers defined different lines of authority. Far from blurring or merging the two areas, these texts reveal either a demarcation between them or a call for such a demarcation to be realized.

3. Local Autonomy, Satrapal Governance, and Central Control

The Persian period materials from Yehud may shed some light on the larger question of the bearing of imperial authority upon the daily operations of local communities. Perhaps the legal relations among the center, the satrapies, and the periphery were not as highly structured and juridically systemic as the Frei hypothesis would have it. Rather than creating and enforcing a tightly defined and coordinated relationship between local and central laws, the Achaemenid authorities may have been content to ensure that their own directives were followed and to allow local communities some latitude to observe their own customs and religious traditions. It also seems likely that the lines between central and local authority were not the same in all regions within the Persian Empire nor constant in various phases of Achaemenid history.[58] The satrapy "Beyond the River" alone contained a great range of *ethnē* and political entities. One must allow for changes in imperial policy not only from reign to reign, but also within the tenure of a single monarch.

In what remains, I would like to make a brief case for the hypothesis rejected by Frei, namely, that the central Persian government, or regional authorities acting on its behalf, permitted local communities to follow their own customs and laws, if so desired, provided that the content and implementation of such statutes did not interfere with their own policies and strategic interests. Dandamaev and Lukonin argue that the Persians themselves distinguished between their royal judicial system administered by Persians and the regional legal systems found in various parts of their empire, Babylon, the Phoenician cities, and Egypt among them.[59] This is not to say that the Achaemenids practiced a laissez-faire policy toward the

---

[58] Tuplin, "Administration of the Achaemenid Empire," 113–37; Berquist, *Judaism,* 87–94, 105–9.

[59] Dandamaev and Lukonin, *Culture and Social Institutions,* 118–30.

subject peoples within their vast empire. Political loyalty, the ongoing movement of trade, the reception of gifts, income from the royal estates, and the regular collection of taxes and tribute were priorities in their regulation of local affairs.[60] Military cooperation in the form of support for garrisons was another active consideration, especially in distant border areas.[61] The Persians did not have to abolish existing structures and create new ones. Rather, existing institutions could be exploited toward Persian ends. To the extent that this larger strategy was successful, it yielded more revenue from the provinces and greater allegiance on the part of local appointees.[62]

The Achaemenid rulers generally allowed communities to maintain, if not revive, their own traditions, laws, and customs.[63] The Persian authorities could impose, of course, their own legal regulations. Darius himself boasts that sundry peoples within his empire obeyed his law.[64] Nevertheless, there

---

[60] Tuplin, "Administration of the Achaemenid Empire," 137–58; Dandamaev and Lukonin, *Culture and Social Institutions,* 177–95, 209–22; W. J. Vogelsang, *The Rise and Organisation of the Achaemenid Empire: The Eastern Iranian Evidence* (SHANE 3; Leiden: Brill, 1992), 245–303; P. Briant, *Histoire de l'Empire perse de Cyrus à Alexandre* (Paris: Fayard, 1996), 399–487; idem, "Bulletin d'histoire achéménide (BHAch) I," *Recherches récentes sur l'Empire achéménide* (ed. M.-F. Boussac; Topoi Supplément 1; Paris: de Boccard, 1997), 82–83; A. Kuhrt, *The Ancient Near East c. 3000—330 BC* (2 vols.; London: Routledge, 1995), 2:676–82, 689–701; J. Wiesehöfer, *Ancient Persia from 550 BC to 650 AD* (London: I. B. Tauris, 1996), 63–65; R. Descat, "Le tribut et l'économie tributaire dans l'Empire achéménide," *Recherches récente sur l'Empire achéménide* (ed. M.-F. Boussac; Topoi Supplément 1; Paris: de Boccard, 1997), 253–62.

[61] Hoglund, *Achaemenid Imperial Administration,* 165–205; Wiesehöfer, *Ancient Persia,* 89–93; J. Betlyon, "Military Operations Other Than War in Persian Period Yehud" (unpublished paper).

[62] Kuhrt, *Ancient Near East,* 696–701.

[63] P. Briant, "Pouvoir central et polycentrisme culturel dans l'empire Achéménide: Quelques réflections et suggestions," in *Sources, Structures and Synthesis: Proceedings of the Groningen 1983 Achaemenid History Workshop* (ed. H. Sancisi-Weerdenburg; Achaemenid History 1; Leiden: Nederlands Instituut voor het Nabije Oosten, 1987), 1–31; Frei, *Reichsidee,* 107–13; K. Koch, "Weltordnung und Reichsidee im alten Iran und ihre Auswirlungen auf die Provinz Jehud," *Reichsidee,* 133–202; Dandamaev and Lukonin, *Culture and Social Institutions,* 116–30. A. Kuhrt argues that these policies were not as generous and widely implemented as some have thought ("The Cyrus Cylinder and Achaemenid Imperial Policy," *JSOT* 25 [1983]: 83–97).

[64] R. G. Kent, *Old Persian: Grammar, Texts, Lexicon* (2d ed.; AOSM 33; New Haven, Conn.: American Oriental Society, 1953), 119 [§§8.1.23–24], 138 [§§3.15–17], 142 [§§4.30–41].

is no compelling evidence to indicate that Darius and his successors made any serious attempt to replace existing structures found within the provinces with one unified Persian administrative structure. It is true that in a few instances the Persian authorities supported local sanctuaries with gifts and endowments. But there is no clear documentation to suggest that such efforts led to any larger attempt to micromanage the daily operations of local communities within the great range of societies found within the enormous Achaemenid empire.[65] Rather, the Persian kings seem to have given local appointees significant leeway to govern their communities in accordance with larger strategic priorities.[66] Achaemenid hegemony was maintained even as local customs were honored. There is even some evidence to suggest that the Persians allowed locals to hold important offices within their territories. But, during most periods, the Persians seem to have restricted entry into the highest offices within their government to members of the Persian aristocracy. The Persian kings preferred to reward good conduct and loyalty from members of other societies by granting honorary titles and material distinctions, rather than by providing open access to the highest levels of martial or political decision making.[67] This practice protected the highest echelon of the Persian elite from unwelcome integration, while encouraging local and regional appointees to manifest loyalty toward their superiors. In the large network of imperial, regional, and local appointments, local power-holders could, and many apparently did, view the Achaemenid king as a guarantor of stability, order, and tradition in no small part because he was also the ultimate guarantor of their own positions.

In discussing the regulations issued by Nehemiah with respect to the service duties of the temple personnel (13:30–31) and the commitments of the community toward the temple (10:1, 34, 35–37), it is, therefore, unnecessary to posit Persian imperial decrees lying behind these measures.[68] Similarly, in discussing the ritual ordering of the Levitical singers for which there was "a rule of the king upon them and a duty" (מצות המלך עליהם

---

[65] E.g., W. Spiegelberg, *Die sogenannte demotische chronik des pap. 215 der Bibliothèque nationale zu Paris* (Leipzig: Hinrichs, 1914), 32–33.

[66] Tuplin, "Administration of the Achaemenid Empire," 111–13; Briant, *Histoire de l'Empire Perse,* 314–44; Wiesehöfer, *Ancient Persia,* 58–59.

[67] Vogelsang, *Rise and Organisation,* 311–15; Cook, *Persian Empire,* 168–73; Briant, *Histoire de l'Empire Perse,* 364–65; Wiesehöfer, *Ancient Persia,* 59.

[68] *Pace* Frei, *Reichsidee,* 97–99. On the reinterpretation and reapplication of pentateuchal law evident in the various commitments made by the people, see D. J. A. Clines, "Nehemiah 10 As an Example of Early Jewish Biblical Exegesis," *JSOT* 21 (1981): 111–17; D. A. Glatt-Gilad, "Reflections on the Structure and Significance of the *ʾamānāh* (Neh 10:29–40)," *ZAW* 112 (2000): 386–95.

ואמנה, Neh 11:23), one does not have to take "the king" to be a Persian monarch.[69] Given the Persian policy of allowing communities to observe their own traditions, it is more likely that the author is alluding to Davidic precedent in establishing offices for the Levitical singers.[70] The authors of Ezra-Nehemiah could present the governor as such a pious leader precisely because of his appeal to older precedent. Nehemiah reinstated the ancient decrees governing the service duties of the priests and Levites. Indeed, it is exceedingly rare for Nehemiah to cite Persian imperial sanction as the basis for any of the policies he implements. He arrives, of course, with the authority to rebuild Jerusalem's city walls and some of its public buildings.[71] But inasmuch as either he or the book's editors appeal to decrees and legislation, they most often cite or allude to older Israelite texts.[72]

---

[69] *Pace* Frei, *Reichsidee,* 21. Note the similar use of אמונה in 1 Chr 9:22, 26, 31 (cf. 2 Chr 31:18) as referring to a permanent, official duty (cf. Old South Arabic *ʾmnt* ["security, protection"], Arabic *ʾamāna* ["security"]).

[70] See most recently the work of J. W. Kleinig, *The Lord's Song: The Basis, Function and Significance of Choral Music in Chronicles* (JSOTSup 156; Sheffield: JSOT Press, 1993), and the references listed there. Frei acknowledges the reference to David and Solomon in Neh 12:45–46 with reference to regulations governing the temple singers, but he thinks that this reference reflects Chronistic composition (*Reichsidee,* 98; "Persian Imperial Authorization," 13). This brings up fundamental issues of source and redaction criticism. In his conception, the Chronicler was not only responsible for the basic composition of Chronicles but also edited some portions of Ezra and Nehemiah. He also regards Neh 11:21–24 as a single insertion into the list of Jerusalem and Judah's residents found within Neh 11. Whatever the complicated history of the composition of Ezra-Nehemiah and in particular the list in Neh 11 (see above), I do not see a significant link between 11:23 and 11:24.

[71] Neh 2:5–9, 18; 5:14; 6:15.

[72] Indeed, one of the major literary motifs in Ezra-Nehemiah has been described as a movement from texts to actualization. See T. Eskenazi, "Ezra-Nehemiah: From Text to Actuality," in *Signs and Wonders: Biblical Texts in Literary Focus* (ed. J. C. Exum; Atlanta: Society of Biblical Literature, 1989), 165–97. The comments of D. J. A. Clines on this matter are also very useful, "The Force of the Text: A Response to Tamara C. Eskenazi's 'Ezra-Nehemiah: From Text to Actuality,'" in *Signs and Wonders: Biblical Texts in Literary Focus* (ed. J. C. Exum; Atlanta: Society of Biblical Literature, 1989), 199–215. On the larger question of the reuse and transformation of older Israelite law, see M. Fishbane, *Biblical Interpretation in Ancient Israel* (Oxford: Clarendon, 1985); B. M. Levinson, "The Human Voice in Divine Revelation: The Problem of Authority in Biblical Law," in *Innovation in Religious Traditions* (ed. M. A. Williams et al.; Religion and Society 31; Berlin: de Gruyter, 1992), 46–61. It should be pointed out, however, that not all of the texts cited or alluded to are "legal" texts (narrowly defined). See G. N. Knoppers, "Sex, Religion, and Politics: The Deuteronomist on Intermarriage," *HAR* 14 (1994): 121–41; T. C.

Nehemiah's social reforms, economic reforms, political appointments, security arrangements, mandatory repopulation of Jerusalem, decrees against intermarriage, firstfruits and tithes enforcement, Sabbath and Sabbatical enforcement, Levitical and priestly support, Levitical and priestly schedules, and wood-offering rulings all are implemented without any reference to Persian imperial authority or legislation.[73] It seems implausible that many of the regulations Yehud's leaders instituted or upheld had to have been individually ratified by the Achaemenid kings.[74]

To be sure, occasional central mediation of or intervention in a local dispute is certainly possible, even probable. It is the merit of Frei's analysis to point to such instances in a variety of different territories within the Achaemenid Empire. Such intervention most likely occurred when a local community requested it or when there was a dispute between groups or communities. One expects that contentious issues involving different parties, such as the (re)construction of a temple, could involve adjudication by regional authorities and governmental officials. In this context, it is interesting that in Ezra-Nehemiah, the opposition to the initiatives spearheaded by Sheshbazzar, Zerubbabel, Jeshua, Ezra, and Nehemiah comes almost entirely from power-holders outside the *gôlâ* community in Yehud.[75] If they were appointed by the Persian authorities, local leaders enjoyed an enormous advantage over their opponents within their own communities. Inasmuch as conflicts exist, they involve competing claims by different regional power-holders, conflicts that have to be addressed by higher authorities precisely because their importance transcends the activities of any one local official.[76]

It is, however, quite another thing to claim that the Persian government had a great interest in authorizing the assembling, formation, inscripturation, and codification of entire law codes. Such an effort, if seriously attempted, would be a massive undertaking, considering the potential number and nature of communities involved. Indeed, if one calculates only

---

Römer and M. Z. Brettler, "Deuteronomy 34 and the Case for a Persian Hexateuch," *JBL* 119 (1999): 401–19.

[73] Neh 5:1–13; 7:1–2, 3, 4–72; 10:1–40; 11:1–2; 13:1–3, 4–9, 10–13, 15–22, 23–27, 30–31.

[74] Such a set of procedures would also be a highly inefficient and unwieldy means, administratively speaking, to run a vast empire.

[75] Indeed, not a small portion of the material found in Ezra-Nehemiah is caught up with these sorts of issues (Ezra 4:4–6, 7–24; 5:2–4, 6–17; 6:1–13; Neh 2:19–20; 3:33–35; 4:1–5; 6:1–14, 17–19; 13:4–5, 7–9).

[76] Whether such conflicts were settled by satrapal officials or by the central authorities is not always clear (Rüterswörden, "Reichsautorisation," 49–61).

the number of temples in ancient Egypt, leaving aside the many different
royal palaces and governmental buildings—each with its own extensive
traditions, customs, endowments, receipts, disbursements, and assorted
records—the task of collecting and collating these texts would not only be
unnecessary and impractical but also well-nigh impossible.[77]

Rather than looking for a highly centralized, constant, and tightly
defined Persian policy to explain the disparate measures taken by local
commissioners, it may be better to recognize the degree to which the Persian government allowed local leaders to be active players in shaping
policies within their communities. Indeed, one should press the matter further by asking whether local officials, such as Nehemiah, sometimes took
advantage of their appointments within the context of a much larger
Achaemenid governmental apparatus to bolster their own positions and
those of their friends and allies.[78] The system of central governance,
regional satrapies, and local officials relied heavily upon the loyalty of
subordinate officials.[79] If the prime duties of such officials were to collect
taxes, uphold loyalty to the Persian authorities, support military garrisons,
and maintain order, does it not seem likely that at least some would exploit
the latitude furnished to them by the Persians to steer their communities
as they themselves saw fit? A variety of measures, some of which might be
regarded by locals as unwelcome or restrictive, could be justified in the
name of maintaining order within the community. If local leaders, including Ezra, wished to rule against intermarriage and could justify such a
policy as a means to consolidate their community in reference to presti-
gious older texts, could they not do so by virtue of the authority vested in
them? One does not have to postulate a Persian interest in or a demand for
the authorization of an entire law code, much less an imperial interest in
the prohibition of mixed marriages, to explain all the actions taken by the
community leaders, Ezra, and Nehemiah. In the Persian Empire, local officials and appointees were themselves participants in the ongoing dynamic
between central authority and regional control.

---

[77] As pointed out by Redford, "So-Called 'Codification,'" in this volume.

[78] Frei also seems to acknowledge that Nehemiah used his appointment from the
Persian crown to introduce and enforce his own decrees within Yehud (*Reichsidee,*
21–22, 34, 46, 98–99). Perhaps Neh 10:1, 35–37 and 11:21–23 should also be cited
in this context (*pace* Frei). See above.

[79] A point emphasized by Vogelsang, *Rise and Organisation,* 314–15.

THE SO-CALLED "CODIFICATION" OF EGYPTIAN LAW UNDER DARIUS I

Donald B. Redford
Pennsylvania State University

Many scholars both early and late have paid homage to the claim—as though in some cases it were an unassailable truth—that Darius the Great was the first to "codify" Egyptian law.[1] The claim, though it arguably enjoys some support in Egyptian sources, is based most commonly on a classical source, specifically Diodorus Siculus.[2] The thesis of the present paper is that the purpose and nature of Darius's "inscripturation" of Egyptian law has been misunderstood and overemphasized.

1. THE LIST OF EGYPTIAN LAWGIVERS IN DIODORUS BOOK 1

Far too much has been made of Diodorus's list of Egyptian lawgivers. The very notion of "lawgiver" is wholly alien to Egyptian tradition.[3] The "ancestors" en bloc or individually were often singled out as having bequeathed written precepts worthy of continued use as standards of living,

---

[1] See, *inter alia,* Alfred Wiedemann, *Ägyptische Geschichte* (Gottha: Perthes, 1884), 681–82; Gaston Maspero, *History of Egypt, Chaldea, Syria, Babylonia and Assyria* (13 vols.; London: Grolier Society, 1900), 9:179; A. T. Olmstead, *History of the Persian Empire* (Chicago: University of Chicago Press, 1948), 142; E. Drioton and J. Vandier, *L'Égypte* (4th ed; Paris: Presses Universitaires de France, 1962), 602; Edda Bresciani, "La satrapia d'Egitto," *SCO* 8 (1958): 153–55; idem, "Ugiahorresnet a Memphi," *EVO* 8 (1985): 1–6; idem, "Egypt, Persian Satrapy," *CHJ* 1:360; Erwin Seidl, *Ägyptische Rechtsgeschichte der Saïten- und Perserzeit* (ÄF 20; Glückstadt: Augustin, 1968), 84; Sergio Donadoni, "L'Egitto achemenide," in *Modes de contact et processus de transformation dans les sociétés anciennes* (Rome: École française de Rome, 1983), 35; Joseph Blenkinsopp, "The Mission of Udjahorresnet and Those of Ezra and Nehemiah," *JBL* 106 (1987): 412–13; J. D. Ray, "Egypt 525–404 B.C.," *CAH*² 4:262; further discussion and bibliography in Pierre Briant, *Histoire de l'Empire Perse de Cyrus à Alexandre* (Leiden: Nederlands Instituut voor het Nabije Oosten, 1996), 490, 973–74.

[2] *Hist.* 1.94.1–95.4.

[3] Cf. Udo Rüterswörden, "Die persische Reichsautorisation der Thora: Fact or Fiction?" *ZABR* 1 (1995): 47–53.

but these fell within the category of worldly wisdom.[4] None encompassed "lawgiving." Each king promulgated royal edicts (*wḏ-nsw*) in accordance with Maᶜat (justice, order, moral rectitude) and would expect as a matter of course that his governance would be characterized as "establishing good laws" (*smn hpw nfrw*).[5] But kings were not normally singled out in the memory of posterity for having drawn up new "codes." Diodorus simply reflects an attempt to "hellenize" an Egyptian institution for foreign consumption, and in a manner no native would recognize.

The criterion of selection for the first three in Diodorus's list is quite artificial and depends largely on Hellenic genre expectations. Menes is included because as first human monarch it was fitting, on a Greek model, that he should have introduced the benefits of civilization to the land.[6] Sasychis (*sic*) would have found a place because of the reputation of the Fourth Dynasty in later folklore as a period of significant text collecting and adjustment of cult prescriptions.[7] Sesoosis, the garbling of *Sesostris,* could

---

[4] Of the many reflections of the esteem in which the ancestors were held, no text rivals the panegyric on ancestral wisdom contained in P.Chester Beatty IV.2.5ff.

[5] *WÄS* 2:488.13 (very common).

[6] Diodorus 1.45; 1.89 (in 94 he confuses the bull "Mnevis" with Menes); see Alan B. Lloyd, *Herodotus Book II: A Commentary* (3 vols.; Leiden: Brill, 1975–1988), 3:10–13; on Hellenic proclivity to speculate on cultural origins, see Harold W. Attridge and Robert A. Oden Jr., *Philo of Byblos: The Phoenician History* (CBQMS 9; Washington, D.C.: Catholic Biblical Association, 1981), 79 n. 41.

[7] As transcribed the personal name clearly derives from *Ššìnq*. See (somewhat confusedly) Anne Burton, *Diodorus Siculus Book I: A Commentary* (Leiden: Brill, 1972), 273–74; for Asychis, see Lloyd, *Herodotus,* 3:88. But the historical Sheshonq (presumably the first of that name is intended) is not at all known for anything remotely resembling "lawgiving." (For a "Sesonchosis" connected with erotic fiction, see *TLG*, 155 [5003]). The position in Diodorus's list, however, and the cultic nature of the alleged "legislation" would favor the case for a confusion with *Souphis,* i.e., the common garbled version of *Khufu:* cf. W. G. Waddell, *Manetho* (LCL; Cambridge: Harvard University Press, 1940), 46. The latter's reign lived on in folklore as a time when several important cultic texts were discovered and edited; cf. P.British Museum 10059:11–13 (Hermann Grapow, Wolfhart Westendorf, and Hildegard Deines, *Grundriss der Medizin der alten Ägypter* [9 vols.; Berlin: Akademie-Verlag, 1954–1973], 5:274); Book of Going Forth by Day, ch. 64 short (Ernest A. W. Budge, *Hieratic Papyri in the British Museum* [London: British Museum, 1912], pl. 41:9–11), ch. 137A, 23, 37–39; Emile Chassinat, *Le temple de Dendara, VI* (Cairo: IFAO, 1965), 173.9–10; Jocelyne Berlandini-Grenier, "Senenmout, stoliste royal, sur une statue-cube avec Néférourê," *BIFAO* 76 (1976): 314 n. 5; in general, Donald B. Redford, *Pharaonic Kinglists, Annals and Daybooks: A Contribution to the Study of the Egyptian Sense of History* (Mississauga, Ont.: Benben, 1986), 220, n. 24.

not be omitted because of this fabulous composite figure's renown in folklore for innovation.[8]

Why Bocchoris should be in the list is baffling. His reign was no more than six years,[9] and no contemporary text celebrates his sagacity in jurisprudence. Yet Diodorus marks him out as a lawgiver who edited the monarchic law and regularized the law on contracts.[10] It is conceivable that at this point Diodorus tapped into a genuine memory of some juridical activity; but the unhistorical use of his reign as a catchall for folklore (prophecy of the ram, a version of the plague-expulsion motif)[11] makes this unlikely.

Both Bocchoris and Amasis share the distinction of being the last significant kings of Egypt before a major invasion and catastrophe and thus objects of sympathy and romance. A political hiatus would have temporarily arrested the additions to archives and in the event stamped the latest documents with the name of the last king of the preceding regime. Amasis is a case in point. Tradition ascribed to his reign acts of state implicitly rooted in written records. The implausible statement that in his reign the number of settlements in Egypt amounted to twenty thousand[12] presupposes census activity. The fragmentary demotic reference in P.D. 6319 (x+iii, 1–2, 5–6)[13] to a king Amasis (?) referring to "all

---

[8] The last word has by no means been said on the origin and nature of the Sesostris legend. Provisionally see, *inter alia,* Kurt Sethe, *Sesostris* (Leipzig: Hinrichs, 1900); Hermann Kees, "Sesostris," PW 2:1861–76; Kurt Lange, *Sesostris, ein ägyptischer König im Mythos, Geschichte und Kunst* (Munich: Hirmer, 1954); Michel Malaise, "Sésostris, pharaon de légende et d'histoire," *ChrEg* 41 (1966): 244–72; Claude Obsomer, *Les campagnes de Sésostris dans Hérodote* (Brussels: Connaissance de l'Egypte ancienne, 1989).

[9] Cf. Donald B. Redford, *From Slave to Pharaoh: The Black Experience in Ancient Egypt* (Baltimore: Baltimore University Press, 2001).

[10] Diodorus 1.65.1; 1.79.1; 1.94.5. Aristide Théodoridès seems to accept the tradition (cf. "The Concept of Law in Ancient Egypt," in *The Legacy of Egypt* [ed. J. R. Harris; Oxford: Oxford University Press, 1971], 319), although Erwin Seidl rejects it (*Ägyptische Rechtsgeschichte,* 53–54).

[11] Redford, *Pharaonic Kinglists,* 283–89.

[12] Herodotus 2.177.1; Pliny the Elder, *Nat.* 5.11.

[13] E. A. E. Reymond, *From Ancient Egyptian Hermetical Writings,* part 2 of *From the Contents of the Suchos Temple in the Fayum* (Vienna: Hollinek, 1977); see also M. Smith, "A Second Dynasty King in a Demotic Papyrus of the Roman Period," *JEA* 66 (1980): 173–74; Joachim-Friedrich Quack, "P. Wien 6319. Eine demotische Übersetzung aus dem Mittelägyptischen," *Enchoria* 19/20 (1992/1993): 124–29; idem, "Der historische Abschnitt des Buches von Tempel," in *Literatur und Politik im pharaonischen und ptolemäischen Ägypten* (ed. J. Assmann and E. Blumenthal;

the temples of Upper Egypt [...], those which have recently (?) fallen to ruin and (those) which are burnt..." also suggests a preoccupation with inventory. The statement[14] that he drew up regulations governing nomarchs implies a focus on that genre of administrative texts that might be called "official instructions" (*tp-rd*) or duty-tables.[15] The tradition of the return of the Phoenix during Amasis's reign[16] may reflect calendrical computation,[17] and the fantastic "crocodile" measurements Aelian reports[18] might point to recorded Nile heights. Finally, and of more than passing interest for the present investigation, Herodotus's reference to the creation of an "income tax" under Amasis[19] signals a concern for fiscal law, and it should be noted that the practice of issuing tax receipts seems to go back to the Saites. In sum, the traditions consistently reflect a broadly based writing-up of legal and quasi-legal texts during the forty-four year regime of the penultimate king of the Twenty-Sixth Dynasty.

The topos of "Darius the Lawgiver," which may in fact be the root cause of the creation of the false set of native lawgivers, finds some historical support in demotic sources.[20] There is scarcely any cogent reason to doubt that a kernel of truth lies within the tradition that the Persian king ordered the writing up of legislation. But who did the writing, and in particular what constituted the "laws" in question?

2. EGYPTIAN LAW (*ḥp*)

The Egyptian lexicon is rich in words and locutions delineating the nature of Egyptian law and legal procedure. Foremost among these is *ḥp,* which

---

Cairo: IFAO, 1999), 267–78. The text, however, is clearly concerned with a "Historische Abschnitt" about much earlier times.

[14] Diodorus 1.95.1.

[15] The best example from the New Kingdom are the instructions for the running of the vizier's office. See G. P. F. van den Boorn, *The Duties of the Vizier* (London: Kegan Paul, 1988).

[16] Tacitus, *Ann.* 6.28; on the bird, see P. Wilson, *A Ptolemaic Lexicon* (Leuven: Uitgeverij Peeters en Department Oosterse Studies, 1997), 316–17.

[17] Note that the midway point in the Sothic cycle occurred shortly before Amasis ascended the throne. That the Egyptians were, by this time, aware of the cycle and its implications seems to follow from the Ptolemaic designation of Isis as "lady of 14 (centuries) who follows her place (through?) 730 complete years" (Lynn E. Rose, "The Sothic Date from the Ptolemaic Temple of Isis at Aswan," *BO* 56 [1999]: 14–34).

[18] Aelian, *Hist. animal.* 17.6.

[19] Herodotus 2.177. The law is seen at work in P.Rylands IX.xvi.1–5.

[20] Wilhelm Spiegelberg, *Die sogenannte demotische Chronik des Pap. 215 der Bibliothèque Nationale zu Paris* (Leipzig: Hinrichs, 1914), 30–32.

functions almost as a generic term[21] at least from the Middle Kingdom on.[22] The Greeks took *ḥp* to be the exact equivalent of νόμος.[23] Its most basic nuance appears to reflect prescription, regulation, procedure, and instruction (for doing something often of a technical nature).[24] Thus Thutmose III is one "who establishes every office required by the departments (of government), every *ḥp* and every instruction [*tp-rd*] being established in its place,"[25] "making laws [*ḥpw*], establishing instructions [*tp-rd*]."[26] Judges perform their tasks "the instructions [*tp-rd*] before them, the laws [*ḥpw*] in their day-books."[27] "The instruction of the palace, the utterance of the maximum security area" are parallel to *ḥpw*.[28] The context can even justify a translation "customary procedure" or "traditional text": "Ye shall say the *ḥtp-di-nsw* exactly like that which is in writing, the invocation in the speech of the ancestors, like that which emerged from the mouth of god.... it is to be done as it should be, as that which is according to the *ḥpw* attested on this stela."[29] An overtone of *obligation* to act in a certain way, rather than a negative nuance, lurks behind the word, brought out best by Coptic *ḥapᵉse–*, "he must (do something)."[30]

Notwithstanding the abstract meaning of custom or pattern of action that clings to the word, mention of *ḥpw* often conjured up for the ancients

---

[21] *WÄS* 2:488–89.

[22] Cf. Paul C. Smither, "A Tax Assessor's Journal of the Middle Kingdom," *JEA* 27 (1941): 17 pl. 9; Merikare P7–8; Ipuwer B53. There is no inherent difficulty in construing the word as Old Egyptian in origin, although it has not yet been found in Old Kingdom texts.

[23] Cf. Diodorus 1.94–95; Charles F. Nims, "The Term *ḥp*, 'Law, Right,'" in Demotic," *JNES* 7 (1948): 244; François Daumas, *Les moyens d'expression en Grecque et en Égyptien* (ASAÉSup 16; Cairo: IFAO, 1952), 234; cf. Alexander Scharff and Erwin Seidl, *Einführung in die Ägyptische Rechtsgeschichte bis zum Ende des neuen Reiches* (Gluckstadt: Augustin, 1957), 60–61.

[24] Cf. Bernadette Menu, *Recherches sur l'histoire juridique, économique et sociale de l'Ancien Égypte* (2 vols.; Versailles, 1982; Cairo: IFAO, 1998), 1:157 n. p; 2:18. Menu has formulated the best definition thus far. "Customary rule, prescription" is not a *weakened* meaning (*pace* van den Boorn, *Vizier,* 168).

[25] *Urk.* IV:1095.9–10.

[26] *Urk.* IV:1045.4–5; cf. 749.14, 936.5, 1187.9–12, 2089.15–16, 2156.6.

[27] Jean-Marie Kruchten, *Le Dékret d'Horemheb* (Brussels: University of Brussels, 1981), 148 (D4).

[28] Alessandra Nibbi, "Remarks on the Two Stelai freom the Wadi Gasus," *JEA* 62 (1976): pl. 10.

[29] *Urk.* IV:121.9–15.

[30] Wolfhart Westendorf, *Koptisches Handwörterbuch* (Heidelberg: C. Winter Universitätsverlag, 1977), 382.

the image of a written document. Ipuwer has some such papyrus copy in mind when he laments: "Really! The *hpw* of the government block [*hnt*] are put outside; and in fact they get walked on in the squares and the poor tear them up in the streets!"[31] The *hp* can be conceived of as a physical object: "his audience (the vizier's) with any petitioner is to be in accordance with this *hp* which is in his hand."[32] The rather specific determinatives of the word as late as Ptolemaic times likewise point to a concrete object, clearly a papyrus.[33] Thoth, patron of writing and archetypal scribe, is closely associated with the *hpw* as the one that inscribes them.[34] The early titles "superintendent of the *hp*"[35] and "custodian of the *hp*"[36] likewise militate in favor of a written (papyrus) document rather than an abstraction. It is also to be noted that the common phrase "like that which conforms to the law"[37] is modelled on (and is found in the same contexts as) "like that which is in writing."[38] Finally, the punishment assigned to a crime is sometimes quoted from a "hieroglyphic text."[39]

2.1. THE SOURCE OF THE LAW

For a nation so concerned about insinuating Ma'at into all aspects of society,[40] the careful identification of the source of legality should come as

---

[31] Ipuwer B53: Wolfgang Helck, *Die 'Admonitions'. Pap. Leiden I 344 recto* (Wiesbaden: Harrassowitz, 1995), 29.

[32] *Urk.* IV:1111.2.

[33] Wilson, *Ptolemaic Lexicon,* 604.

[34] *WÄS* 2:488.13, 19; cf. Patrick Boylan, *Thoth, the Hermes of Egypt* (Oxford: Oxford University Press, 1922), 89; cf. also Hathor and Sakhmet: Siegfried Schott, *Bücher und Bibliotheken im alten Ägypten* (Wiesbaden: Harrassowitz, 1990), 288; J. Couyat and P. Montet, *Les inscriptions hiéroglyphiques et hiératiques de l'Ouâdi Hammamat* (Cairo: IFAO, 1912), no. 12.2, line 7: "the likeness of Thoth with respect to the laws of the Eternal Lord."

[35] H. O. Lange and H. Schäfer, *Grab- und Denksteine des mittleren Reiches* (4 vols.; Cairo: IFAO, 1902–1925), 3:46.

[36] Smither, "Tax Assessors' Journal," 17 pl. 9. This individual was also "scribe of the cadastre," a *written* record; cf. van den Boorn, *Vizier,* 166.

[37] *Mi ntt r hp* (*WÄS* 2:488.25).

[38] *Mi nty r sš;* cf. Donald B. Redford, "Scribe and Speaker," in *Writing and Speech in Israelite and Ancient Near Eastern Prophecy* (ed. E. Ben Zvi and M. H. Floyd; SBLSymS 10; Atlanta: Society of Biblical Literature, 2000), 166.

[39] KRI 5:363 (P.Lee 2.5).

[40] Cf. H. Goedicke and E. F. Wente, *Ostraka Michaelides* (Wiesbaden: Harrassowitz, 1962), pl. 50, no. 47 recto 2–3; *Urk.* IV:1387.13 ("laws of justice"); IV:969, 1271.14 ("fair laws").

no surprise. In general the Egyptians postulated a divine underpinning to all law. We have already noted the role of Thoth in writing laws, and the divine decrees that emerged from his pen, especially in the first millennium,[41] point out the increasing recourse in those times to the juridical role of the gods. This often took the form of a *Gottesentscheidung* through oracle delivered by the god's barque in processional, and issuing in a "(favorable) decision to the summons,"[42] or of a private letter laid before the god.[43] Presumably those passages justifying the sentence of a court by alluding to what the gods "said"[44] refer to such oracular pronouncements, rather than to some (divine) law code.[45]

When we turn to the persona of Pharaoh as the source of law, we are on firmer ground. Much of ancient Egyptian legislation was characterized as "the law [*ḥp*] of Pharaoh, l.p.h,"[46] directly ascribed to the king,[47] or to

---

[41] *Edfu* IV:181 (A. Barucq, "Les textes cosmogoniques d'Edfou d'après les manuscrits laissés par Maurice Alliot," *BIFAO* 64 [1964]: 130); Harold H. Nelson, "Certain Reliefs at Karnak and Medinet-Habu and the Ritual of Amenophis I," *JNES* 8 (1949): 220, fig. 18:9–11; H. Junker, *Das Götterdekret über Abaton* (Vienna, 1913), 7, 25; Alexandre Moret, *Catalogue du Musée Guimet: Galerie égyptienne: Stèles, bas-reliefs, monuments divers* (Annales du Musée Guimet, 32; Paris, 1909), 80 (C.40); cf. also Diodorus 1.94.1 (Hermes gave the law to Menes).

[42] *Wḏt n cš:* Richard A. Parker, *A Saite Oracle Papyrus in the Brooklyn Museum* (Providence: Brown University Press, 1962), 12; see Erwin Seidl, "Die Gottesentscheidungen der Saïten- und Perserzeit," in *Essays in Honor of C. Bradford Welles* (New Haven, Conn.: American Society of Papyrologists, 1966), 59–65; also D. Berg, "The Genre of Non-juridical Oracles (*ḥr.tw*) in Ancient Egypt" (Ph.D. diss., Toronto, 1988); the existence of a special "Oracle Scribe" (*sš by3yt*) points up the frequency and regularity of such juridical decisions: see Parker, *Saite Oracle Papyrus*, pl. 2, lines 7–8.

[43] George R. Hughes, "A Demotic Letter to Thoth," *JNES* 17 (1958): 1–12.

[44] Cf. P.Amherst 20.7: "the great sentence of death shall be inflicted on him, of which the gods said 'do it to him!'" Cf. KRI 5:362.13.

[45] But cf. KRI 5:363 (P.Lee 2.5), which substitutes "hieroglyphic text" for "the gods."

[46] P.Boulaq X.11; KRI 5:450.5.

[47] Cf. "I am one that enforces [*smn*] the laws of/for the king, who gives instruction to the entourage" (*Urk.* IV:2089.15–16); "conversant with the character of the Lord of the Two Lands, who grasps his laws and does not frustrate his doctrine" (*Urk.* IV:1421.1–1423.2); "enrich your officials in order that they may enforce your laws" (Merikare P iv.7–8, in Wolfgang Helck, *Die Lehre für König Merikare* [Wiesbaden: Harrassowitz, 1977], 24); "superintendent of the laws of the Perfect God in the chamber of administering justice" (M. Moursi, "Die Stele des Vezirs Re-hotep," *MDAIK* 37 [1981]: 322, fig. 1, lines 5–6); "conversant with the Council of 30 in

"him that is in the palace"[48] or simply "the palace."[49] A substantial part of this "royal" law fell under the rubric of royal decrees, *wḏ-nsw*,[50] sometimes qualified as *ḥp* in the same passage.[51] Both in theory and practice a *wḏ-nsw* could be any statement embodying a directive, opinion, or sentiment that emerged from the king's mouth.[52] In many cases, perhaps indeed most, these were statements issued in favor of the endowment, immunity, or exemption of an individual or institution and could eventually result in the bestowal of a "(royal) charter."[53] They could also embody a royal initiative, in which case the formula often used was, "he made it as his monument for his father (god X), making for him a. . . ."[54] Even royal communications of a simple letter format could qualify under the heading *wḏ-nsw*.[55] Royal directives to an individual by the king employed the

---

interpreting [*sšm*] the laws of his lord" (Alan H. Gardiner, *The Admonitions of an Egyptian Sage* [Leiden, 1909; repr., Hildesheim: Georg Olms, 1969, 1990], 50).

[48] *Urk.* IV:903.13.

[49] *WÄS* 2:488.9; Kruchten, *Dékret d'Horemheb*, 148, D4 "laws of the Porte"; KRI 1:9.5 "laws of the palace"; CCG 42226 h 5 "laws of the palace, regulations of those who lived aforetime" (cf. *Urk.* IV:969.9–10); for the *pr-nsw*, "the king's house," as a metonym for the source of law, see van den Boorn, *Vizier,* 74–75, 322.

[50] *WÄS* 1:396.19.

[51] G. A. Reisner, "Inscribed Monuments from Gebel Barkal," *ZÄS* 69 (1933): pl. 8, line x+8; *Urk.* IV:1815.15–17; P.Anastasi I.9.2.

[52] Hans Goedicke, "Diplomatical Studies in the Old Kingdom," *JARCE* 3 (1964): 34–35; idem, *Königliche Dokumente aus dem Alten Reich* (Wiesbaden: Harrassowitz, 1967), 10–12; Henry George Fischer, "A Feminine Example of *wḏ ḥm·k* 'Thy Majesty Commands' in the Fourth Dynasty," *JEA* 61 (1975): 246–47.

[53] *c-nsw* (*WÄS* 1:158.19). This oft-discussed term, favored by Old Kingdom nomenclature, designates an "enabling" document of immense legal force: *Urk.* I:2.9–11, "she made a will for her children, drawn up in their favor and covered by [*n*] a royal charter, (with copies) in every office"; Goedicke, *Königliche Dokumente,* figs. 17 and 28, "N's charter does not exist," i.e., N has no legal claim; cf. Paule Posener-Krieger and Jean Louis de Cenival, *The Abu Sir Papyri* (London: British Museum, 1968), pl. 73(E) ("any charter-holders or craftsmen notwithstanding"); cf. also PT 408a–409a, 467a–c. See further Wolfgang Helck, *Altägyptische Aktenkunde des 3. und 2. Jahrtausends v. Chr.* (Munich: Deutscher Kunstverlag, 1974); Nigel Strudwick, *The Administration of Egypt in the Old Kingdom* (London: Routledge, 1985), 210–11.

[54] Sayed Tawfik, "*ir·n·f m mnw·f* als Weihformel. Gebrauch und Bedeutung," *MDAIK* 27 (1971): 227–34.

[55] *Urk.* I:60.14, 61.17–18, 128.4, 137.16–17, 138.10–12; Kurt Sethe, *Ägyptische Lesestucke* (Leipzig: Hinrichs, 1929), 70 (no. 14), 76 (no. 17b); William Christopher Hayes, *A Papyrus of the Late Middle Kingdom in the Brooklyn Museum (Papyrus*

metonymy of the palace and were given special legal force by the phrase "what was said (var. authorized or commanded) in the Majesty of the Palace,"[56] or "decree issued from the Majesty of the Palace."[57]

Two other words that help to define the king's role as source of the law are *sḫrw* and *sbꜣyt*. The former is often rendered "plan," but it not infrequently approximates "executive decision." In fact, the phrase *iri sḫrw*, "to make executive decisions," means "to govern,"[58] and *sḫrw n hpw* comes close to "(due) process of law."[59] *Sbꜣyt*, "teaching," has wide use in contexts that promote the king as a source of wisdom. Courtiers will often describe themselves as pupils of the monarch, who have hearkened to his teaching.[60] Examples that survive, such as the Instruction for Merikare, the Instruction for the Vizier, and the general section of the Horemheb Decree, suggest that royal disquisitions approach the status of "doctrine," in which basic moral and legal principles of equity might be promulgated.[61] In light of the frequency of the phrase *smn hpw*[62] in royal texts and epithets, one wonders whether the delivery of a *sbꜣyt* did not assume a more formal aspect at the outset of a reign.[63]

Brooklyn 35.1446) (New York: Brooklyn Museum, 1955), 78; P.Anastasi IV.10.8–10 (called *wbꜣ*, "letter" in 11,4); cf. also *Urk.* 4:208.10 (daily arrival of *wḏ-nsws*).

56 *Urk.* I:62.1, 63.2–3; 4:194.1–2, 325.17, 409.5, 651, 1021; KRI 2:710.9; var. "authorized in the residence," *Urk.* I:66.3; Rudolph Anthes, *Die Felseninschriften von Hatnub* (Leipzig: Hinrichs, 1928), 22, pl. 12 no. 7.

57 *Urk.* IV:1618; Nauri 29 (KRI 1:50.12–13).

58 Cf. Alan H. Gardiner, *Late Egyptian Stories* (Brussels: Edition de la Fondation Egyptologique Reine Elisabeth, 1931), 19:1, 37:12–13; idem, "The Gods of Thebes As Guarantors of Personal Property," *JEA* 48 (1962): 66 line 3, n. 6; Georges Posener, *Annuaire du Collège de France* 68e Année (1968–1969): 401–2; Michèle Broze, *Mythe et roman en Égypte ancienne: Les aventures d'Horus et Seth dans le Papyrus Chester Beatty I* (Leuven: Peeters, 1996), 21; Westendorf, *Koptisches Handwörterbuch,* 336.

59 Cf. Ramesses IV's words: "whenever I presided in court, justice was exact, and the process of law was adhered to" (*mn*) (Alan H. Gardiner, "A Pharaonic Encomium," *JEA* 41 [1955]: 30–31).

60 Denise M. Doxey, *Egyptian Non-royal Epithets in the Middle Kingdom: A Social and Historical Analysis* (Leiden : Brill, 1998), 120–21.

61 Aristide Théodoridès, *Vivre de Maât: Travaux sur le droit égyptien ancien* (Brussels: Societe belge d'etudes orientales, 1995), 8 and n. 21, 15–17.

62 *WÄS* 2:488.13. The literal rendering is "to make firm the law," but the nuance hovers between promulgation and enforcement.

63 Those passages which deal with the discretionary rights of individuals sound like general, royal "doctrine." Cf. KRI 5:450.5: " 'Let burial goods be released!' so

There is some evidence for the existence of local law, independent of that of Pharaoh. The threat "his case will not be judged as an inhabitant of his town" militates in favor of parochial jurisdiction.[64] One might similarly argue from such expressions as "the law of Upper Egypt"[65] or "the law of market-gardeners"[66] that local law was recognized. It has been noted that, while Pharaoh (i.e., the government) took a keen interest in the legal affairs of Deir el-Medina, legal procedure within the community was fluid and adaptable[67] and conformed to what is called "the custom of this place."[68]

2.2. The Publication of Law

There exists, outside the more specific uses of *ḥpw* noted above, a number of more general contexts. These include such locutions as "the laws of Egypt,"[69] "the laws of the Two Banks,"[70] "the laws of the land,"[71] or simply "the laws."[72] One wonders whether these phrases constitute a catchall for any regulations, local or central, or whether they betray the existence of a formal, *codified* body of legislation. The problem becomes acute in those

---

says the law of Pharaoh my good lord"; KRI 6:740.4–5: "Thus speaks Pharaoh, l.p.h: 'let everyman do what he wants with his (own) property'"; KRI 6:740.13–14: "Thus speaks Pharaoh l.p.h: 'give every woman's dowry to her'"; CCG 42208c, 14: "inasmuch as the words of the great god are: 'let everyman dispose of his (own) property'." One does not have to conjure up edict or code for such general dicta: Eberhard Otto, "Prolegomena zur Frage der Gesetzgebung und Rechtsprechung in Ägypten," *MDAIK* 14 (1956): 153.

[64] PT 485c; cf. *kîma âli,* "according to the (custom/law of) the city" in Akkadian; W. F. Leemans, "Aperçu sur les textes juridiques d'Emar," *JESHO* 31 (1988): 224.

[65] P.Kahun 22.2–3.

[66] George Möller, *Hieratische Paläographie* (3 vols.; Leipzig: Hinrich, 1909–1912), 1:6, 14.

[67] A. G. McDowell, *Jurisdiction in the Workmen's Community of Deir el-Medina* (Leiden: Nederlands Instituut voor het Nabije Oosten, 1990), 235–49.

[68] Alan H. Gardiner and Jaroslav Černý, *Hieratic Ostraca* (Oxford: Griffith Institute, 1957), pl. 46A, 2 verso.

[69] *Urk.* IV:2157.7 (*Tꜣ-mry*), 2144.8 (*Kmt*); cf. J. D. Ray, *The Archive of Hor: Texts from Excavations* (2 vols.; London: Egypt Exploration Society, 1976), vol. 2, text 6, vs. 6 (*pꜣ ḥp n Kmt*).

[70] *Urk.* IV:2114.16.

[71] Sethe, *Lesestücke,* no. 81.21–22; *WÄS* 2:488.10.

[72] George R. Hughes, *Saite Demotic Land Leases* (Chicago: University of Chicago Press, 1956), 70 sec. q.

citations in demotic coming from the fifth century and later, as it would be conceivable that they might bear upon the alleged codification of Darius. But *hp* in the Late Period is rather loosely used. It can mean, with *n,* simply "in the right"[73] or "to have just claim to,"[74] or in the negative (*mn mtw.i hp*) "I have no right/claim."[75] In contracts *hr nꜣ hpw nty hry,* "according to the *hpw* which are above," simply refers to the conditions of that specific agreement laid out earlier in the text.[76] "To do the *hp*" to someone, used as early as the Middle Kingdom, means to mete out the punishment prescribed (cf. our "I'll have the law on you!").[77] Because of the authoritative and irrevocable nature of the word, *hp* can even spill over into other categories: a "*hp* of writing" can mean a potent magic spell.[78]

The evidence, though more extensive than one might have expected, is yet inadequate to help us decide whether *hpw* ever refers to codified law. For one thing, one looks in vain for any word or phrase in the Egyptian language that conveys the idea of *codification.* For another, as we have seen, statements of legal principles within the realm of jurisprudence belong within the categories of *shrw* and *shꜣyt,* not code. Examples of *hpw* that have been vouchsafed to us fall within the category of circumstantial applications of the law, not of statements of principle.[79]

No matter how firmly implanted law and custom was in the collective oral tradition of the Egyptian community,[80] the archivist penchant of the scribal class ensured that all legislation was committed to writing at once. In fact the act of writing a *wḏ-nsw* and sealing it in the king's presence was part

---

[73] Ray, *Archive of Hor,* 92–93, n. e.

[74] S. R. K. Glanville, *A Theban Archive of the Reign of Ptolemy I, Soter,* vol. 1 of *Catalogue of Demotic Papyri in the British Museum* (London: British Museum, 1939), 6, n. g.

[75] Wolja Erichsen, *Demotisches Glossar* (Copenhagen: Munksgaard, 1954), 274; Nims, "The Term *hp,*" 247–60.

[76] Michel Malinine, *Choix de textes juridiques en hiératique anormal et en démotique* (part 1; Paris: Librairie Ancienne Honore Champion, 1953), 94 n. 16. Cf. *pꜣ hp n pꜣ sh,* "the regulations of the document" (Erichsen, *Demotisches Glossar,* ad loc.).

[77] Wolfgang Helck, *Historisch-biographische Inschriften der 2. Zwischenzeit* (Wiesbaden: Harrassowitz, 1975), 18; Hayes, *Papyrus of the Late Middle Kingdom,* 47; David Randall-MacIver and A. C. Mace, *El Amrah and Abydos* (London: Egypt Exploration Fund, 1902), pl. 29; Kruchten, *Décret d'Horemheb,* 46–47 (1.16), 217 nn. 58–59. Cf. Nims, "The Term *hp,*" 246.

[78] I Khamois iii.35–36; II Khamois vi.14.

[79] Geneviève Husson and Dominique Valbelle, *L'État et les institutions en Égypte des premiers pharaons aux empéreurs romains* (Paris: Armand Colin, 1992), 123.

[80] On oral tradition in ancient Egypt, see Redford, "Scribe and Speaker," 145–218.

of the law-making process,[81] and the very shape of the text of the decree reproduced the original sheet of papyrus on which it had been taken down.[82] By the close of the Old Kingdom the state archives contained a wealth (850 years' worth, in fact) of legal and quasi-legal documentation: decrees, annals, royal work-orders (*wpt-nsw*), charters (*c*), property-transfers (*imyt-pr*), census records (*ṯnwt*), conscription orders (*srw*), notices and rescripts (*mḏꜣwt*), duty-tables (*sšm ꜣꜣwt*), salary sheets (*sšm n swt*), service regulation books (*sšm r imy-st c*), tax documents (*mḏd*), receipts (*sšm ꜣwt*) and inventories (*ipwt*).[83] From the restoration of the Middle Kingdom the archives expanded many fold by the addition of such genres as daybooks of landed institutions (*hrwyt*), the land cadastre (*ḫwdt*), communiques (*wstyw*), royal encyclicals (*wstnw*), inspectors' reports (*siptiw*), work regulations (*sḥnwt*), indictments (*sḫꜣw*), trial transcripts (*smtr*), and depositions (*ḏdt.n N*).[84] This vast mass of material covered a "law" that was not only represented in the archives but was also "published" on public stelae and "seen to be done" by enforcement.[85] And there is some indication the populace was treated to public readings of legal texts (for example, treaties).[86]

---

[81] Goedicke, *Königliche Dokumente,* 10–14; PT 491a; cf. *Urk.* I:64.1, 65.2, 66.10; IV:1116.13: "it is he (the vizier) that seals [every] edict [of the king]"; Otto, "Prolegomena zur Frage der Gesetzgebung," 154–55.

[82] Goedicke, *Königliche Dokumente,* 7–8; idem, "Diplomatical Studies," 39; Helck, *Altägyptische Aktenkunde.*

[83] For these terms, see Posener-Krieger and de Cenival, *Abu Sir Papyri;* Paule Posener-Krieger, *Les Archives du temple funéraire de Neferirkare-Kakai* (Cairo: IFAO, 1976), passim; Dimitri Meeks, *Année lexicographique* (3 vols.; Paris: Librairie Cybele, 1980–1982); Schott, *Bücher und Bibliotheken.*

[84] See Meeks, *Année lexicographique;* and Schott, *Bücher und Bibliotheken.* Also Wolfgang Helck, *Zur Verwaltung des Mittleren und Neuen Reiches* (Leiden: Brill, 1958); Redford, *Pharaonic Kinglists;* van den Boorn, *Vizier.*

[85] Texts are explicit on this point. The stela of Koptos B (Goedicke, *Königliche Dokumente,* pl. 8, 48) was set up "for the support staff of this township to see, so that they will not take these priests by impressment for any work of the king's house"; cf. Koptos R (ibid., pl. 28, col. 5–7): "make copies of this decree and cause that they be [circulated] to every nomarch of Upper Egypt, and set it on a sandstone stela at the gate of [every temple] where your monuments are, so that the sons of the sons of the people may see it"; cf. Koptos L (ibid., pl. 17, col. 8–9): "you shall act in concert with N, and fix this order, which has been made in many copies, in writing"; cf. *Urk.* IV:833.15–17, "the king himself issued the command to put (this) in writing, in accordance with the minutes of the council for proceeding with this monument, on public view (lit. in the face of those on earth)."

[86] Cf. the case of the Egypto-Hittite treaty, read periodically to their respective courts by Ramesses II and Hattusilis III. See Redford, "Scribe and Speaker," 159–63; cf. Gary Beckman, *Hittite Diplomatic Texts* (Atlanta: Scholars Press, 1995), 91.

The law was not only written down with care but also classified and filed according to a "système raisonée." The (royal) residence, temples, and other land-owning institutions and towns in the provinces all abounded in libraries and scriptoria. From the Old Kingdom *pr-mḏꜣt,* "house of rescripts (later more generally 'books'),"[87] with its own classification system and postal service (*sic*), to the multiplicity of "offices" (*ḫꜣ*)[88] of the New Kingdom, legal and related documents were filed, reproduced, and dispatched to numerous provincial locations. The center of all this scriptorial activity was the "office of the vizier"[89] with its attached "office of the vizier's archives."[90] Here documents were "classified" (*ḥbs*)[91] or "unclassified" (*nn st ḥbs*)[92] by "librarians" (*iryw-irw*)[93] and available for the vizier to consult. The specific contents included "the register of criminal(s) who are in the Great Prison,"[94]

---

[87] *WÄS* 2:187.8. The core of this library consisted of the annals (*LD* 3:194.27), decrees (Wolfgang Helck, *Untersuchungen zu den Beamtentiteln des ägyptischen Alten Reiches* [Gluckstadt: Augustin, 1954], 71), and inventories (Auguste Mariette, *Abydos* [Paris: Imprimerie National, 1880] 2:2, 9c); it possessed its own "inspector of scribes," "inspector-seal-bearer," and "superintendent of seal-bearers" (Helck, *Untersuchungen,* 71) and contained the royal secretariat (Helck, *Verwaltung,* 277; see also Strudwick, *Administration of Egypt,* 199–216). The *pr-mḏꜣt ḫ-nsw* was a repository of census-lists, lists of workers, and similar documentation (Helck, *Untersuchungen,* 71–72). The term *pr-mḏꜣt* had already become a general generic designation before the close of the third millennium and (especially with the addition of *nṯr*) had begun to approximate a religious archive: P.Chester Beatty VIII, recto 4.3; Neferhotep 6; U. Luft, "Zur Einleitung der Liebesgedichte auf Papyrus Chester Beatty I," *ZÄS* 99 (1973): 109–10.

[88] For *ḫꜣ n sš,* "writing office," see *WÄS* 3:479.2. The word is of ancient origin: the *ḫꜣw* of which Ipuwer speaks (6,7) clearly contained registers and charters; cf. "the department of writings (*st* [*n nꜣ*] *sšw*)" containing chests of conscription lists: P.Anastasi I.12.1. Cf. also P.Rylands IX.iv.9 (*pꜣ cwy n sš,* an official's office). A civil case might be disputed in a "writing office" (Michel Malinine, "Une affaire concernant un partage (Pap. Vienne D 12003 et D 12004)," *RdE* 25 [1973]: 207 n. w and pl. 10:12). The "office of Pharaoh's correspondence" is a veritable secretarial pool: see the depiction in the tomb of Tjay (PM 1:38; Jean Leclant, "Fouilles et travaux en Égypte et au Soúdan, 1989–1990," *Or* 60 (1991): 224.

[89] For a detailed treatment of the workings of this office, see van den Boorn, *Vizier.*

[90] P.Abbott 7.16.

[91] *Urk.* IV:1110.5.

[92] *Urk.* IV:1109.12.

[93] *Urk.* IV:1109.15, 1110.6.

[94] *Urk.* IV:1109.3; Hayes, *Papyrus of the Late Middle Kingdom,* 65–66; Stephen Quirke, *The Administration of Egypt in the Late Middle Kingdom* (Whitstable: SIA, 1990), 127–54.

the land cadastre (*ḫwdt*),[95] property-transfers (under the vizier's seal),[96] depositions of petitioners,[97] trial transcripts,[98] provincial reports,[99] tax documents,[100] royal decrees,[101] and work regulations.[102] There was probably additional material, the genre terms for which have not survived. In addition, the vizier's office would have had copies of, or at the least had access to, documents normally stored in the granary-office, the treasury, the army barracks/stables, the office of Pharaoh's correspondence,[103] and even the temples.[104] Each archival

---

[95] Cf. *Urk.* IV:1110–1111; 1113.15.

[96] *Urk.* IV:1111.6–7; cf. Pierre Lacau, *Une stèle juridique de Karnak* (Cairo: IFAO, 1949), line 15.

[97] *Urk.* IV:1111.14–1112.3.

[98] Cf. P. Abbott 7, 16; P. Leopold II,iv.3.

[99] *Urk.* IV:1112.9–11.

[100] *Urk.* IV:1114.9–11.

[101] *Urk.* IV:1116.13.

[102] *WÄS* 4:216–18; KRI 2:358.5–6; 361.5.9; Gardiner and Černý, *Hieratic Ostraca,* pl. 17, 1.1.

[103] Broadly speaking, the contents of these archives would have mirrored categories already passed in review: conscription-lists of soldiers, workers, and cultivators; inventories; tax assessments; registers of grain receipts; records of imposts; and quotas and letters. See in particular Helck, *Verwaltung;* idem, *Wirtschaftsgeschichte des alten Ägypten in 3. und 2. Jahrtausend v. Chr.* (Leiden: Brill, 1975); Sally L. D. Katary, *Land Tenure in the Ramesside Period* (London: Kegan Paul, 1989); David A. Warburton, *State and Economy in Ancient Egypt: Fiscal Vocabulary of the New Kingdom* (OBO 151; Fribourg: Universitätsverlag, 1997); Menu, *Recherches sur l'histoire juridique,* vol. 2.

[104] For a sketch of the contents of temple libraries, see Redford, *Pharaonic Kinglists,* 215–23. In the New Kingdom the distinction between the terms *pr-mḏȝt* and *ist n sšw* ("chamber of writings") tends to become blurred: together they have assumed a high-flown status designating that most secret of library-scriptoria, the *pr-cnḫ,* "the House of Life": A. H. Gardiner, "The House of Life," *JEA* 24 (1938): 157–79; Philippe Derchain, *Papyrus Salt 825 (B. M. 10051), rituel pour la conservation de la vie en Égypte* (Brussels: Royal Academy, 1965), 60–61; Jean-Claude Goyon, *Confirmation du pouvoir au nouvel an* (Cairo: IFAO, 1972), 104–5; 106 n. 213; Wilson, *Ptolemaic Lexikon,* 351; cf. P.Anastasi I.11.5 ("the house of books which is hidden and whose Ennead is not seen"). For the "chamber of writings" described as "(the writings of) the House of Life" containing "the hidden things of heaven and all the secrets of earth," see Redford, "The Earliest Years of Ramesses II and the Building of the Ramesside Court at Luxor," *JEA* 57 (1971): 113; cf. *Urk.* IV:364.1–6; KRI 3:296 (a temple school); P.Chester Beatty VIII, recto 4.3 (repository of magic spells), P.Anastasi I.1.2 (scriptorium).

office was run by librarians (*sȝw sšw*) under a "chief librarian"(*ḥry sȝw-sšw*).[105]

One document not mentioned above, but of importance for the present discussion, is the journal or daybook (*hrwyt*). This was a running record of events, income, and disbursements in the day-to-day operation of an institution, arranged calendrically.[106] The word appears several times in a legal context, the clearest being the passage in the Horemheb decree wherein the king states, "I brought to their (the judges') attention the instructions and the laws in [their] daybooks."[107] The word is used elsewhere with respect to depositions, credentials, and affidavits made on a certain day and presumably filed calendrically.[108] *Hrwyt* survives into the first millennium under the form *hȝw*[109] and alternates with *md* ("document") and *sḫ* ("writing") as a term for supporting documentation that the litigant brings to court.[110] That it was possible for later jurors to refer back in time to precedents under earlier regimes militates strongly

---

[105] *WÄS* 3:418.10–11; 478.18–23. Good examples are P.Turin A:2.10; P.Chester Beatty V.2.1–2 ("of the granary of Pharaoh"); P.Anastasi V.37; P.Sallier I.3.5; 3.11; 4.5; 5.4 and passim ("of the treasury of Pharaoh"); Edouard Naville, *Inscriptions historique ... de Paynodgem,* line 15 and passim; Berlin 6747; Marie-Pierre Foissy-Aufrère, ed., *Egypte et Provence: Civilisation, survivances et "Cabinets de curiosités"* (Avignon: Fondation du Muséum Calvet, 1985), inv. A.82 ("of the Treasury of the House of Amun"); P.Bologna 1094:11.9 ("of the army"); Helck, *Verwaltung,* 190–91.

[106] See Redford, *Pharaonic Kinglists,* 97–126. The criterion of listing according to calendar-date is paramount: *hrwyt* can therefore apply to any list arranged sequentially by year-month-day, even a "death-register" (cf. Kim Ryholt, *The Story of Petese Son of Petetum* [Copenhagen: Casten Niebuhr Institute of Near East Studies, University of Copenhagen, Museum Tusculanum Press, 1999], 2.24, cf. 28). The semantic range encompasses the formal listing of the names and death-dates of humankind preserved before Osiris (cf. the "Life-book": Redford, *Pharaonic Kinglists,* 84).

[107] *Urk.* IV:2156.6; Kruchten, *Décret de Horemheb,* 154–55.

[108] Cf. Jaroslav Černý, "The Will of Naunakhte and Related Documents," *JEA* 31 (1945): pl. 8, 1.1ff.: "Regnal Year 3, fourth month of *akhet,* day 5. On this day a *hrwyt* was made by the citoyenne N before the court"; there follows a list of the apportionment of her property to her children. An addition to the text a year later refers to the document as "the writing which N made," and the external docket identifies it as "the document of *hrwyt* which N made of her property" (cf. also p. 32, n. a).

[109] *LD* 3:255. This is not to be understood in any way as "une sorte de diplome d'investiture," as Jean-Marie Kruchten would have it (*Les annales des prêtres de Karnak (XXI–XXIII dynasties) et autres textes contemporains* [OLA 32; Leuven: Departement Oriëntalistiek, 1989], 257).

[110] Cf. Malinine, *Choix de textes juridiques,* 1:13(16), 60, 74; cf. 48 n. 20.

in favor of *ḥpw m ḥrwyt* being construed as a collection of dated precedents.[111] Altering them in any way was a great crime: "do not falsify the *ḥrwyt!* That's (an act of) great hostility deserving of death; for they are serious affidavits (taken) under oath, and would be under investigation by the Reporter."[112]

3. THE CONTRIBUTION OF DYNASTIES TWENTY-FIVE AND TWENTY-SIX

Of all the terms passed in review above, none appears to correspond to what we would call a law code. Statutes, documents relating to the market, rules and regulations, law journals, tax assessments, the land cadastre, and related files—all abound. But where is what would have been, at least in the view of us moderns, of immediate use to the judges, namely, a digest?

The two centuries immediately preceding the Persian conquest of Egypt witnessed a notable change in the country's relationship with its own past. During this period Egyptian intellectual life is characterized by a wholesale delving into the past for suitable models, and not only in the realm of art, but also from archival records.[113] The latter had come through the millennia remarkably well; apart from whatever destruction of documents had attended the outgoing Old Kingdom—and later survivals prove that a considerable amount of material had escaped—Egyptian archives in general exhibit an uninterrupted continuum into the fourth century B.C.E. Statutes of earlier kings could be consulted and validated: "Now My Majesty has caused that the decrees for their exemption by former kings be adhered to."[114] The land cadastre of Amenemhet I (twentieth century

---

[111] Cf. Gardiner and Černý, *Hieratic Ostraca,* pl. xlvi, no. 2, in which the court scribe can cite an earlier case for the edification of the vizier; Lacau, *Une stèle juridique,* passim, where allusions to earlier precedents abound. The "*ḥȝw* of the necropolis" was a journal incorporating legal cases (among other things): P.Berlin 10496 rs.

[112] Amenemope xxi.9.

[113] On "Saite" archaism, see F. K. Jienitz, "Die saïtische Renaissance," in Elena Cassin et al., *Die erste Halfte des I. Jahrhunderts,* vol. 3 of *Die altorientalischen Reiche* (Fischer Weltgeschichte 4; Frankfurt: Fischer, 1967), 256–82; Helmut Brunner, "Zum Verständnis der archaisierenden Tendenzen in der ägyptischen Spätzeit," *Saeculum* 21 (1970): 151–56; idem, "Archaismus," *LÄ* 1:386–95; Edna R. Russmann, *The Representation of the King in the 25th Dynasty* (New York: Brooklyn Museum, 1974); W. Stevenson Smith and William Kelly Simpson, *The Art and Architecture of Ancient Egypt* (New Haven, Conn.: Yale University Press, 1983), 239–47; Peter Der Manuelian, *Living in the Past: Studies in Archaism of the Egyptian Twenty-Sixth Dynasty* (London: Routledge, 1994).

[114] Goedicke, *Königliche Dokumente,* Coptos C, col. 12.

B.C.E.) was drawn up "according to what is in writing, inventoried according to what is in ancient [texts],"[115] and provincial magistrates could boast "[I enforced] the laws of antiquity."[116] Texts of "antiquity" could also be adduced as *Vorlagen* of such disparate genres as mathematical papyri,[117] tax-lists of municipal benevolences,[118] ground-plans of buildings,[119] medical prescriptions,[120] recherché orthography,[121] hemerologies,[122] administrative records of the necropolis,[123] regulations (*hpw*) for temple decoration and festival prescriptions,[124] and even genealogies. Osorkon, the high priest of Amun during the ninth-century civil war, could boast (probably quite honestly) that "regular decisions in the Privy Chamber were taken [through] his knowledge of all the pol[icy decisions] which had accumulated throughout the generations of former kings."[125] Similarly the worthy Hory (ca. 800 B.C.E.) was "skilled in the laws of the palace, the regulations of the ancestors."[126]

Saite "archaism," though popularly associated with the field of art, also manifested itself in language, orthography, and texts.[127] The two centuries from 711 to 525 B.C.E. are characterized by a diligent search in libraries for old texts and a resuscitation of obsolete phraseology and formulas.[128]

---

[115] Adrian de Buck, *Egyptian Readingbook* (Leiden: Nederlands Intituut voor het Nabije Oosten, 1948), nos. 68:11–12, 70:11–14.

[116] Alan H. Gardiner, "The Inscriptions from the Tomb of Sirenpowet I," *ZÄS* 45 (1908): pl. 7:8; *Urk.* 7:2.12; cf. Cairo 42226, h, 9.

[117] Gay Robins and Charles Shute, *The Rhind Mathematical Papyrus* (New York: Dover, 1987), pl. 1.

[118] *Urk.* IV:1120.5.

[119] *Dendera* VI:158–59.

[120] P.Ebers 47.16; P.Berlin 3038:15.1ff.

[121] *Urk.* IV:1082.2–5; cf. 406.10–11.

[122] Abd el-Mohsen Bakir, *The Cairo Calendar* (Cairo: Government Press, 1966), pl. i.1.

[123] Jaroslav Černý, *A Community of Workmen at Thebes in the Ramesside Period* (Cairo: IFAO, 1973), 18.

[124] *Edfu* V.126–27; VII.27.9–10; cf. *Esna* III.287; *Dendera* VII.111.

[125] Epigraphic Survey, *The Bubastite Portal,* vol. 3 of *Reliefs and Inscriptions at Karnak* (Chicago: Oriental Institute, 1954), pl. 21, col. 4; cf. pl. 18, col. 35: punishment of the rebels was meted out "according to a charter of the ancestors." Cf. the expression "lawfully, according to what is in ancient writings" (*WÄS* 2:488.8, "Belegstellen").

[126] Cairo 42226, h, 5.

[127] See Der Manuelian, *Living in the Past.*

[128] John H. Taylor, *Egypt and Nubia* (London: British Museum , 1991), 44 n. 53 (shawabti formula); G. Daressy, "Inscriptions des carrieres de Tourah et Mâsarah,"

From this activity there emerged a recopying of Pyramid Texts[129] and a major redaction of the Book of Going Forth by Day.[130] Saite biographical texts dwell heavily on temple rebuilding and general cultic restoration, which is presented as a pious act undertaken at Pharaoh's behest or voluntarily to please him. The "House of Life," that archive of ancient texts, likewise figures in the record of refurbished monuments,[131] and its scribes are called upon to carve inscriptions.[132]

This vital interest the Saites displayed toward ancient texts as models extended also to the realm of law. We have already seen some of the indications from Amasis's reign (see above), but these are anticipated by earlier evidence. Montuemhat (ca. 655 B.C.E.) boasts of "restoring regulations which had fallen into neglect."[133] Ahmose son of Nes-Atum,[134] in an unpublished statue-inscription from Mendes,[135] makes a significant statement about his early career under Necho II: "I am a royal servant who does good, a righteous man, one who paid attention to (lit. seized, i.e., adhered to[?]) the texts of.... [136] See! I was not inattentive! See! there was none whom I expelled from his land, there was none whom I deprived of his paternal inheritance.... I paid attention to the documents of the palace,[137] and I never

---

ASAÉ 11 (1911): 260 (obsolete Old Kingdom regnal year dating); cf. P. Montet, "Inscriptions de basse époque trouvés à Tanis," *Kêmi* 8 (1946): 40, pl. 3:4; Battiscombe Gunn, "The Inscribed Sarcophagi in the Serapeum," *ASAÉ* 26 (1926): 92–94 (obsolete syntax); Jean-Pierre Corteggiani, "Une stéle héliopolitaine d'époque saïte," in *Hommages à la mémorie de Serge Sauneron (1927–1976)* (2 vols.; Cairo: IFAO, 1979), 1:129–30, and R. el-Sayed, *Documents relatifs à Sais et ses divinités* (Cairo: IFAO, 1975), 125 (archaic lexical choices).

[129] L. Habachi, "Sais and Its Monuments," *ASAÉ* 42 (1942): 389–90.

[130] M. Mosher Jr., review of U. Verhoeven, *Das saïtische Totenbuch der Iatesnakht, BO* 56 (1999): 636–39.

[131] Cf. Louvre A 93 (E. Jelinková-Reymond, "Quelques recherches sur les reformes d'Amasis," *ASAÉ* 54 [1954]: 275–87); Vatican no. 158 (Posener, *La première domination perse en Egypte,* 6).

[132] P.Rylands IX, xiii.15–xiv.1; Gardiner, "House of Life," 165–66.

[133] Jean Leclant, *Montouemhât: Quatrième Prophète d'Amon, Prince de la Ville* (Cairo: IFAO, 1961), p. 200, col. 19 and textual note.

[134] For a bibliography of the inscriptions left by this general, see Pierre-Marie Chevereux, *Prosopographie des cadres militaires égyptiens de la Basse Époque* (Paris: n.p., 1985), 89–90 (Doc. 115); see also Emma Swan Hall and Bernard V. Bothmer, eds., *Mendes* (2 vols.; New York: Brooklyn Museum, 1976), pl. 18, no. 45.

[135] To be published by the present writer in *The Royal Necropolis,* vol. 1 of *The Excavations of Mendes* (Winona Lake, Ind.: Eisenbrauns, 2001).

[136] Unknown locution.

[137] Cf. Malinine, *Choix de textes juridiques,* 60 line 28.

neglected anything that had happened aforetime." This passage suggests that Ahmose diligently consulted, and perhaps collated, archival material containing earlier texts bearing upon property law. The Saite juridical corpus is, in fact, replete with deeds, contracts, and leases having to do with landed property. The fruits of this implied application of legal minds to problems of jurisprudence appears in what has been claimed to be a "conscious conceptualization of legal relations" during the Twenty-Sixth Dynasty.[138] And it was during this same period that the introduction of new terminology and formulas points to a legal awareness of volition as a factor in contracts.[139]

In short, insofar as the history of jurisprudence is concerned, the Saite period stands out as a time of great advance. Property law, contract law, and tax law were brought to a peak of refinement and based on ancient precedent and modern adaptation. Egypt entered the last quarter of the sixth century B.C.E. with perhaps the most sophisticated legal system in the world. It may now be asked what Darius, a late arrival on the scene whose ancestors had but recently emerged from breechcloth, wanted with this law? He could not use it or transplant it, and probably barely understood it. In view of the far more sophisticated classification of Egyptian archives, Darius was doing Egyptians no favor by having their laws written out—again!—and in a distinctly inferior and "user-unfriendly" format. And if he ever contemplated such a concept as "authorization" (whatever that might mean in the present historical context), he was indulging in meaningless self-delusion. For he could scarcely withhold "authorization" from the vast body of social and commercial regulation of the Egyptian community, which would simply have ignored him; and if he chose to rescind selected statutes of earlier kings of Egypt, he was doing no more than any pharaoh might have done under the circumstances.[140]

---

[138] Bernadette Menu, "Les Actes de vente en Egypte ancienne, particulièrement sous les rois Kouchites et Saïtes," *JEA* 74 (1988): 164.

[139] Janet H. Johnson, "The Persians and the Continuity of Egyptian Culture," in *Continuity and Change: Proceedings of the Last Achaemenid History Workshop* (ed. H. Sancisi-Weerdenburg et al.; Achaemenid History 8; Leiden: Nederlands Instituut voor het Nabije Oosten, 1994), 154–55.

[140] Peter Frei ("Persian Imperial Authorization: A Summary," 2.4.1.1) unnecessarily complicates the issue by introducing the notion of (Achaemenid) *imperial* authorization in the case involving the purification of Neith's temple at Sais. But in fact, by reporting a crisis and eliciting a royal *directive* (*wd*), Udjahorresne was doing nothing more than what any Egyptian grandee would have done at any period of Egypt's history.

4. THE PERICOPE IN THE DEMOTIC CHRONICLE

The brief notice on the recto of the Demotic Chronicle is not as straightforward as it looks.[141] At first glance the tripartite trope used by the writer appears to have a non-Egyptian cast: soldiers, priests, and scribes as the totality of the intelligentsia sounds a little odd,[142] and the tripartite division of the law into pharaonic, temple, and popular does not exactly comprehend the gamut of Egyptian legislation. But on closer inspection the motif approximates the "collegium" of the royal entourage in Late Period folklore. These are usually identified as consisting of three groups: guards, generals, and great men,[143] or councilors (*qnbtyw*), generals, and great men.[144] Elsewhere, both in fiction and day-to-day records, priests are well-represented. In the tale in P.Vandier lector-priests constitute the majority of the court and, in fact, become the major agents in the furtherance of the plot,[145] while Piankhy divides power-wielding authority around Pharaoh into three parts: gods (i.e., priests), dukes (*ḥꜣwtyw*), and people.[146] In the Late Period the imposition of legally binding oaths is inextricably linked to temples, and it is in the sacred precincts that trials take place, priests presiding as judges.[147]

As for the three types of law the colloquy was supposed to produce, "the law of Pharaoh" and "of the people" corresponds, as we have seen, to statutory and local law respectively,[148] but what of "temple law"? Far from any form of "Canon Law"[149] or "documents ... conservés dans les

---

[141] Spiegelberg, *Demotische Chronik,* 30–32.

[142] It does not correspond to Late Egyptian idiom; cf. "scribes and wisemen" (Gardiner, *Late Egyptian Stories,* 21.3; 87.5); "magistrates, soldiers, and officers" (ibid., 88:11–14).

[143] H. S. Smith and W. J. Tait, *Saqqara Demotic Papyri,* vol. I (London: Egypt Exploration Society, 1983), text no. 1, col. 9:6; no. 2, col. x + 1:3–4; similarly A. Volten, *Ägypter und Amazonen* (Vienna, 1962), 24, lines 6–7.

[144] Onkhsheshonqy ii.14–15; II Khamois 2.29; cf. 5.25, "nobles and people."

[145] Georges Posener, *Le Papyrus Vandier* (Cairo: IFAO, 1985), passim.

[146] Gebel Barkal no. 26, col. 22–23: Reisner, "Inscribed Monuments," ad loc.

[147] See the literature cited in Cary J. Martin, "The Child Born in Elephantine: Papyrus Dodgson Revisited," in *Acta Demotica* (Pisa: Giardini, 1994) = *EVO* 17 (1994): 211; Bernadette Menu, "Les juges égyptiens sous les derniers dynasties indigènes," in *Acta Demotica,* 213–24. On the continuing power of the "church" and "clergy" as late as the Ptolemaic period, see Werner Huss, "Some Thoughts on the Subject 'State' and 'Church' in Ptolemaic Egypt," in *Life in a Multi-cultural Society: Egypt from Cambyses to Constantine and Beyond* (ed. J. H. Johnson; SAOC 51; Chicago: Oriental Institute, 1992), 159–63.

[148] Bresciani, "La satrapia d'Egitto," 157.

[149] *Pace* Olmstead, *History,* 142.

maisons de vie,"[150] the term *ḥp* when associated (as it often is) with temples, refers to secular regulations governing the operations of a landed estate.[151] It thus would cover directives regulating food supply for offerings,[152] paraphernalia for ointment production,[153] temple personnel and their duties,[154] craftsmen training,[155] and especially endowments (usually royal).[156] The latter were invariably written up in a hieroglyphic text, carved on temple walls in a prominent place where they could be consulted easily. And it was not acceptable to suffer their erasure, either through natural weathering or human agency. In this connection Amun lauds the temple Hatshepsut built for him: "My temple, it has been newly reborn in fine limestone of Tura, refurbished for the hereafter by this work! The dilapidation (suffered by) former kings was in accordance with my wish, through the working of an ordinance for an earlier dispensation. But shall I indeed erase *your* laws (made) on my behalf? ... It is a happy god whose laws are inscribed!"[157]

Not enough evidence has survived to sketch an economic history of the temple community in Egypt during the period from ca. 711 to 525 B.C.E., but circumstantial evidence suggests a growing prosperity. P.Rylands IX (vi.16–18) suggests that temples during the Saite period were exempt from taxation. Business documents of sales of landed property direct the

---

[150] Briant, *Histoire de l'empire perse,* 490. The contents of the "House of Life" constituted the *Bꜣw Rꜥ* or the *Bꜣw ntr* ("Manifestations of Re [var. the god]"), a collective term covering secret, mystical works—all highly classified—of magic, esoteric information, ritual, cult prescription, and medicine (Redford, *Pharaonic Kinglists,* 92; Schott, *Bücher und Bibliotheken,* nos. 120–21).

[151] Cf. *Urk.* IV:1151: "the laws in the temples"; Couyat and Montet, *Les inscriptions hiéroglyphiques,* no. 12.2, line 7: "the laws of the Eternal Lord"; KRI 2:626.6: "Amun, perfect of laws"; even such locutions as "the laws of the temple's principal naos" probably is a high-flown reference to such regulations (cf. Ricardo A. Caminos, *Literary Fragments in the Hieratic Script* [Oxford: Griffith Institute, 1956], pl. 21.10.3).

[152] *Urk.* IV:1045.3–6.

[153] *Urk.* IV:352.10.

[154] *Urk.* IV:1187.9–12.

[155] Gustave Lefebvre, *Histoire des grands prêtres d'Amon de Karnak* (Paris: Geuthner, 1929), 259.

[156] *Ḥtp-ntr,* lit. "god's-offering"; see now M. Römer, *Gottes- und Priesterherrschaft in Ägypten am Ende des Neuen Reiches* (Wiesbaden: Harrassowitz, 1994), §385.

[157] Pierre Lacau and Henri Chevrier, *Une chapelle d'Hatshepsout à Karnak* (Cairo: IFAO, 1977), 1:124–25.

transfer taxes on such transactions into the temple treasury,[158] a practice
that continued in spite of the Persian occupation.[159] A substantial number
of biographical texts of the Twenty-Sixth Dynasty deal, as we have seen,
with the refurbishing of temples, and it is during the same period that the
temple economy experiences a bifurcation in personnel roles between
prebendary and functioning priesthoods, the former often absentee. The
"prophets" and *we'eb*s of former times, moreover, had gravitated increasingly into ritual functions, leaving the "superintendent of stores" (*imy-r šn*),
the *lesonis*-priest, as the all-important manager of temple business.[160] Now
the new ordering of the Pherendates correspondence indicates quite
clearly the rigorous control with which the Persians intended to "rein in"
the Egyptian temple administration.[161] They were well aware of the wealth

---

[158] S. P. Vleeming, "The Tithe of Scribes (and) Representatives," in *Life in a Multi-
cultural Society: Egypt from Cambyses to Constantine and Beyond* (ed. Janet H.
Johnson; SAOC 51; Chicago: Oriental Institute, 1992), 343.

[159] Malinine, *Choix de textes juridiques,* no. XI, line 3 (511 B.C.E.).

[160] On the *lesonis*-priest, see Hermann Kees, *Das Priestertum im ägyptischen
Staat vom Neuen Reich bis zur Spätzeit* (Leiden: Brill, 1953), 217 and n. 2; Erhart
Graefe, *Untersuchungen zur Verwaltung und Geschichte des Institution der Gottes
gemahlin des Amun* (Wiesbaden: Harrassowitz, 1981), vol. 2, sec. 25d; Françoise
de Cenival, *Les associations réligieuses en Égypte d'après les documents démotiques*
(Cairo: IFAO, 1972), 154–59; B. Muhs, "Demotic and Greek Ostraca in the Third
Century B.C.," in *Life in a Multi-cultural Society: Egypt from Cambyses to Constantine and Beyond* (ed. Janet H. Johnson; SAOC 51; Chicago: Oriental Institute, 1992),
250; Günter Vittmann, "Zu fremden und hellenisierten Ägyptern," in
Egyptian Religion: The Last Thousand Years (ed. W. Clarysse; Leuven: Peeters,
1998), 1238. By Ptolemaic times the Greeks could, with justification though impre-
cisely, render the term "temple overseer" and "chief priest" (W. Otto, *Priester und
Tempeln in hellenistischen Ägypten* [Leipzig, 1905], 39; Daumas, *Les moyens d'expressions,* 183; D. J. Thompson, *Memphis under the Ptolemies* [Princeton, N.J.:
Princeton University Press, 1988], 111).

[161] Wilhelm Spiegelberg, *Drei demotische Schreiben aus der Korrespondenz des
Pherendates* (Berlin: Akademie der Wissenschaften, 1928), 610; K.-T. Zauzich,
"Lesonis," *LÄ* 3:1008–9; M. Chauveau, "La chronologie de la correspondence dite
'de Phéréndates,'" *RdE* 50 (1999): 269–71. In the frontier reach of Elephantine,
Pherendates' authority was rigorous: cf. *TAD* 4:D7.39. Yet Persian control could not
have been as universally tight as the Pherendates' correspondence might suggest.
At Teudjoy in the ninth year of Darius I the dismissal and appointment of the *lesonis* was wholly in Egyptian hands (P.Rylands IX.ii.8–9). It might be pointed out in
this regard that, through the accidence of preservation, a preponderance of papyrus
sources bearing upon the Persian period in Egypt comes from Elephantine. But the
cataract was a sensitive *frontier* region, where expectation of a Kushite attack
remained high (cf. Lazlo Török, *The Kingdom of Kush: Handbook of the Napatan-*

of the temples and the capability of the landed estates to *create* wealth. Like the Ptolemies afterwards, it behooved Darius to learn all he could about the regulations within which the temples operated. This, I submit, is the underlying motivation on both his and Cambyses' part to cultivate the priestly establishment at Sais (premier city under the Saite regime),[162] as well as the Apis cult.[163] Undergoing formal investiture as Pharaoh would likewise strengthen the Great King's hand in dealing with the priests.[164]

Meroitic Civilization [Leiden: Brill, 1996], 374–78) and where Persian administration was guided by security needs not felt elsewhere. It would be unwise, therefore, to generalize the application of the contents of the papyri as valid for the rest of Egypt.

[162] About all we know about the relations of Cambyses and Darius with Sais derives from the statue inscription of Udjahorresne, a former secretary of state and an admiral: Posener, *La première domination perse en Egypte*, 1–26; cf. Alan B. Lloyd, "The Inscription of Udjaḥorresnet: A Collaborator's Testament," *JEA* 68 (1982): 166–80; U. Rossler-Köhler, "Zur Textcomposition der naolphoren Statue des Udjahorresnet/Vatikan luv. Nr. 196," *GM* 85 (1985): 43–54; Blenkinsopp, "Mission of Udjahorresnet," 409–21; Frei, "Persian Imperial Authorization," 2.4.1.1; Bresciani, "Ugiahorresnet," 1–6; Verner, "La tombe d'Oudjahorresnet et le cimetière saïto-perse d'Abousir," *BIFAO* 89 (1989): 283–90. It seems to me extremely doubtful, in the light of the discussion above (pp. 150–53) that Udjahorresne's mission had anything to do with the alleged codification (J. Quaegebauer, "Sur la 'loi sacrée' dans l'Égypte gréco-romaine," *Ancient Society* 11–12 [1980–1981]: 227–40; Briant, *Histoire de l'Empire Perse*, 489–90). Much more likely, in my view, is a connection between Udjahorresne's perambulations and the later tradition that "books and writings" and "new writings" were brought to Egypt under Darius (Richard A. Parker, *A Vienna Demotic Papyrus on Eclipses and Solar Omina* [Providence: Brown University Press, 1958], A iv.7–10, pl. III).

[163] On the overriding political importance during the first millennium B.C.E. of the Apis cult (and therefore the Memphite priesthood), see Redford, *Pharaonic Kinglists*, 298–99. The official stela commemorating the Apis buried in year 4 of Darius I formally acknowledges the Persian king in stock formulas (Posener, *La première domination perse en Egypte*, pl. III), but general Ahmose, celebrant of the obsequies, speaks as though a foreign administration did not exist: "I instilled the fear of you (Apis) in the hearts of everybody, including the aliens of every foreign land who were in Egypt.... (for) I despatched messengers quickly to the southland as well as the northland, making every mayor of the towns and townships come with their gifts to your embalming chamber" (Jean Vercoutter, *Textes biographiques du Sérapéum de Memphis* [Paris: Champion, 1962], text H, 4–6, pl. viii).

[164] On the assumption of the pharaonic role by Cambyses and Darius, see Alan B. Lloyd, "The Late Period, 664–323 BC," in *Ancient Egypt, a Social History* (Cambridge: Cambridge University Press, 1983), 288–99; Briant, *Histoire de l'Empire Perse*, 494–97; Ray, "Egypt 525–404 B.C.," 4:258.

To sum up: the writing-up of Egyptian law at Darius's behest, if it occurred as the Demotic Chronicle describes, was no "authorization," much less a "codification" of Egyptian legislation. It would have been, quite simply, the translation into Aramaic,[165] the new language of imperial administration, of regulations governing those parts of Egyptian society productive of wealth. It served as a means of instructing the new authority in its attempt to control that wealth through tapping into the laws and statutes of the administration of the pharaohs, the lay-community, and *especially* the temples.

ADDENDUM

Over the past decade or so some scholars have cautiously opined that the so-called law code of Hermopolis[166] is a later reflection of the Darian process of codification.[167] This would be both tempting and ingenious, were it not for the contents and style of the document. The themes addressed by the (albeit fragmentary) papyrus may be listed as follows: (1) land and property leases, (2) annuity law, (3) house ownership, (4) the "building code" and problems arising therefrom, (5) inheritance law, (6) cemetery regulations. All this smacks of a parochial purview, the customary regulations governing life in a medium-sized community. In much of the document the paragraphs can be construed as reductions from specific cases, and thus a *Vorlage* may be postulated of a collection of dated precedents, that is, *hpw m hrwyt**. One detects a certain *didactic* intent in the inclusion of *models* for the writing-up of summonses and leases. In short, the Hermopolis papyrus would best be construed as a *Manual*[168] pertaining to life in a rural community, intersected by waterways and flanked by farmland, with a cemetery close by. In this light, and in view of its third-century B.C.E. date, it seems

---

[165] Bresciani, "La satrapia d'Egitto," 155.

[166] Girgis Mattha and George R. Hughes, *The Demotic Legal Code of Hermopolis West* (Cairo: IFAO, 1975); K. Donker van Heel, *The Legal Manual of Hermopolis* (Leiden: Brill, 1990). For commentary, see esp. Pieter W. Pestman, "Een juridisch 'Handboek' uit het Oude Egypte," *Phoenix* 25 (1979): 25–35; S. Grunert, "Das demotische Rechtsbuch von Hermopolis-West," *Das Altertum* 26 (1980): 96–110; Schafik Allam, "Réflexions sur le 'code legal' d'Hermopolis dans l'Égypt ancienne," *ChrEg* 61 (1986): 50–75; idem, "Traces de 'codification' en Égypte ancienne (à la basse époque)," *RIDA* 3d series, 40 (1993): 11–26.

[167] Sources listed in Briant, *Histoire de l'Empire Perse,* 972–73.

[168] Similar, in fact, to the "directions" governing certain aspects of property and inheritence: cf. A. S. Hunt and C. C. Edgar, *Select Papyri,* vol. 2 (LCL 282; Cambridge: Harvard University Press, 1934), §206.

plausible to classify the Hermopolis manual as part of the "instructional" literature solicited by the incoming Macedonian/Ptolemaic regime in order to familiarize itself with the ways of the land.[169]

---

[169] Manetho's *Aegyptiaca* is the best known work of this sort (Waddell, *Manetho*); behind it lies, arguably, a demotic original (Redford, *Pharaonic Kinglists,* 213–30; idem, "Textual Sources for the Hyksos Period," in *The Hyksos: New Historical and Archaeological Perspectives* (ed. E. Oren; Philadelphia: University Museum, 1997), 22–24; see also Hunt and Edgar, *Select Papyri,* §411 (cultic information); Plutarch, *Is. Os.* 28 (cultic information); B. P. Grenfell and A. S. Hunt, *The Hibeh Papyri* (2 vols.; London: Egypt Exploration Fund, 1906), 1:27 (cultic calendar). Transactions done "according to native laws" were of great concern to the Ptolemaic administration (Hunt and Edgar, *Select Papyri,* 2:217–19, §72).

"PERSIAN IMPERIAL AUTHORIZATION": SOME QUESTION MARKS

Jean Louis Ska
Pontifical Biblical Institute

1. THE THEORY

The discussion about Persian imperial authorization started some sixteen years ago with the publication of Peter Frei's article in which he tried to explain the policy of the Persian Empire toward the many different nations subject to its authority.[1] The Persian Empire was more flexible than the Assyrian and Babylonian empires and usually granted relative autonomy to the provinces. In the Persian Empire local laws were not only recognised and approved by the central government but were moreover considered as "imperial laws."[2]

Two points must be underlined in this theory:

(1) Local laws receive a new juridical "status," namely, that of "imperial laws."

(2) This imperial law is valid throughout the empire. One can naturally suppose that the norm was enforced only for those directly concerned by it.[3]

---

[1] "Zentralgewalt und Lokalautonomie im Achämenidenreich," in Peter Frei and Klaus Koch, *Reichsidee und Reichsorganisation im Perserreich* (OBO 55; Fribourg: Universitätsverlag, 1984; 2d ed., 1996), 5–131; idem, "Die persische Reichsautorisation: Ein Überblick," *ZABR* 1 (1995): 1–35 (= "Persian Imperial Authorization: A Summary," pp. 5–40 in this volume); cf. Reinhard Gregor Kratz, *Translatio imperii: Untersuchungen zu den aramäischen Danielerzählungen und ihrem theologiegeschichtlichen Umfeld* (WMANT 63; Neukirchen-Vluyn: Neukirchener Verlag, 1991), 225–60.

[2] Frei, "Persian Imperial Authorization," 7: "[By imperial authorization I understand] a process by which the norms established by a local authority are not only approved and accepted by a central authority but adopted as its own. The local norms are thereby established and protected within the framework of the entire state association, that is, the empire, as higher-ranking norms binding on all."

[3] For instance, if one considers the Pentateuch as the "imperial law" for the Jews, this law applied only to the Jews in the Persian Empire.

2. THE FORMATION OF THE PENTATEUCH AND IMPERIAL AUTHORIZATION

Some exegetes resorted to this theory to interpret the formation of the Pentateuch in its present form. These exegetes belong for the most part to the so-called "Heidelberg School"; they are Frank Crüsemann, Erhard Blum, and Rainer Albertz.[4] Some introductions to the Pentateuch and some studies on the same topic adopted the theory.[5]

---

[4] Frank Crüsemann, "Le Pentateuque, une Tora. Prolégomènes et interprétation de sa forme finale," in *Le Pentateuque en question* (ed. A. de Pury; Genève: Labor et Fides, 1989), 339–60, esp. 350–52; idem, *Die Torah: Theologie und Sozialgeschichte des alttestamentlichen Gesetzes* (Munich: Kaiser, 1992), 387–93; 404–7 = *The Torah: Theology and History of Old Testament Law* (trans. A. W. Mahnke; Edinburgh: T&T Clark, 1996), 334–39, 349–51; Erhard Blum, *Studien zur Komposition des Pentateuch* (BZAW 189; Berlin: de Gruyter, 1990), 345–60; Odil Hannes Steck, *Der Abschluß der Prophetie im Alten Testament* (Neukirchen-Vluyn: Neukirchener Verlag, 1991), 17–20 (with bibliography); Rainer Albertz, *Vom Exil bis zu den Makkabäern*, vol. 2 of *Religionsgeschichte in alttestamentlicher Zeit* (ATD 8.2; Göttingen: Vandenhoeck & Ruprecht, 1992), 497–539 = *From the Exile to the Maccabees*, vol. 2 of *A History of Israelite Religion in the Old Testament Period* (OTL; Louisville: Westminster/John Knox, 1994), 466–80; Jonathan E. Dyck, *The Theocratic Ideology of the Chronicler* (BibInt 33; Leiden: Brill, 1998), 96–101. For a critical presentation of the theory, see, e.g., Norbert Lohfink, "Gab es eine deuteronomistiche Bewegung?" in *Jeremia und die "deuteronomistische Bewegung"* (ed. W. Groß; BBB 98; Weinheim: Beltz Athänäeum, 1995), 313–82, esp. 369–70 = *Studien zum Deuteronomium und zur deuteronomistischen Literatur,* vol. 3 (SBAB 20; Stuttgart: Katholisches Bibelwerk, 1995), 65–142, esp. 128–30. For previous attempts in this direction, see, e.g., Hans Heinrich Schaeder, *Ezra der Schreiber* (BHT 5; Tübingen: Mohr Siebeck, 1930); idem, "Das persische Weltreich," in *Der Mensch im Orient und Okzident* (Breslau [Wrocław]: Korn, 1940–1941; Munich: Kaiser, 1960), 71: "Es ist mir unverzweifelhaft, daß nicht erst die Verkündigung, sondern schon die Kodifizierung des mosaischen Gesetzes auf Veranlassung der persischen Reichsregierung zurückgeht—auf dieselbe Initiative des Königs Dareios, die das ägyptische Rechtsbuch hervorrief"; J. Maxwell Miller and John H. Hayes, *A History of Ancient Israel and Judah* (Philadelphia: Fortress, 1986), 450–56, 462–65. The real "ancestor" of the theory is, however, Eduard Meyer, *Die Entstehung des Judenthums: Eine historische Untersuchung* (Halle: Niemeyer, 1896), 65–66: "Die Einführung eines derartigen Gesetzbuchs [das Gesetzbuch Ezras] ist nur möglich, *wenn es vom Reich sanktionirt, wenn es königliches Gesetz geworden ist*" (66; italics mine). According to Meyer, this is confirmed by Ezra 7:26; see also the last sentence of his book: "Das Judenthum ist im Namen des Perserkönigs und kraft der Autorität seines Reichs geschaffen worden, und so reichen die Wirkungen des Achämenidenreichs gewaltig wie wenig anderes noch unmittelbar in unsere Gegenwart hinein" (243). Cf. Blum, *Studien*, 346 n. 44; and Udo Rüterswörden, "Die persische Reichsautorisation der Thora: Fact or Fiction?" *ZABR* 1 (1995): 47–61 (51).

[5] For instance, Joseph Blenkinsopp, *The Pentateuch: An Introduction to the First Five Books of the Bible* (ABRL; New York: Doubleday, 1992), 239–42; Erich Zenger,

According to these scholars, the Pentateuch would be the "imperial authorization" for the Jews living in the Persian Empire, especially in the province of Yehud (Judea). The Persian authorities needed a legal document containing the basic customs and laws of the community living in Judea to grant political and religious autonomy on a clear juridical basis to this province. This decision prompted the different groups, especially the priesthood of Jerusalem and the lay institution of the "elders," to reach a compromise. The elders were responsible for the so-called Deuteronomistic composition of the Pentateuch (KD), and the priesthood stood naturally behind the Priestly composition (KP).[6] Encouraged or constrained by the circumstances, the two groups presented a common document combining the two compositions. The document complied with the requirements of the Persian authorities and, at the same time, was acceptable to the main representative groups of the province of Judea. The result of this compromise is our Pentateuch, or a text very close to it, which became the text of the Persian imperial authorization for the province of Judea. In other words, the Persian legal foundation of the province of Judea was the Pentateuch.

This procedure explains why so many contradictions in the Pentateuch were in no way removed. These contradictions can be explained in a satisfactory way only when one admits the external intervention of the Persian authorities, which obliged the different groups to come to an agreement. They could present only one text if they wanted the relative autonomy granted by Persia. Therefore, they arranged the texts most of the time side by side, without making much effort to harmonize them. The text is one, because it is meant to be the "constitutional text" of one community, but it retains all the peculiarities of the different groups that composed it.

Crüsemann adds an interesting element to the theory. For him, the Pentateuch reflects the legal mentality of the Persians, for whom a written law could not be abrogated. He refers to texts such as Esth 1:19; 8:8; Dan 6:9, 13, 16 [Eng. 6:8, 12, 15] to support his theory. Because of this conception, the several legal codes of the Pentateuch had to be transmitted integrally without any change. They were written texts and for this reason irrevocable.[7]

"Die Bücher der Tora/des Pentateuch," in *Einleitung in das Alte Testament* (ed. E. Zenger; Stuttgart: Kohlhammer, 1995; 2d ed., 1996), 39–44. In the third edition (1998), Zenger takes into account the criticisms expressed against the theory and modifies his presentation (81–84). See also David M. Carr, *Reading the Fractures of Genesis: Historical and Literary Approaches* (Louisville: Westminster/John Knox, 1996), 327–33.

[6] This is a summary of Blum's theory.

[7] Crüsemann, "Le Pentateuque, Une Tora," 351–52; idem, *The Torah,* 349–50 (*Die Torah,* 404–5).

3. Some Problems with the Theory

The theory, after a first flush of enthusiasm, came under soft or sharp criticism from several sides.[8] Some of these criticisms are related to the theory itself, and others to its application to the formation of the Pentateuch.

3.1. The Documentation about Persian Imperial Authorization

3.1.1. The Documentation Is Not Really Unified

The examples proposed by Frei belong to different genres: he quotes written documents unearthed by archaeologists and biblical texts coming either from "historical books" (Ezra 7; Neh 11:23) or from literary (and fictional) compositions (Daniel, Esther). The nonbiblical documents treat several questions: a regulation about the construction of a temple, the trilingual inscription in the Letoon (Xanthus, in Lycia, Asia Minor); a collection of Egyptian laws compiled under King Darius I (586–522 b.c.e.) in two different languages, namely demotic and Aramaic; a regulation about the liturgical celebration of the Feast of Passover in the Jewish colony of Elephantine (Egypt) around 419–418 b.c.e.; the inscription from Sardis forbidding the worshipers of Zeus to participate in other Asian cultic ceremonies ("mysteries"); a border regulation between Miletus and Myus, and so forth. The documentation is very variegated and not really unified. Regulations concerning whole nations are rare and come mostly from biblical texts (Ezra, Nehemiah); the only exception is the compilation of Egyptian laws required by Darius I. But even in this case the purpose of the undertaking is not very clear. Did the Persian authorities promulgate these laws as "Persian imperial

---

[8] See especially Rüterswörden, "Reichsautorisation," 47–61; Josef Wiesehöfer, " 'Reichsgesetz' oder 'Einzelfallgerechtigkeit'? Bemerkungen zu P. Freis These von der Achämenidischen 'Reichsautorisation,' " *ZABR* 1 (1995): 36–46; Eckart Otto, "Die nachpriesterschriftliche Pentateuchredaktion im Buch Exodus," in *Studies in the Book of Exodus: Redaction-Reception-Interpretation* (ed. M. Vervenne; BETL 126; Leuven: Peeters, 1996), 61–111, esp. 66–70; Jean Louis Ska, *Introduction à la lecture du Pentateuque: Clés pour l'interprétation des cinq premiers livres de la Bible* (Le livre et le rouleau; Paris: Cerf, 2000), 310–21; Pierre Briant, "Histoire impériale et histoire régionale: À propos de l'histoire de Juda dans l'empire achéménide," in *Congress Volume: Oslo, 1998* (ed. A. Lemaire and M. Sæbø; VTSup 80; Leiden: Brill, 2000), 235–45, esp. 240–41. For a summary of the criticisms and objections, see Zenger, *Einleitung*³, 82; James W. Watts, *Reading Law: The Rhetorical Shaping of the Pentateuch* (Biblical Seminar 59; Sheffield: Sheffield Academic Press, 1999), 137–43 (rather favorable to the theory); for the history of Judea during the Persian period, see the recent study by Charles Edward Carter, *The Emergence of Yehud in the Persian Period: A Social and Demographic Study* (JSOTSup 294; Sheffield: Sheffield Academic Press, 1999).

law for Egypt"? Or did the collection serve as archives for consultation in case of conflicts? It is reasonable to think that the king of Persia (or his administration) kept for himself (or for itself) the power to enforce the laws or not. In antiquity the ruler is more important than the rule.

3.1.2. Local or Imperial Laws and Regulations?

According to Frei, the regulations or laws became "Persian laws." But not a single document mentions this in an explicit and unambiguous way. Most of the time, it seems simpler to think that these documents were local regulations approved by the local (Persian) authorities, the satraps, but never became "imperial laws." The approval of the Persian authorities did not mean that the documents had a special value in the rest of the empire. The documents could bear, so to speak, the imperial seal, but this only meant that the local Persian authority had approved it and considered the operation as legitimate.[9] They had no special value either for the emperor or for the rest of the empire.

The case of the Egyptian laws compiled by Darius I around 519–503 B.C.E. might be different because, for once, the authority involved is the king of Persia himself.[10] A careful analysis of the documentation, however, obliges us to reconsider Frei's opinion in this case as well.[11] According to Rüterswörden, the purpose of the text is to legitimate old Egyptian rights in the Hellenistic (Ptolemaic) period. It is difficult to glean any information about Persian juridical activity in Egypt from this document.[12] According to Wiesehöfer, it is better not to speak of a "codification of Egyptian laws." Darius only wanted to have at hand some documentation about the financial rights of Egyptian temples. Cambyses, his predecessor, had become unpopular because of his fiscal policy with respect to Egyptian sanctuaries. Darius adopted a "softer" policy; for this reason he reestablished the rights of the temples according to older regulations. These regulations were written down to give them permanent value. The measure was once again local, and we are far from the redaction of an "Egyptian law code."[13]

---

[9] See the analysis of all the documents given by Wiesehöfer, "Reichsgesetz," 36–46.

[10] Demotic papyrus 215, Paris National Library; see Wilhelm Spiegelberg, *Die sogenannte demotische Chronik des Pap. 215 der Bibliothèque Nationale zu Paris* (Leipzig: Hinrich, 1914).

[11] See Wiesehöfer, "Reichsgesetz," 38–41; Rüterswörden, "Reichsautorisation," 52–53.

[12] Rüterswörden, "Reichsautorisation," 53. The same holds true, still according to Rüterswörden, for the information given by Diodorus (1.94–95).

[13] Wiesehöfer, "Reichsgesetz," 38–41.

3.1.3. The Letters from Elephantine

The letters from the Jewish community in Elephantine (Egypt) create several problems.[14] On the island of Elephantine different military communities lived together. A Jewish temple was built close to an Egyptian temple dedicated to the god Khnum. After a conflict between the Egyptian and the Jewish communities, the Jewish temple or altar was destroyed. Perhaps the Egyptians were upset because the Jews used to offer sheep and rams on the altar, and the usual representation of the god Khnum is a statue with the head of a ram. The Jewish community, however, was unhappy about this outcome and tried to reverse it. They appealed to the Persian administration, which punished the culprits and, some time afterward, arrived at a compromise. The Jewish community was allowed to rebuild its altar but could offer only incense and meal-offerings on it, no sacrifices (holocausts). The Persian authorities in Jerusalem intervened to reach this solution. Now, how could the Persian authorities in Trans-Euphrates[15] not only allow but encourage the reconstruction of a shrine, a measure that is in clear contradiction with the norms that they must have themselves promulgated in the Pentateuch as "imperial law," at least according to the theory of imperial authorization?[16]

3.1.4. Ezra 7:11–26

It is obviously impossible to treat within this short article all the interpretive problems in Ezra 7:11–26.[17] Two points, however, are of interest

---

[14] Rüterswörden, "Reichsautorisation," 59–60. For the text, see Bezalel Porten, *Archives from Elephantine: The Life of an Ancient Jewish Military Colony* (Berkeley and Los Angeles: University of California Press, 1968), 286; idem, *The Elephantine Papyri in English: Three Millennia of Cross-Cultural Continuity and Change* (DMOA 22; Leiden: Brill, 1996), 148–51; Pierre Grelot, *Documents araméens d'Égypte* (LAPO 5; Paris: Cerf, 1972), 415–18; Pierre Briant, "Ethno-classe dominante et populations soumises dans l'Empire Achéménide: le cas de l'Égypte," in *Method and Theory: Proceedings of the London 1985 Achaemenid History Workshop* (ed. A. Kuhrt and H. Sancisi-Weerdenburg; Achaemenid History 3; Leiden: Nederlands Instituut voor het Nabije Oosten, 1988), 144–47.

[15] The province of Judea (Yehud) belonged to the satrapy of Trans-Euphrates.

[16] On this point, I must correct a statement I made in *Introduction,* 317–18. Yehud and Egypt do not belong to the same satrapy, of course. In the case of the conflict mentioned in these Elephantine letters, the Persian authorities in the satrapy of Trans-Euphrates intervene in favor of the reconstruction of the altar. These are the authorities who must have promulgated the Pentateuch as "imperial law." They should know that this measure is in contradiction to the text of this imperial authorization.

[17] See, e.g., Blum, *Studien,* 350–51, n. 64; Kratz, *Translatio imperii,* 254–55; Crüsemann, *The Torah,* 335–39; Zenger, *Einleitung*³, 81–2; Ska, *Introduction,* 314–20.

for our purpose. First, the text supposes an equivalence between the "law of God and the law of the king" (7:26). Second, there is the problem of whether the "law" mentioned in Ezra 7 can be identified with our Pentateuch. There are several objections to the latter hypothesis. The most important one, in my opinion, is that some of the sanctions laid down by Artaxerxes' firman do not correspond to the more common sanctions in the civil, criminal, and cultic laws found in the Pentateuch. The text of Ezra 7:26 reads: "All who will not obey the law of your God and the law of the king, let judgment be strictly executed on them, whether for death or for banishment or for confiscation of their goods or for imprisonment."[18] Some terms are unclear, for instance, the word לִשְׁרֹשׁוּ (Qere: לִשְׁרֹשִׁי) translated in the NRSV by "banishment."[19] Others prefer to see in this term a Persian word (*sransha,* "corporal punishment") and propose to translate by "bastinado," "beating," or other similar terms.[20] Be that as it may, it is preferable not to base any interpretation on this difficult term.

The translation of the other terms in the list, such as death, confiscation of goods (or fines), and imprisonment, is less problematic. As for the interpretation of the text, the last term is the most surprising of all. Nowhere do the laws of the Pentateuch mention imprisonment as a punishment for a crime. אֲסוּרִין ("prison" or, better, "custody," Hebrew: מִשְׁמָר) is mentioned only twice in these laws, not as punishment, however, but as a measure taken to keep somebody under guard until judgment is passed on him (Lev 24:12; Num 15:34). If the "law of the king" is identical with the Pentateuch, how can we explain that this law introduces sanctions unknown to Israel's legislation? Moreover, more usual sanctions such as stoning are not mentioned in Ezra 7:26. And, after all, the more usual way of concluding a law code in the Pentateuch is not to list a series of severe sanctions but rather to seal the legislation with blessings and curses (Lev 26; Deut 28; cf. Exod 23:20–33, which contains a conditioned promise of assistance).

One could object that Ezra 7 is not identical with the Pentateuch and that it does not even intend to summarize it. But if the "law of the king" mentioned there is an equivalent of the "law of God" and of the Pentateuch, it remains somewhat startling that the text of Ezra 7 should differ from the Pentateuch on such important points as sanctions.

---

[18] Translation of the NRSV.

[19] From the word "root"; the meaning would be "being rooted out"; see *BDB,* 1117; *HAL,* 1796.

[20] See Godfrey Rolles Driver, *Aramaic Documents of the Fifth Century B.C.* (abridged and rev. ed.; Oxford: Clarendon, 1957), 47; cf. TOB ("bastonnade"); NAB ("corporal punishment").

3.2. PERSIAN IMPERIAL AUTHORIZATION AND THE PENTATEUCH

3.2.1. Law and Narrative[21]

The Persian authorities were mostly interested in political, military, and financial affairs. What mattered for them was the loyalty of the provinces, the security of the empire, and the regular payment of taxes. Most of the examples given by Frei are in fact juridical texts. The Pentateuch, however, is not merely a juridical text. Why are there so many narrative texts in the Pentateuch? Besides, the Pentateuch is by far the longest instance of a possible "imperial authorization." Is it reasonable to think that such a long, composite, and heterogeneous text was meant to be the reference document about the juridical status of Israel in the eyes of the Persian authorities?

3.2.2. The Juridical Value and Utility of the Pentateuch[22]

The complexity of the Pentateuch is well known. Everyone is aware of the multiple contradictions between the laws, in particular between similar laws present in the three main codes (the Covenant Code, the Holiness Laws, and the Deuteronomic Code). This obliges us to raise a question about the practical value of the Pentateuch as "Persian authorization." How could judges decide in particular cases? Which law was to apply? One can easily imagine the confusion and the endless conflicts that could be created by a document such as the Pentateuch because of its lack of clarity and its incoherence. The Persian authorities, on the other hand, had a rather precise and literal understanding of law, which is difficult to reconcile with the nature of the Pentateuch in its present form.

3.2.3. The Theology of the Pentateuch and the Imperial Authorization

There are no references, either explicit or implicit, to imperial authorization in the Pentateuch,[23] and it is nowhere said that the Persian authorities issued the document.[24] It must even be said that some basic ideas developed in the Pentateuch are rather in contradiction with the idea of an imperial authorization. Israel's law comes from God, not

---

[21] Hans-Christoph Schmitt, "Die Suche nach der Identität des Jahweglaubens im nachexilischen Israel: Bemerkungen zur theologischen Intention des Pentateuch," in *Pluralismus und Identität* (ed. J. Mehlhausen; Munich: Kaiser, 1995), 259–78 (266); Ska, *Introduction,* 316. See also Ulrich Kellermann, "Erwägungen zum Ezragesetz," *ZAW* 80 (1968): 373–85 (377–78).

[22] Ska, *Introduction,* 316.

[23] See Zenger, *Einleitung*[3], 82.

[24] Schmitt, "Suche nach Identität," 264.

from a human authority, and is transmitted only by Moses.[25] The Pentateuch is a theological document about Israel's identity, not exactly a political compromise.

This criticism requires some nuances.[26] Religion and politics are often mixed, and there are many ways of covering political interest with a religious "coating." It remains true, however, that there are no allusions to imperial authorization within the Pentateuch. Moreover, the Pentateuch affirms that all the laws were promulgated in the desert, in a "legal and political void," so to speak, since the desert is literally a "no man's land." In the desert, Israel is completely independent, but also without monarchy and territory, the two main conditions for political autonomy in antiquity. This does not mean, however, that Israel could not admit that her laws could be approved or ratified later by foreign powers. The above objection is therefore weaker than the others.

3.2.4. Problems with Certain Texts

Some texts contained in the Pentateuch may have raised the suspicion or even the hostility of the Persian authorities. For instance, according to Gen 15:18, the land promised to Abraham goes from the stream of Egypt to the Euphrates. This is a rather ambitious view. The wars of conquest described in Num 21, 25, and 31 could have raised some perplexities in Persian minds. And what could or would the Persian authorities have said when reading texts such as Deut 7 (Israel must destroy all the nations occupying the land); Deut 20 (the rules for war); Deut 17:14–20 (the king or ruler must be chosen among the people of Israel); Deut 26:19; 28:1 (YHWH promises to place Israel above all other nations)? The Balaam oracles (Num 22–24) contain a certain number of affirmations about the future of Israel upon which the Persians could frown.[27]

3.2.5. An Aramaic Version of the Pentateuch?

A last problem regards the language of the "authorization."[28] Our Pentateuch is written in Hebrew, and there is no trace of an Aramaic copy of it. The problem is twofold. First, the Persian authorities surely needed for their own purposes a copy of the texts in the diplomatic language of the time, namely, Aramaic. The collection of laws compiled for Darius I was available in two copies, one in demotic and the other in Aramaic. The

---

[25] Schmitt, "Suche nach Identität," 267; Watts, *Reading Law,* 140 n. 26, thinks that such Persian documents did not necessarily make explicit who promulgated them.

[26] Cf. Watts, *Reading Law,* 143 n. 38.

[27] Ska, *Introduction,* 316–17.

[28] Cf. Schmitt, "Suche nach Identität," 264–65.

inscription from the Letoon exists in Lycian, Greek, and Aramaic. Why is there no Aramaic version of the Pentateuch? This seems puzzling, especially since an important "political" text such as Ezra 7:12–26 is written in Aramaic. Second, the simple fact that the Pentateuch was written in Hebrew and not in the more commonly used language of the time, namely, Aramaic, proves that the Second Temple community was more eager to reestablish solid links with the past, even in the choice of the language, than to comply with the requirements of the foreign government of the time.

4. The Pentateuch and the Archives of the Second Temple Community

I would like to defend the thesis that the Pentateuch contains the "official and national archives/library"[29] of the Second Temple community. As a written text, the Pentateuch acquires the quality of a normative and irrevocable document about Israel's origins and juridical organization.

4.1. Written Texts in the Ancient Near East

The point that must be underlined in this context is the value of written texts in antiquity, and particularly in the ancient Near East.[30] *Verba volant, scripta manent,* according to an old Latin saying. Similar affirmations can be found in the Bible.[31] Job 19:23–24, for instance, is very clear in this respect: "O that my words were written down! O that they were inscribed in a book [בספר]! O that with an iron pen and with lead they were engraved on a rock forever [בצור לעד]!"[32] The word "forever" [לעד]

---

[29] Authors usually distinguish between "archives" and "libraries." "Archives" contain administrative records (lists of wares, contracts, letters, etc.) preserved mostly for administrative purposes; "libraries" contain literary works (scrolls or books). An "archive" is the result of administrative necessities; a "library" is more the product of a free choice. But the distinction is perhaps too sharp. Written works were not meant to be accessible to a wide public, since only a minority of the population could read or have access to costly written materials. Anyway, the problem of the preservation of the different kinds of writings was the same. See André Lemaire, "Writing and Writing Material," *ABD* 6:999–1008 (1004); Philip R. Davies, *Scribes and Schools: The Canonization of the Hebrew Scriptures* (Louisville: Westminster/John Knox, 1998), 85–7.

[30] See Ska, *Introduction,* 247–52.

[31] See texts such as Job 19:23–24; Isa 30:8; Esth 1:19; 8:8; Dan 6:9, 13, 16 [Eng. 6:8, 12, 15]; cf. Isa 8:1, 16; Jer 17:1; 36:2, 32. According to Crüsemann, the idea of royal orders being irrevocable because they are written is typical of the Persian legal mentality (see n. 7).

[32] Translation of the NRSV.

appears in Isa 30:8 too (לְעַד עַד־עוֹלָם).[33] The idea that a written text, especially of a ruling issued by a king, cannot "pass away" and is therefore irrevocable appears in texts such as Esth 1:19; 8:8; Dan 6:9, 13, 16 [Eng. 6:8, 12, 15].[34] In Deut 31:19, 21, 26 Moses affirms that written texts are "testimonies" (עֵד) against future generations' unfaithfulness. In the first two verses, the written text is Moses' song; in the third, it is the "law." In the Pentateuch itself, it is repeated that the law has been "written down" by Moses himself (Exod 24:4, 7; Deut 31:9, 24).

This short inquiry has shown that written words have a special value because they can survive longer than those who utter them. Writing gives an enduring quality to ephemeral elements such as spoken words. This is the main reason why some "words" were written down: in antiquity, the first purpose of written texts was not to be read—too few people could read and consult written material—but to be *preserved*.[35] Ancient texts were not "published" because there was no real "public" to read them.[36] This is the case with the Pentateuch as we have it in its present form. In the postexilic period oral tradition was no longer capable of meeting the needs of the community, and hence it became necessary to write down the most essential parts of Israel's "documents" about its past. Not all the reasons for this change are clear, and we are often left with surmise and supposition. Some of the reasons may be material, others more cultural.

4.2. MATERIAL REASONS

4.2.1. New Writing Material and New Script

Two changes took place in the Persian period with respect to the material conditions of writing. Several scholars have noticed a slow passage from papyrus to skins during this time (sixth to fourth century

---

[33] Some scholars correct the text and read "as witness" (לְעֵד) instead of "forever" (לְעַד). Be that as it may, the idea of "permanence" is still present in the text.

[34] See the Aramaic expression דִי־לָא תֶעְדֵא ("which will not pass away") in Dan 6:9, 13 [Eng. 6:8, 12].

[35] See Dale Patrick, *Old Testament Law* (Atlanta: John Knox, 1985), 185–204. About literacy in Israel, see especially David W. Jamieson-Drake, *Scribes and Schools in Monarchic Judah: A Socio-archaeological Approach* (JSOTSup 109; Sheffield: Sheffield Academic Press, 1991); Christine Schams, *Jewish Scribes in the Second Temple Period* (JSOTSup 291; Sheffield: Sheffield Academic Press, 1998).

[36] This fact does not exclude the possibility that official texts could be read publicly on certain occasions. See Watts, *Reading Law,* and the review of this work by Eckart Otto, *ZABR* 5 (1999): 353–57.

B.C.E.).[37] The use of this new material became more and more widespread. On the other hand, the use of Aramaic script ("square Hebrew" script) progressively replaced the Paleo-Hebrew one. The new script was used mostly for official documents. The adoption of new writing material and of a new script made it possible or even necessary to rewrite or copy older texts afresh. In this context, it also became possible to edit, rework, and adapt these texts to new situations and new preoccupations. Older traditions may have been integrated and new texts or redactional layers may have been inserted in order to create a more comprehensive literary document that could meet the needs of the postexilic community.

4.2.2. Archives and Libraries[38]

Archives and libraries are well known in the ancient Near East. Royal palaces had archives and libraries, as probably did some temples as well.[39] In the Persian period there are sufficient examples of this practice. The letters from Elephantine sent by the Jewish military colony to the Persian authorities in Samaria and in Jerusalem were kept in an "archive," where they were found later. In two places the Bible itself refers to the existence of archives in Jerusalem. The texts are late but may preserve older traditions.

According to 2 Macc 2:13, "[Nehemiah] founded a library [βιβλιοθήκα] and collected the books about the kings and prophets, and the writings of David, and letters of kings about votive offerings." It is surprising that the Law is not mentioned in this list. It was perhaps not necessary—or even allowed—to introduce a book of the Law into this new library because the book of the Law was kept in the temple.[40] The archives of the temple had been previously ransacked and the books burnt by Antiochus IV Epiphanes (175–164 B.C.E.), according to 1 Macc 1:56. Afterwards Judas Maccabeus "collected all the books that had been lost on account of the war" (2 Macc 2:14). The data can be questioned, of course, but it remains the case that 2 Macc 2:13 connects the foundation of a library to

---

[37] See Menahem Haran, "Book-Scrolls at the Beginning of the Second Temple Period: The Transition from Papyrus to Skins," *HUCA* 54 (1983): 111–22; Lemaire, "Writing and Writing Material," 6:1003; the Greek Historian Diodorus Siculus, in his *Bibliotheca Historica,* mentions the "royal parchments [skins]" (βασιλικαὶ διφθέρα, 2.32.4) used by the Persian court and Persian officials.

[38] See Lemaire, "Writing and Writing Material," 6:1004–5; Davies, *Scribes and Schools,* 85–87.

[39] 2 Kgs 22 tells about the famous discovery of a scroll of the law in the Jerusalem temple under King Josiah.

[40] About this text, see Davies, *Scribes and Schools,* 187–88.

Nehemiah's activity. The text implies that the "rebuilding" of the postexilic community required not only the reconstruction of Jerusalem and of the temple but also the constitution of a library.

4.3. CULTURAL REASONS

4.3.1. The Exile and Its Consequences

The fall of Samaria in 722 B.C.E. and of Jerusalem in 586 B.C.E. caused a deep break in the civil and religious life of the two kingdoms. One can even surmise that Sennacherib's invasion of Judah in 701 B.C.E. had already had dire and drastic effects on the life of the kingdom of the south.[41] These breaks had their effect on the traditions of the past as well. It is difficult to know with precision which traditions had already been written down when Jerusalem was destroyed by the Babylonians in 586 B.C.E. and even more difficult to determine their exact content. Nonetheless, one thing is certain, namely, that the Assyrian and Babylonian invasions from the eighth till the beginning of the sixth century B.C.E. deeply affected the people's consciousness of their identity.

One point may have a special bearing on our understanding of the composition of the Pentateuch. The need to write down and keep in a written form the traditions of the past became more urgent in the postexilic period. Oral tradition can be maintained in a stable and homogeneous society.[42] However, because of the movements of population and the social disruptions caused by the invasions, the society of Israel was no longer capable of transmitting a unified and common oral tradition about its past. When the different groups of exiled people started coming back from Babylon and establishing themselves again in Judea, the conflict between the returnees and those who had remained in the country soon became acute.[43]

---

[41] For a summary of this period, see, e.g., Eckart Otto, *Das Deuteronomium: politische Theologie und Rechtsreform in Juda und Assyrien* (BZAW 284; Berlin: de Gruyter, 1999), 364–78; for more details, see Hermann Spieckermann, *Juda unter Assur in der Sargonidenzeit* (FRLANT 129; Göttingen: Vandenhoeck & Ruprecht, 1982); Francolino J. Gonçalves, *L'expédition de Sennachérib en Palestine dans la littérature hébraïque ancienne* (EB 7; Paris: Gabalda, 1986).

[42] See Patricia G. Kirkpatrick, *The Old Testament and Folklore Study* (JSOTSup 62; Sheffield: Sheffield Academic Press, 1988).

[43] See esp. Hans M. Barstad, *The Babylonian Captivity of the Book of Isaiah: "Exilic" Judah and the Provenance of Isaiah 40–55* (Oslo: Novus forlag—The Institute for Comparative Research in Human Culture, 1997); Lester L. Grabbe, ed., *Leading Captivity Captive: "The Exile" As History and Ideology* (JSOTSup 278; European Seminar in Historical Methodology 2; Sheffield: Sheffield Academic Press,

Whether one group prevailed over the other(s) or divergent traditions were reconciled and amalgamated to form a new common document approved by a majority of the population is a question that can remain open for the moment.[44] What is certain, however, is that the postexilic community needed a solid ideological basis if it wanted to survive within the Persian Empire. For at least two reasons this ideological basis had to have a rather strong religious dimension. First, religion and politics could not be separated at that time.[45] Second, the postexilic community became explicitly what is often called a theocracy.[46] After the return from the exile, it soon appeared clearly that the monarchy could not be reestablished and, therefore, the community had to renounce political independence.[47] Without monarchy and without territory or, more precisely, without full territorial autonomy, the community tried to recompose its identity and its unity around its faith and its religious institutions, especially the temple.[48]

The modern theory of the *Bürger-Tempel-Gemeinde* ("citizen-temple community"), proposed by the Latvian scholar Joel P. Weinberg, has often been used to understand better the situation in which the Pentateuch in its present form came into existence.[49] According to this theory, the Persian

---

1998). About the identity of the different groups, see esp. Brooks Schramm, *The Opponents of the Third Isaiah: Reconstructing the Cultic History of the Restoration* (JSOTSup 193; Sheffield: Sheffield Academic Press, 1994); Thomas Willi, *Juda-Jehud-Israel* (FAT 12; Tübingen: Mohr Siebeck, 1995); Carter, *Emergence of Yehud*, 307–16.

[44] The first opinion is defended by Eckart Otto, e.g., in "Kritik der Pentateuchkomposition," *TRu* 60 (1995): 163–91; idem, "Die nachpriesterschriftliche Redaktion im Buch Exodus," in *The Book of Exodus: Redaction-Reception-Interpretation* (ed. M. Vervenne; BETL 126; Leuven: Peeters, 1996), 61–111; Ska, *Introduction*, 265–73. The second opinion is defended by the "Heidelberg School"; see Blum, *Komposition des Pentateuch*, 333–60; Albertz, *Vom Exil*, 497–539 (*From the Exile*, 464–95).

[45] "Indeed, religion and its symbolism have a power that often transcends that of the state, and remains one of the most potent forces for social stability (and even for promoting social change)" (Carter, *Emergence of Yehud*, 316).

[46] See, among others, Steck, *Abschluß der Prophetie*, 15 n. 13. The idea is already present in Wellhausen's work.

[47] Miller and Hayes, *History*, 445–46; Paolo Sacchi, *Storia del Secondo Tempio: Israele tra VI secolo a.C. e I secolo d.C.* (Turin: Società Editrice Internazionale, 1994), 73–76; Carter, *Emergence of Yehud*, 39–50.

[48] See Jean Louis Ska, "Exode 19,3b–6 et l'identité de l'Israël postexilique," in *The Book of Exodus: Redaction-Reception-Interpretation* (ed. M. Vervenne; BETL 126; Leuven: Peeters, 1996), 289–317; Sacchi, *Storia*, 89–104.

[49] Joel P. Weinberg, "Demographische Notizen zur Geschichte der nachexilischen Gemeinde in Juda," *Klio* 54 (1972): 45–59; idem, *The Citizen-Temple Community* (JSOTSup 151; Sheffield: Sheffield Academic Press, 1992); for a critical

authorities granted some privileges to sanctuaries and the personnel serving in them. Temples and shrines were, understandably, not only religious but also economic, commercial, and financial centers. Administration of the shrines was entrusted to a small group, which can be identified with the main priestly families and some of the main representatives of the laity or the landlords (probably "the elders"). Other aspects of the theory can be left aside for the moment, such as the economic aspects or the details about the political organization of the community. The citizen-temple community, which is not identical with the whole community, tended of course to defend its privileges. I believe this behavior could be the cause of strong tensions between different groups. It could also elucidate the reasons why the ruling class fostered a certain spirit of "exclusivism" notable, for instance, in the books of Ezra and Nehemiah, but also in certain parts of the Pentateuch, such as the laws of purity in the book of Leviticus (Lev 11–15) or in Deut 7.

This theory has recently come under attack. The criticisms are summarized by Charles E. Carter, who adds some of his own objections to them.[50] The main problems are three. First, Weinberg suggests a considerable increase of the population under Ezra and Nehemiah. To reach this conclusion, he must take at face value texts such as the lists in Ezra 2 and Neh 7, lists of cities in Neh 3 and 11:25–35, and the account of tax remission for temple functionaries in Ezra 7:24.[51] Second, there is no clear

---

presentation of the theory, see Wilhelm Schottroff, "Zur Sozialgeschichte Israels in der Perserzeit," *VF* 27 (1982): 46–68, esp. 61–62; Klaus Koch, "Weltordnung und Reichsidee im alten Iran und ihre Auswirkungen auf die Provinz Jehud," in Peter Frei and Klaus Koch, *Reichsidee und Reichsorganisation im Perserreich* (OBO 55; Fribourg: Universitätsverlag, 1984), 134–337, esp. 203–4; Helmut Utzschneider, *Das Heiligtum und das Gesetz: Studien zur Bedeutung der sinaitischen Heiligtumstexte (Ex 25–40; Lev 8–9)* (OBO 77; Göttingen: Vandenhoeck & Ruprecht, 1988), 292–95, 333; Manfred Oeming, *Das Wahre Israel: Die »Genealogische Vorhalle« 1Chronik 1–9* (BWANT 128; Stuttgart: Kohlhammer, 1990), 68–69; Joseph Blenkinsopp, "A Jewish Sect of the Persian Period," *CBQ* 52 (1990): 5–20; idem, "Temple and Society in Achaemenid Judah," in *Second Temple Studies 1: Persian Period* (ed. P. R. Davies; JSOTSup 117; Sheffield: Sheffield Academic Press, 1991), 22–53; Paul Dion, "The Civic-and-Temple Community of Persian Period Judea: Neglected Insights from Eastern Europe," *JNES* 50 (1991): 281–87; David L. Petersen, "Israelite Prophecy: Change versus Continuity," in *Congress Volume: Leuven, 1989* (ed. J. A. Emerton; VTSup 43; Leiden: Brill, 1991), 191–203 (197–203); Steck, *Abschluß der Prophetie,* 14 n. 10; Dyck, *Theocratic Ideology,* 101–9; Ska, *Introduction,* 323–25.

[50] Carter, *Emergence of Yehud,* 294–307.

[51] See Carter (ibid., 297–301), who quotes among others Hugh G. M. Williamson, "Judah and the Jews," in *Studies in Persian History: Essays in Memory of David M.*

evidence that there was a "two-governor system" in the province of Yehud. According to Weinberg, there was, prior to Nehemiah's mission, a political governor in Samaria and a governor of the citizen-temple community in Jerusalem. After Nehemiah, the priesthood gained influence and both offices were merged. In other words, the governor of the citizen-temple community also became the governor of the province of Yehud. This reconstruction has been contested by specialists in the field.[52] Third, some scholars challenge the centrality of the temple in the economy of Yehud during the Persian period.[53] All in all, the authorities mentioned by Carter and Carter himself tend to dispense with the theory and assign the temple the same role as in preexilic times, namely, as a "symbol of social order."[54]

It is not possible to discuss these problems at length. Nonetheless, in my opinion, these scholars tend to undervalue the importance of one essential fact about postexilic Judea, namely, that the temple was the only important indigenous institution after the return from the exile, since the monarchy could not be restored. We may have to add many nuances to Weinberg's theory, especially in some concrete details, but it holds true that the postexilic community was rebuilt and survived around the temple and not around a royal palace. The civil government was in the hands of foreign, that is, Persian authorities. Moreover, biblical texts insist on the fact that Ezra's and Nehemiah's missions were explicitly approved by Persian authorities. Many exegetical and historical problems are linked with those two figures. Nonetheless it is difficult to imagine the reconstruction of the temple and of the city of Jerusalem without any approval by the (local) Persian authorities. The problem of the two-governor system is perhaps less important. We must note, however, that some of the Elephantine letters were addressed both to the Persian governor of Samaria and to the high priest of Jerusalem. Others were addressed to the Persian governor of

---

Lewis (ed. M. Brosius and A. Kuhrt; AH 11; Leiden: Nederlands Instituut van het Nabije Oosten, 1998), 143–63 (154–56).

[52] See Carter, *Emergence of Yehud,* 301–4, who quotes Peter R. Bedford, "On Models and Texts: A Response to Blenkinsopp and Petersen," in *Second Temple Studies 1: Persian Period* (ed. P. R. Davies; JSOTSup 117; Sheffield: Sheffield Academic Press, 1991), 154–62; Williamson, "Judah and the Jews," 156–58.

[53] See Bedford, "On Models and Texts," 158; Richard A. Horsley, "Empire, Temple, and Community—But No Bourgeoisie! A Response to Blenkinsopp and Petersen," in *Second Temple Studies 1: Persian Period* (ed. P. R. Davies; JSOTSup 117; Sheffield: Sheffield Academic Press, 1991), 163–74 (169–70).

[54] Horsley, "Empire, Temple, and Community," 170, quoted by Carter, *Emergence of Yehud,* 306.

Yehud.[55] Finally, even if one has to admit that the temple was not the major source of income and that the main social division was not between the citizen-temple community and "the populace," but between a "social and political elite" and the peasantry,[56] the temple remains one of the key elements in defining the identity of the postexilic community. For instance, the "people of the land" are those who are excluded from the reconstruction of the temple (Ezra 4:1–4).

4.3.2. Israel, Moses, and the Desert

In these particular circumstances, Moses emerged as a central figure. The real founder of Israel was older than the monarchy and even older than the entrance into the land. What could appear as a shortcoming or a weakness became a real advantage because "Israel" had to make do without monarchy and territory. Israel needed to prove that it was more ancient than the monarchy and even than the possession of the land. Therefore the desert became Israel's real "birthplace," and Moses Israel's true founder. The desert is literally a "no man's land," and Moses' authority cannot be identified with any usual form of civil power.[57] It can be safely affirmed that, thanks to Moses, Israel was born before the monarchy and before the entrance into the land, and could then survive after the disappearance of the monarchy (and without it) and without full possession of the land. Moses is also the only figure who can unify the different groups and different tendencies within the postexilic community, especially the priestly

---

[55] See letter no. 102, lines 1, 17–19, 28; letter no. 103 contains the answer of both the Persian governor of Yehud (Bagavahya) and of Samaria (Daliyeh).

[56] Carter, *Emergence of Yehud,* 306; Horsley, "Empire, Temple, and Community," 170.

[57] Philo of Alexandria considered Moses a king (*Mos.* 1.4), and the Jewish tradition followed him; in modern times, Johann Pedersen (*Israel: Its Life and Culture,* vols. 3–4 [Copenhagen: Branner, 1940], 662–63) has the same idea, as does Joshua R. Porter (*Moses and Monarchy: A Study in the Biblical Tradition of Moses* [Oxford: Oxford University Press, 1963]). Moses, however, cannot be a real king since he lacks all the normal symbols of royalty, such as throne, sceptre, guards, army, palace, capital, and he does not found a dynasty. See Jean Louis Ska, "La scrittura era parola di Dio, scolpita sulle tavole (Es 32,16). Autorità, rivelazione e ispirazione nelle leggi del Pentateuco," in *Spirito di Dio e Sacre Scritture nell'autotestimonianza della Bibbia* (ed. E. Manicardi and A. Pitta; Ricerche Storico-Bibliche 1–2; Bologna: Dehoniane, 2000), 7–23 (19–21). Instead, Moses is rather like a prophet. His career begins with a typical prophetic vocation (Exod 3–4), and the last words of the book of Deuteronomy, in a kind of epitaph, acclaim him as the "greatest among all prophets" (Deut 34:10–12). On the postexilic Moses, see Crüsemann, *The Torah,* 102–7 (*Die Torah,* 126–31).

families and the landlords or the civil and lay authorities of Judah. "What connected them was really 'Moses,' that is, the Pentateuch as the book and work of Moses", says Crüsemann.[58]

These reasons can explain why the Pentateuch remains open-ended and finishes before the entrance into the land. Israel had to survive with the sole help of the institutions inaugurated in the desert, because Israel had to live in another "desert," the political situation of the postexilic community within the Persian Empire.

4.3.3. Israel's Ancestors and Neighbors

The postexilic community had to grapple with another problem besides the institutional one solved by the figure of Moses, namely, the thorny problem of "membership." They had to determine who was a member of Israel and who could not be part of the chosen people. The book of Genesis answers the question through genealogies and narratives. Genesis determines the place of Israel in the universe (Gen 1–11) and then traces Israel's genealogical tree (Gen 12–50). The first book of the Bible explains, too, Israel's relationships with its neighbors, especially in Gen 12–36, while the Joseph story mainly describes problems and conflicts within the people.[59]

Seen from this perspective, the origin of the Pentateuch is to be found more in the inner necessities of the Second Temple community than in any explicit requirement coming from the Persian authorities. The Persian authorities were ready to concede relative autonomy to the province of Yehud. This decision made it possible for the postexilic community living in Jerusalem and Judea to start a new life on a new basis. But this possibility required from the community itself a great effort to redefine in clear terms its identity and conditions of existence. This was done, not to comply with the requirements of the Persian authorities, but to meet the needs of the community itself.

Among the needs of this community, I would like especially to mention the strong desire to show continuity with the past. Whether there was ever a real preexilic "Israel" is a question hotly debated today, but it has

---

[58] *The Torah,* 105 (*Die Torah,* 129). See also 107 (*Die Torah,* 131): "In the postexilic period Moses was just an image, but an extremely effective one for the correlation of tradition and autonomy. He stood for the possibility and necessity to bring together the interests and traditions of divergent groups, especially between priests and laity."

[59] See Erhard Blum, *Die Komposition der Vätergeschichte* (WMANT 57; Neukirchen-Vluyn: Neukirchener Verlag, 1984), 478–506; Ska, *Introduction,* 265–67, 323–25.

no direct bearing on our study.[60] It is patent that the postexilic community wanted to be the unique heir of its preexilic predecessor(s), and this was the only way to provide a decent future for those who belonged to "Israel" and could prove they belonged to it.[61]

5. CONCLUSION

Not everything has been said about Persian imperial authorization, Ezra 7, and the citizen-temple community, of course, and many problems are still awaiting a solution. It seems to me, however, that the hypothesis of Persian imperial authorization has helped us to clarify certain points about the origin of the Pentateuch. It might be better to abandon the theory as such because of the reasons enumerated above. But the discussion has been useful in many ways, and this should not be forgotten.

EXCURSUS: PERSIAN IMPERIAL AUTHORIZATION AND THE
INTELLECTUAL HISTORY OF CENTRAL EUROPEAN EXEGESIS

The theory of Persian imperial authorization is one of the many theories about the Pentateuch that originated in the past two centuries in Europe, especially in Germany, and bear similar characteristics. One of their peculiarities is the propensity to link literary phenomena with institutions, either political or religious.[62]

One well-known and conspicuous example of this tendency is the work of Hermann Gunkel. His study of oral tradition and *Formgeschichte* is based on two pillars, namely, "literary genre" and "*Sitz im Leben*."[63] Every "literary genre" has a

---

[60] See, for a summary of the discussion, Carter, *Emergence of Yehud,* 307–16, who mentions the positions held by Thompson, Davies, Ahlström, and Lemche.

[61] Ska, *Introduction,* 265–68; cf. Dyck, *Theocratic Ideology,* 124 (about the Chronicler): "The perspective from which the Chronicler [writes is] clearly *post-exilic* but by presenting the exile as but a brief interruption in the history of 'all Israel' the Chronicler intended to demonstrate that a broader understanding of Israel (in comparison to Ezra-Nehemiah) was possible in his own day."

[62] It may be of interest that Peter Frei himself says that the model for his theory is the Swiss constitution. See Frei, *Reichsidee,* 15 n. 17. The Swiss federal constitution "guarantees" the rights of the differents cantons.

[63] Martin J. Buss, "The Idea of Sitz im Leben: History and Critique," *ZAW* 90 (1978): 157–70; idem, *Biblical Form Criticism in Its Context* (JSOTSup 274; Sheffield: Sheffield Academic Press, 1999). For an intellectual biography of H. Gunkel, see Werner Klatt, *Hermann Gunkel: zu seiner Theologie der Religionsgeschichte und*

Sitz im Leben, which often means an institutional setting, such as family (clan), cult, or juridical procedures. The *Sitz im Leben* is not just an "existential context" or a "setting in (daily) life." It implies an institutional and public dimension.[64]

Coming back to the Pentateuch, we can observe the same phenomenon. My purpose, to be sure, is not to evaluate or to criticize the theories, but only to draw up a short history of exegesis and, in particular, to underline some interesting recurrent elements in studies on the Pentateuch during the past two centuries. We can start with de Wette's work on Deuteronomy published in 1805.[65]

De Wette's well-known thesis is indeed one of the major discoveries in recent pentateuchal studies. For the sake of clarity, let us summarize it in a few words: for de Wette, Deuteronomy was, in its original kernel, the fundamental text of Josiah's reform in 622 B.C.E. This discovery had so much success, in my opinion, because this scholar could for the first time link a major text of the Pentateuch with a historical fact. The enduring success of de Wette's theory is due to another element, namely, that the historical fact was a cultic and political reform that had official and institutional consequences and that affected Jerusalem's and Judea's public life. Deuteronomy was a document promulgated by a king and his officials and became the blueprint of a religious and administrative reform. De Wette's study had long-lasting effects on pentateuchal studies for several reasons. One of them is, again in my opinion, that de Wette was a pioneer in the search for connections between the Pentateuchal sources and Israel's religious and political institutions. Several authors followed him along this path.

De Wette's thesis was first taken over by Julius Wellhausen in his *Prolegomena zur Geschichte Israels.*[66] Wellhausen himself distinguished three main phases in the composition of the Pentateuch and connected the three of them with institutional moments in Israel's history. The first sources of the Pentateuch (especially

---

zur Entstehung der formgeschichtlichen Methode (Göttingen: Vandenhoeck & Ruprecht, 1969); Rudolf Smend, *Deutsche Alttestamentler in drei Jahrhunderten* (Göttingen: Vandenhoeck & Ruprecht, 1989), 160–81.

[64] Recent folklore studies have challenged the idea that, in oral tradition, literary genre and *Sitz im Leben* are fixed entities. They are much more flexible than Gunkel and his disciples believed them to be. See Kirkpatrick, *Old Testament and Folklore Study,* 76–97.

[65] Wilhelm Martin Leberecht de Wette, *Dissertatio critica qua Deuterononium diversum a prioribus Pentateuchi libris, alius cuiusdam recentioris auctoris opus esse demonstratur* (Iena, 1805). For more details on the author and his background, see John W. Rogerson, *W. M. L. de Wette: Founder of Biblical Criticism. An Intellectual Biography* (JSOTSup 126; Sheffield: Sheffield Academic Press, 1992); Smend, *Deutsche Alttestamentler,* 38–52.

[66] Julius Wellhausen, *Prolegomena zur Geschichte Israels* (Berlin: Reimer, 1878; 3d ed., 1886) = *Prolegomena to the History of Israel, with a reprint of the article Israel from the Encyclopaedia Britannica* (preface by W. Robertson Smith; Reprints and Translations Series; Atlanta: Scholars Press, 1994). For more details on Wellhausen's life and career, see Smend, *Deutsche Alttestamentler,* 99–113.

the Jahwist) were written at the beginning of the united monarchy, under David and Solomon. Deuteronomy was, as for de Wette, the document of Josiah's religious and juridical reform. The Priestly texts were written to buttress the organization of the Second Temple community. In linking texts with institutions, Wellhausen was clearly a disciple of de Wette.

Martin Noth worked along the same lines. For him, however, the Pentateuch was older than the united monarchy and originated during the period of the judges, in an oral tradition, which transmitted the "five themes" common to the twelve tribes. These themes are the exodus, the sojourn in the desert, the entrance into the land, the promises to the patriarchs, and the legal tradition of Mount Sinai.[67] At this point Martin Noth asked an interesting and characteristic question: What is the institution of the twelve tribes that can support this common oral tradition? His answer was the famous theory of the "amphictyony" that he had developed some years earlier.[68] Here again, one can observe that Noth felt the need for an institution to support the existence of texts or oral traditions.

Martin Noth was more of a historian, whereas Gerhard von Rad, who is often associated with him, was rather a theologian. In his renowned work on the "form-critical problem of the Hexateuch," he developed the theory of two main blocks of tradition at the oral stage which were afterwards integrated into the Yahwist's work.[69] The first block contains historical traditions that have their kernel in the "historical creeds" (Deut 26:5b–9; 6:20–23; cf. Josh 24:2b–13). The second block corresponds to Israel's "legal" tradition and is to be found mainly in the so-called "Sinai pericope" (Exod 19–24). Since von Rad was a theologian, he naturally connected these two "streams" of oral tradition with religious institutions. The historical traditions are recited during the feast of harvest at Gilgal (cf. Deut 26:2–3; Josh 4:19–24), while the legal tradition is rooted in the regular celebration of the covenant at Shechem during the Feast of the Booths (Deut 31:9–13; Josh 24:25–26).[70]

---

[67] Martin Noth, *Überlieferungsgeschichte des Pentateuch* (Stuttgart: Kohlhammer, 1948) = *A History of Pentateuchal Traditions* (Englewood Cliffs, N.J.: Prentice-Hall, 1972; Chico: Scholars Press, 1981). For more details on Noth's intellectual background, see Smend, *Deutsche Alttestamentler,* 255–75.

[68] Martin Noth, *Das System der zwölf Stämme Israels* (BWANT 52; Stuttgart: Kohlhammer, 1930). See Noth, *Pentateuchal Traditions,* 42–45, 54, 252–59 and passim. It is well known that Noth had little sympathy for the Nazi ideology. It is therefore interesting that for him the Pentateuch came to be, in its essential parts, when Israel formed a confederation and not yet a "state" because, according to him, the state usually limits the people's freedom and creativity (*Pentateuchal Traditions,* 42–45).

[69] Gerhard von Rad, *Das formgeschichtliche Problem des Hexateuch* (BWANT 78; Stuttgart: Kohlhammer, 1938) = *Gesammelte Studien zum Alten Testament* (TB 8; Munich: Kaiser, 1958), 9–86 = "The Form-Critical Problem of the Hexateuch," in *The Problem of the Hexateuch and Other Essays* (New York: McGraw-Hill, 1966), 1–78. On von Rad's intellectual horizon, see Smend, *Deutsche Alttestamentler,* 226–54.

[70] For more details on the intellectual background of these theories, see Ska, *Introduction,* 152–75.

The theory of "Persian imperial authorization" is most probably a further example of the same way of thinking. Since the Pentateuch in its present form was compiled or composed in the postexilic period, it became necessary to find a post-exilic institution that could make possible the redaction of this important document. And since "Israel," that is, the postexilic community, was ruled by a foreign power, it was natural to look for a public and official support coming from this foreign power.

These reflections, as such, do not at all invalidate the theory but may help us understand better the reason(s) why it came to be. As a last note, it can be added that the historical origin for linking literary documents to institutions can be sought in an old cultural phenomenon. For centuries, before the rise of our modern democracies, artists in general and writers in particular could live only if supported and protected by kings, princes, or rich and powerful "patrons." Some of these "patrons" were also church or ecclesiastical authorities. Moreover, certain authors worked under the express command of their "patrons" as, for instance, did the chroniclers and secretaries (chancellors) of the court. It is probable that scholars such as de Wette, Wellhausen, and the other aforementioned scholars had this background in mind, or something very similar, when they worked out their theories.

BIBLIOGRAPHY

Ackroyd, Peter R. "The Chronicler As Exegete." *JSOT* 2 (1977): 2–32.

Aharoni, Yohanan. *The Land of the Bible.* Rev. ed. by Anson Rainey. Philadelphia: Westminster, 1979.

Albertz, Rainer. *From the Exile to the Maccabees.* Vol. 2 of *A History of Religion in the Old Testament Period.* OTL. Louisville: Westminster/John Knox, 1994. Translation of *Vom Exil bis zu den Makkabäern.* Vol. 2 of *Religionsgeschichte in alttestamentlicher Zeit.* ATD 8.2. Göttingen: Vandenhoeck & Ruprecht, 1992.

Allam, Schafik. "Réflexions sur le 'code legal' d'Hermopolis dans l'Égypt ancienne." *ChrEg* 61 (1986): 50–75.

——. "Richter." Pages 245–47 in vol. 5 of *Lexikon der Ägyptologie.* Edited by Wolfgang Helck et al. Wiesbaden: Harrassowitz, 1975–1992.

——. "Traces de 'codification' en Égypte ancienne (à la basse époque)." *RIDA* 3d series, 40 (1993): 11–26.

Anthes, Rudolph. *Die Felseninschriften von Hatnub.* Leipzig: Hinrichs, 1928.

Attridge, Harold W., and Robert A. Oden Jr. *Philo of Byblos: The Phoenician History.* CBQMS 9. Washington, D.C.: Catholic Biblical Association, 1981.

Aubert, Jean-François. *Traité de droit constitutionnel Suisse.* 3 vols. Neuchatel: Editions Ides et Calendes, 1967–1982.

Bakir, Abd el-Mohsen. *The Cairo Calendar.* Cairo: Government Press, 1966.

Balcer, Jack Martin. "The Athenian Episkopos and the Achaemenid's 'King's Eye'." *AJP* 98 (1977): 252–63.

——. "Ionia and Sparta under the Achaemenid Empire. The Sixth and Fifth Centuries B.C. Tribute, Taxation and Assessment." Pages 1–27 in *Le tribut dans l'empire Perse: Actes de la Table ronde de Paris 12–13 Décembre 1986.* Edited by Pierre Briant and Clarisse Heffenschmidt. Travaux de l'Institut d'Études Iraniennes de l'Université de la Sorbonne Nouvelle 13. Paris: Peeters, 1989.

———. *Sparda by the Bitter Sea: Imperial Interaction in Western Anatolia.* BJS 52. Chico, Calif.: Scholars Press, 1984.

Bar-Kochva, Bezalel. *Pseudo-Hecataeus,* On the Jews: *Legitimizing the Jewish Diaspora.* Hellenistic Culture and Society 21. Berkeley and Los Angeles: University of California Press, 1996.

Barstad, Hans M. *The Babylonian Captivity of the Book of Isaiah: "Exilic" Judah and the Provenance of Isaiah 40–55.* Oslo: Novus forlag—The Institute for Comparative Research in Human Culture, 1997.

Barucq, A. "Les textes cosmogoniques d'Edfou d'après les manuscrits laissés par Maurice Alliot." *BIFAO* 64 (1964): 125–68.

Beckman, Gary. *Hittite Diplomatic Texts.* Atlanta: Scholars Press, 1995.

Bedford, Peter R. "On Models and Texts: A Response to Blenkinsopp and Petersen." Pages 154–62 in *Second Temple Studies 1: Persian Period.* Edited by P. R. Davies. JSOTSup 117. Sheffield: Sheffield Academic Press, 1991.

Berg, D. "The Genre of Non-juridical Oracles (*ḫr.tw*) in Ancient Egypt." Ph.D. diss., Toronto, 1988.

Berlandini-Grenier, Jocelyne. "Senenmout, stoliste royal, sur une statue-cube avec Néférourê." *BIFAO* 76 (1976): 314.

Berquist, Jon L. *Judaism in Persia's Shadow: A Social and Historical Approach.* Minneapolis: Fortress, 1995.

Betlyon, J. "Military Operations Other Than War in Persian Period Yehud." Unpublished paper.

Blenkinsopp, Joseph. *Ezra-Nehemiah: A Commentary.* OTL. Philadelphia: Westminster, 1988.

———. "A Jewish Sect of the Persian Period." *CBQ* 52 (1990): 5–20.

———. "The Mission of Udjahorresnet and Those of Ezra and Nehemiah." *JBL* 106 (1987): 409–21.

———. *The Pentateuch: An Introduction to the First Five Books of the Bible.* ABRL. New York: Doubleday, 1992.

———. "Temple and Society in Achaemenid Judah." Pages 22–53 in *Second Temple Studies 1: Persian Period.* Edited by P. R. Davies. JSOTSup 117. Sheffield: Sheffield Academic Press, 1991.

Bloom, John. "Ancient Near Eastern Temple Assemblies." Ph.D. diss., Annenberg Research Institute, 1992.

Blum, Erhard. *Die Komposition der Vätergeschichte.* WMANT 57. Neukirchen-Vluyn: Neukirchener Verlag, 1984.

―――. *Studien zur Komposition des Pentateuch.* Berlin: de Gruyter, 1990.

Bolin, Thomas M. "The Temple of יהו at Elephantine and Persian Religious Policy." Pages 127–42 in *The Triumph of Elohim: From Yahwisms to Judaisms.* Edited by D. Edelman. Grand Rapids, Mich.: Eerdmans, 1995.

Bontty, Monica M. "Conflict Management in Ancient Egypt: Law As a Social Phenomenon." Ph.D. diss., University of California, Los Angeles, 1997.

Boorn, G. P. F. van den. *The Duties of the Vizier.* London: Kegan Paul, 1988.

Bottéro, Jean. "The 'Code' of Ḥammurabi." Pages 156–84 in *Mesopotamia: Writing, Reasoning, and the Gods.* Edited by J. Bottéro. Translated by Z. Bahrani and M. Van de Mieroop. Chicago: University of Chicago Press, 1992.

Boyce, Mary. *The Early Period.* Vol. 1 of *A History of Zoroastrianism.* Leiden: Brill, 1996.

Boylan, Patrick. *Thoth, the Hermes of Egypt.* Oxford: Oxford University Press, 1922.

Brandstein, W., and M. Mayrhofer. *Handbuch des Altpersischen.* Wiesbaden: Harrassowitz, 1964.

Bresciani, Edda. "Egypt, Persian Satrapy." Pages 358–72 in *Introduction; The Persian Period.* Vol. 1 of *The Cambridge History of Judaism.* Cambridge: Cambridge University Press, 1984.

―――. "The Persian Occupation of Egypt." Pages 502–28 in *The Median and Achaemenian Periods.* Vol. 2 of *The Cambridge History of Iran.* Edited by Ilya Gershevitz. Cambridge: Cambridge University Press, 1985.

―――. "La satrapia d'Egitto." *SCO* 8 (1958): 132–88.

―――. "Ugiahorresnet a Memphi." *EVO* 8 (1985): 1–6.

Briant, Pierre. "Bulletin d'histoire achéménide (BHAch) I." Pages 82–83 in *Recherches récentes sur l'Empire achéménide.* Edited by M.-F. Boussac. Topoi Supplément 1. Paris: de Boccard, 1997.

―――. "Ethno-classe dominante et populations soumises dans l'Empire Achéménide: le cas de l'Égypte." Pages 144–47 in *Method and Theory: Proceedings of the London 1985 Achaemenid History Workshop.* Edited by A. Kuhrt and H. Sancisi-Weerdenburg. AH 3. Leiden: Nederlands Instituut voor het Nabije Oosten, 1988.

————. *Histoire de l'Empire Perse de Cyrus à Alexandre.* Paris: Fayard, 1996.

————. "Histoire impériale et histoire régionale: À propos de l'histoire de Juda dans l'empire achéménide." Pages 235–45 in *Congress Volume: Oslo, 1998.* Edited by A. Lemaire and M. Sæbø. VTSup 80. Leiden: Brill, 2000.

————. "Pouvoir central et polycentrisme culturel dans l'Empire achéménide." Pages 1–31 in *Sources, Structures and Synthesis: Proceedings of the Groningen 1983 Achaemenid History Workshop.* Edited by Heleen Sancisi-Weerdenburg. AH 1. Leiden: Nederlands Instituut voor het Nabije Oosten, 1987.

————. "Social and Legal Institutions in Achaemenid Iran." Pages 517–28 in volume 1 of *Civilizations of the Ancient Near East.* Edited by J. Sasson. 4 vols. New York: Scribner, 1995.

Broze, Michèle. *Mythe et roman en Égypte ancienne: Les aventures d'Horus et Seth dans le Papyrus Chester Beatty I.* Leuven: Peeters, 1996.

Brunner, Helmut. "Archaismus." Pages 386–95 in vol. 1 of *Lexikon der Ägyptologie.* Edited by Wolfgang Helck et al. Wiesbaden: Harrassowitz, 1972.

————. "Zum Verständnis der archaisierenden Tendenzen in der ägyptischen Spätzeit." *Saeculum* 21 (1970): 151–61.

Bryce, T. R. "Political Unity in Lycia during the 'Dynastic' Period." *JNES* 42 (1983): 31–42.

Bucci, Onorato. "L'attività legislativa del sovrano achemenide e gli Archivi reali persiani." *RIDA* 3d series, 25 (1978): 11–93.

Buck, Adrian de. *Egyptian Readingbook.* Leiden: Nederlands Intituut voor het Nabije Oosten, 1948.

Burton, Anne. *Diodorus Siculus Book I: A Commentary.* Leiden: Brill, 1972.

Buss, Martin J. *Biblical Form Criticism in Its Context.* JSOTSup 274. Sheffield: Sheffield Academic Press, 1999.

————. "The Idea of Sitz im Leben: History and Critique." *ZAW* 90 (1978): 157–70.

————. "Legal Science and Legislation." Pages 88–90 in *Theory and Method in Biblical and Cuneiform Law: Revisions, Interpolation, and Development.* Edited by B. M. Levinson. JSOTSup 181. Sheffield: Sheffield Academic Press, 1994.

Cameron, George G. *Persepolis Treasury Tablets*. Chicago: University of Chicago Press, 1948.

Caminos, Ricardo A. *Literary Fragments in the Hieratic Script*. Oxford: Griffith Institute, 1956.

Cardascia, G. "La Coutume dans les Droits Cunéiformes." *Receuils de la Societé Jean Bolin* (1990): 61–69.

Carr, David M. *Reading the Fractures of Genesis: Historical and Literary Approaches*. Louisville: Westminster/John Knox, 1996.

Carter, Charles Edward. *The Emergence of Yehud in the Persian Period: A Social and Demographic Study*. JSOTSup 294. Sheffield: Sheffield Academic Press, 1999.

Cenival, Françoise de. *Les associations religieuses en Égypte d'après les documents démotiques*. Cairo: IFAO, 1972.

Cenival, Jean Louis de. *The Abu Sir Papyri*. London: British Museum, 1968.

Černý, Jaroslav. *A Community of Workmen at Thebes in the Ramesside Period*. Cairo: IFAO, 1973.

———. "The Will of Naunakhte and Related Documents." *JEA* 31 (1945): 29–53.

Chassinat, Emile. *Le temple de Dendara, VI*. Cairo: Institut français d'archéologie orientale, 1965.

———. *Le Temple d'Edfou*. Paris and Cairo: Institut français d'archéologie orientale, 1960–.

Chaumont, M.-L. "Un nouveau gouverneur de Sardes à l'époque achéménide d'après une inscription récemment découverte." *Syria* 67 (1990): 579–608.

Chauveau, M. "La chronologie de la correspondence dite 'de Phéréndates'." *RdE* 50 (1999): 269–71.

Chevereux, Pierre-Marie. *Prosopographie des cadres militaires égyptiens de la Basse Epoque*. Paris: n.p., 1985.

Clines, David J. A. *Ezra, Nehemiah, Esther*. NCB. Grand Rapids, Mich.: Eerdmans, 1984.

———. "The Force of the Text: A Response to Tamara C. Eskenazi's 'Ezra-Nehemiah: From Text to Actuality'." Pages 199–215 of *Signs and Wonders: Biblical Texts in Literary Focus*. Edited by J. C. Exum. Atlanta: Society of Biblical Literature, 1989.

Bibliography

————. "Nehemiah 10 As an Example of Early Jewish Biblical Exegesis." *JSOT* 21 (1981): 111–17.

Cook, John M. *The Persian Empire*. London: J. M. Dent, 1983.

Corsaro, Mauro. "Autonomia cittadina e fiscalità regia ecc." Pages 61–75 in *Le tribut dans l'empire Perse: Actes de la Table ronde de Paris 12–13 Décembre 1986*. Edited by Pierre Briant and Clarisse Heffenschmidt. Travaux de l'Institut d'Études Iraniennes de l'Université de la Sorbonne Nouvelle 13. Paris: Peeters, 1989.

————. "Tassazione regia e tassazione cittadina dagli Achemenidi ai re ellenistici: alcune osservazioni." *REA* 87 (1985): 73–95.

Corsten, Thomas. "Herodot 1 131 und die Einführung des Anahita-Kultes in Lydien." *StIr* 26 (1991): 163–80.

Corteggiani, Jean-Pierre. "Une stéle héliopolitaine d'époque saïte." Pages 115–53 in vol. 1 of *Hommages à la mémoire de Serge Sauneron (1927–1976)*. 2 vols. Cairo: IFAO, 1979.

Couyat, J., and P. Montet. *Les inscriptions hiéroglyphiques et hiératiques de l'Ouâdi Hammamat*. Cairo: IFAO, 1912.

Crampa, Jonas. *The Greek Inscriptions*. Vol. 3, parts 1–2 of *Labraunda: Swedish Excavations and Researches*. Stockholm: Svenska Institut i Athen, 1969–1972.

Cross, F. M. *From Epic to Canon: History and Literature in Ancient Israel*. Baltimore: Johns Hopkins University Press, 1998.

Crüsemann, Frank. "Israel in der Perserzeit. Eine Skizze in Auseinandersetzung mit Max Weber." Pages 205–32 in *Max Webers Sicht des antiken Christentums: Interpretation und Kritik*. Edited by W. Schluchter. Frankfurt: Suhrkamp, 1985.

————. "Le Pentateuque, une Tora: Prolégomènes à l'interprétation de sa forme finale." Pages 339–60 in *Le Pentateuque en Question*. Edited by A. de Pury. Geneva: Labor et Fides, 1989.

————. *The Torah: Theology and Social History of Old Testament Law*. Translated by W. Mahnke. Minneapolis: Fortress, 1996. Translation of *Die Torah: Theologie und Sozialgeschichte des alttestamentlichen Gesetzes*. Munich: Kaiser, 1992.

Cruz-Uribe, Eugene. "Cambyses and the Temples in Egypt." Unpublished paper.

Dandamaev, Muhammad A. "Achaemenid Imperial Policies and Provincial Governments." *Iranica Antiqua* 34 (1999): 269–82.

————. *A Political History of the Achaemenid Empire*. Leiden: Brill, 1989.

Dandamaev, Muhammad A., and Vladimir G. Lukonin. *The Culture and Social Institutions of Ancient Iran*. Cambridge: Cambridge University Press, 1989.

Daressy, G. "Inscriptions des carrieres de Tourah et Mâsarah." *ASAÉ* 11 (1911): 257–68.

Daumas, François. *Les moyens d'expression en Grecque et en Egyptien*. ASAÉSup 16. Cairo, 1952.

Davies, Philip R. "Minimalists and Maximalists." *BAR* 26.2 (2000): 24–27, 72–73.

————. *Scribes and Schools: The Canonization of the Hebrew Scriptures*. Louisville: Westminster/John Knox, 1998.

Derchain, Philippe. *Papyrus Salt 825 (B. M. 10051): rituel pour la conservation de la vie en Égypte*. Brussels: Royal Academy, 1965.

Descat, Raymond. "Darius, le roi kapēlos." Pages 161–66 in *Continuity and Change: Proceedings of the Last Achaemenid History Workshop, April 6–8, 1990, Ann Arbor, Michigan*. Edited by H. Sancisi-Weerdenburg, A. Kuhrt, and M. Cool Root. AH 8. Leiden: Nederlands Instituut voor het Nabije Oosten, 1994.

————. "Le tribut et l'économie tributaire dans l'Empire achéménide." Pages 253–62 in *Recherches récente sur l'Empire achéménide*. Edited by M.-F. Boussac. Topoi Supplément 1. Paris: de Boccard, 1997.

Dion, Paul. "The Civic-and-Temple Community of Persian Period Judea: Neglected Insights from Eastern Europe." *JNES* 50 (1991): 281–87.

Donadoni, Sergio. "L'Egitto achemenide." Pages 27–43 in *Modes de contact et processus de transformation dans les sociétés anciennes*. Rome: École française de Rome, 1983.

Dossin, G. "L'inscription de fondation de Iaḫdun-Lim, roi de Mari." *Syria* 32 (1955): 4.

Doxey, Denise M. *Egyptian Non-royal Epithets in the Middle Kingdom: A Social and Historical Analysis*. Leiden: Brill, 1998.

Driver, Godfrey Rolles. *Aramaic Documents of the Fifth Century B.C.* Abridged and rev. ed. Oxford: Clarendon, 1957.

Drioton, E., and J. Vandier. *L'Egypte*. 4th edition. Paris: Presses Universitaires de France, 1962.

Dupont-Sommer, André. "La stèle trilingue récemment découverte à Xanthos: Le texte araméen." *CRAI* (1974): 132–49.

Dyck, Jonathan E. *The Theocratic Ideology of the Chronicler.* BibInt 33. Leiden: Brill, 1998.

Epigraphic Survey. *The Bubastite Portal.* Vol. 3 of *Reliefs and Inscriptions at Karnak.* Chicago: Oriental Institute, 1954.

Erichsen, Wolja. *Demotisches Glossar.* Copenhagen: Munksgaard, 1954.

Eskenazi, Tamara C. "Ezra-Nehemiah: From Text to Actuality." Pages 165–97 in *Signs and Wonders: Biblical Texts in Literary Focus.* Edited by J. C. Exum. Atlanta: Society of Biblical Literature, 1989.

Falk, Ze'ev. "Ezra VII 26." *VT* 9 (1959): 88–89.

Fensham, F. Charles. *The Books of Ezra and Nehemiah.* NICOT. Grand Rapids, Mich.: Eerdmans, 1982.

Finkelstein, Jacob J. "Ammiṣaduqa's Edict and the Babylonian 'Law Codes'." *JCS* 15 (1961): 91–104.

————. "Some New *Misharum* Material and Its Implications." Pages 233–46 in *Studies in Honor of Benno Landsberger.* Edited by H. G. Guterbock and T. Jacobsen. AS 16. Chicago: University of Chicago Press, 1966.

Fischer, Henry George. "A Feminine Example of *wḏ ḥm·k* 'Thy Majesty Commands' in the Fourth Dynasty." *JEA* 61 (1975): 246–47.

Fishbane, Michael. *Biblical Interpretation in Ancient Israel.* Oxford: Clarendon, 1985.

Foissy-Aufrère, Marie-Pierre, ed. *Egypte et Provence: Civilisation, survivances et "Cabinets de curiosités."* Avignon: Fondation du Muséum Calvet, 1985.

Folmer, M. L. *The Aramaic Language in the Achaemenid Period: A Study in Linguistic Variation.* OLA 68. Leuven: Peeters, 1995.

Fornara, Charles W. *Archaic Times to the End of the Peloponnesian War.* 2d ed. Translated Documents of Greece and Rome 1. Cambridge: Cambridge University Press, 1983.

Frei, Peter. "Die persische Reichsautorisation: Ein Überblick." *ZABR* 1 (1995): 1–35. Translated as "Persian Imperial Authorization: A Summary," pp. 5–40 in this volume.

————. "Zentralgewalt und Lokalautonomie im Achämenidenreich." Pages 8–131 in Peter Frei and Klaus Koch, *Reichsidee und Reichsorganisation im Perserreich.* OBO 55. Fribourg: Universitätsverlag, 1984; 2d ed., 1996.

————. "Zentralgewalt und Lokalautonomie im achämenidischen Kleinasien." *Transeu* 2 (1990): 157–71.

Frei, Peter, and Klaus Koch. *Reichsidee und Reichsorganisation im Perserreich.* OBO 55. Fribourg: Universitätsverlag, 1984; 2d ed., 1996.

Fried, Lisbeth S. "The Political Struggle in Fifth Century Judah." *Transeu* 24 (forthcoming 2002).

—. *The Priest and the Great King: Temple-Palace Relations in the Persian Empire.* Biblical and Judaic Studies from the University of California, San Diego. Winona Lake, Ind.: Eisenbrauns, forthcoming (= "The Rise to Power of the Judaean Priesthood: The Impact of the Achaemenid Empire." Ph.D. diss., New York University, 2000).

Frye, Richard·N. *The Heritage of Persia.* Costa Mesa, Calif.: Mazda, 1993.

—. *The History of Ancient Iran.* Munich: C. H. Beck, 1984.

Galling, Kurt. *Studien zur Geschichte Israels im persischen Zeitalter.* Tübingen: Mohr Siebeck, 1964.

Gardiner, Alan H. *The Admonitions of an Egyptian Sage.* Leiden: 1909. Repr., Hildesheim: Georg Olms, 1969, 1990.

—. "The Gods of Thebes As Guarantors of Personal Property." *JEA* 48 (1962): 57–69.

—. "The House of Life." *JEA* 24 (1938): 157–79.

—. "The Inscriptions from the Tomb of Sirenpowet I." *ZÄS* 45 (1908): 123–40.

—. *Late Egyptian Stories.* Brussels: Edition de la Fondation Egyptologique Reine Elisabeth, 1931.

—. "A Pharaonic Encomium." *JEA* 41 (1955): 30–31.

Gardiner, Alan H., and Jaroslav Černý. *Hieratic Ostraca.* Oxford: Griffith Institute, 1957.

Gerleman, Gillis. *Esther.* BKAT 21. Neukirchen-Vluyn: Neukirchener Verlag, 1973.

Gitin, Seymour, and Mordecai Cogan. "A New Type of Dedicatory Inscription from Ekron." *IEJ* 49 (1999): 193–202.

Glanville, S. R. K. *A Theban Archive of the Reign of Ptolemy I, Soter.* Vol. 1 of *Catalogue of Demotic Papyri in the British Museum.* London: British Museum, 1939.

Glatt-Gilad, David. "Reflections on the Structure and Significance of the ꜣᵃmānāh (Neh 10:29–40)." *ZAW* 112 (2000): 386–95.

Goedicke, Hans. "Diplomatical Studies in the Old Kingdom." *JARCE* 3 (1964): 31–42.

———. *Königliche Dokumente aus dem Alten Reich.* Wiesbaden: Harrassowitz, 1967.

Goedicke, Hans, and E. F. Wente. *Ostraka Michaelides.* Wiesbaden: Harrassowitz, 1962.

Gonçalves, Francolino J. *L'expédition de Sennachérib en Palestine dans la littérature hébraïque ancienne.* ÉB 7. Paris: Gabalda, 1986.

Goyon, Jean-Claude. *Confirmation du pouvoir au nouvel an.* Cairo: IFAO, 1972.

Grabbe, Lester L. *Ezra-Nehemiah.* Old Testament Readings. New York: Routledge, 1998.

———. "Jewish Historiography and Scripture in the Hellenistic Period." Pages 129–55 in *Did Moses Speak Attic? Jewish Historiography and Scripture in the Hellenistic Period.* Edited by L. L. Grabbe. JSOTSup 317. European Seminar in Historical Methodology 3. Sheffield: Sheffield Academic Press, 2000.

———. "The Jews in Egypt." Pages 372–400 in *Introduction; The Persian Period.* Vol. 1 of *The Cambridge History of Judaism.* Edited by W. D. Davies and L. Finkelstein. Cambridge: Cambridge University Press, 1984.

———. *Judaic Religion in the Second Temple Period: Belief and Practice from the Exile to Yavneh.* London: Routledge, 2000.

———. *The Persian and Greek Periods.* Vol. 1 of *Judaism from Cyrus to Hadrian.* Philadelphia: Fortress, 1992.

———. *Priests, Prophets, Diviners, Sages: A Socio-historical Study of Religious Specialists in Ancient Israel.* Valley Forge, Pa.: Trinity Press International, 1995.

———. "Reconstructing History from the Book of Ezra." Pages 98–107 in *Second Temple Studies 1: Persian Period.* Edited by P. R. Davies. JSOTSup 117. Sheffield: JSOT Press, 1991.

———. "What Was Ezra's Mission?" Pages 286–99 in *Second Temple Studies 2: Temple and Community in the Persian Period.* Edited by T. C. Eskenazi and K. H. Richards. JSOTSup 175. Sheffield: JSOT Press, 1994.

———, ed. *Leading Captivity Captive: 'The Exile' As History and Ideology.* JSOTSup 278; European Seminar in Historical Methodology 2. Sheffield: Sheffield Academic Press, 1998.

Graefe, Erhart. *Untersuchungen zur Verwaltung und Geschichte des Institution der Gottes gemahlin des Amun.* 2 vols. Wiesbaden: Harrassowtiz, 1981.

Grapow, Hermann, Wolfhart Westendorf, and Hildegard Deines. *Grundriss der Medizin der alten Ägypter.* 9 vols. Berlin: Akademie-Verlag, 1954–1973.

Grayson, A. Kirk. "Chronicle 7: The Nabonidus Chronicle." *Assyrian and Babylonian Chronicles.* Winona Lake, Ind.: Eisenbrauns, 2000.

Greenfield, Jonas C. "The Aramaic Legal Texts of the Achaemenian Period." *Transeu* 3 (1990): 85–92.

Greengus, Samuel. "Legal and Social Institutions of Ancient Mesopotamia." Pages 469–84 in vol. 1 of *Civilizations of the Ancient Near East.* Edited by J. Sasson. 4 vols. New York: Scribner, 1995.

———. "Some Issues Relating to the Comparability of Laws and the Coherence of the Legal Tradition." Pages 60–87 in *Theory and Method in Biblical and Cuneiform Law: Revisions, Interpolation, and Development.* Edited by B. M. Levinson. JSOTSup 181. Sheffield: Sheffield Academic Press, 1994.

Grelot, Pierre. *Documents araméens d'Égypt.* LAPO 5. Paris: Cerf, 1972.

———. "Le Papyrus pascal d'Éléphantine: essai de restauration." *VT* 17 (1967): 201–7.

Grenfell, B. P., and A. S. Hunt. *The Hibeh Papyri.* 2 vols. London: Egypt Exploration Fund, 1906.

Griffith, Francis L. "The Petition of Peteesi." In vol. 3 of *Catalogue of the Demotic Papyri in the John Rylands Library, Manchester.* Edited by F. L. Griffith. John Rylands Library 9. Manchester and London: John Rylands University Library of Manchester, 1909.

Gruen, Eric. *Heritage and Hellenism: The Reinvention of Jewish Tradition.* Hellenistic Culture and Society 30. Berkeley and Los Angeles: University of California Press, 1998.

Grunert, S. "Das demotische Rechtsbuch von Hermopolis-West." *Das Altertum* 26 (1980): 96–110.

Gschnitzer, Fritz. "Eine persische Kultstiftung in Sardeis." Pages 45–54 in *Im Bannkreis des Alten Orients: Studien … Karl Oberhuber zum 70 Geburtstag gewidmet.* Edited by Wolfgang Meid and Helga Trenkwalder. Innsbrucker Beiträge zur Kulturwissenschaft 24. Innsbruck: Institut fur Sprachwissenschaft der Universität Innsbruck, 1986.

Gunn, Battiscombe. "The Inscribed Sarcophagi in the Serapeum." *ASAÉ* 26 (1926): 92–94.

Habachi, L. "Sais and Its Monuments." *ASAÉ* 42 (1942): 369–416.

Hahn, István. "Zur Frage der Sklavensteuer im frühen Hellenismus." Pages 56–64 in *Antike Abhängigkeitsformen in den griechischen Gebieten ohne Polisstruktur und den romischen Provinzen*. Edited by Heinz Kreissig und Friedmar Kühnert. Schriften zur Geschichte und Kultur der Antike 25. Berlin: Akademie-Verlag, 1985.

Hall, Emma Swan, and Bernard V. Bothmer, eds. *Mendes*. 2 vols. New York: Brooklyn Museum, 1976.

Hallock, Richard T. "The Evidence of the Persepolis Tablets." Pages 588–609 in *The Median and Achaemenian Periods*. Vol. 2 of *The Cambridge History of Iran*. Edited by Ilya Gershevitz. Cambridge: Cambridge University Press, 1985.

———. *Persepolis Fortification Tablets*. Chicago: University of Chicago Press, 1969.

Hangartner, Yvo. *Grundzüge des schweizerischen Staatsrechts*. 2 vols. Zürich: Schulthess, 1980–1982.

Hansen, O. "The Purported Letter of Darius to Gadates." *Rheinisches Museon* 129 (1986): 95–96.

Haran, Menahem. "Book-Scrolls at the Beginning of the Second Temple Period: The Transition from Papyrus to Skins." *HUCA* 54 (1983): 111–22.

Harris, Rivkah. *Ancient Sippar: A Demographic Study of an Old-Babylonian City, 1894–1595 B.C.* Istanbul: Nederlands Historisch-Archaeologisch Instituut te Istanbul, 1975.

———. "The *nadītu* Laws of the Code of Hammurapi in Praxis." *Or* 30 (1961): 163–69.

———. "On the Process of Secularization under Hammurapi." *JCS* 15 (1961): 117–20.

Hayes, William Christopher. *A Papyrus of the Late Middle Kingdom in the Brooklyn Museum (Papyrus Brooklyn 35.1446)*. New York: Brooklyn Museum, 1955.

Heel, K. Donker van. *The Legal Manual of Hermopolis*. Leiden: Brill, 1990.

Helck, Wolfgang. *Die 'Admonitions'. Pap. Leiden I 344 Recto*. Wiesbaden: Harrassowitz, 1995.

————. *Altägyptische Aktenkunde des 3. und 2. Jahrtausends v. Chr.* Munich: Deutscher Kunstverlag, 1974.

————. *Historisch-biographische Inschriften der 2. Zwischenzeit.* Wiesbaden: Harrassowitz, 1975.

————. *Die Lehre für König Merikare.* Wiesbaden: Harrassowitz, 1977.

————. *Untersuchungen zu den Beamtentiteln des ägyptischen Alten Reiches.* Glückstadt: Augustin, 1954.

————. *Wirtschaftsgeschichte des alten Ägypten in 3. und 2. Jahrtausend v. Chr.* Leiden: Brill, 1975.

————. *Zur Verwaltung des Mittleren und Neuen Reiches.* Leiden: Brill, 1958.

Heltzer, Michael. "The Flogging and Plucking of Beards in the Achaemenid Empire and the Chronology of Nehemiah." *AMI* 28 (1995–1996): 305–7.

————. "The Right of Ezra to Demand Obedience to 'the Laws of the King' from Gentiles of the V Satrapy." *ZABR* 4 (1998): 192–96.

Hoglund, Kenneth G. *Achaemenid Imperial Administration in Syria-Palestine and the Missions of Ezra and Nehemiah.* SBLDS 125. Atlanta: Scholars Press, 1992.

Holm-Rasmussen, Torben. "Collaboration in Early Achaemenid Egypt: A New Approach." Pages 29–38 in *Studies in Ancient History and Numismatics Presented to Rudi Thomsen.* Edited by Aksel Damsgaard-Madsen. Aarhus: Aarhus University Press, 1988.

Hornblower, Simon. *Mausolus.* Oxford: Clarendon, 1982.

Horsley, Richard A. "Empire, Temple, and Community—But No Bourgeoisie! A Response to Blenkinsopp and Petersen." Pages 163–74 in *Second Temple Studies 1: Persian Period.* Edited by P. R. Davies. JSOTSup 117. Sheffield: Sheffield Academic Press, 1991.

Hout, M. van den. "Studies in Early Greek Letter-Writing." *Mnemosyne* 2 (1949): 19–41, 138–53.

Houtman, Cornelis. "Ezra and the Law: Observations on the Supposed Relation between Ezra and the Pentateuch." *OtSt* 21 (1981): 91–115.

Hughes, George R. "A Demotic Letter to Thoth." *JNES* 17 (1958): 1–12.

————. *Saite Demotic Land Leases.* Chicago: University of Chicago Press, 1956.

————. "The So-Called Pherendates Correspondence." Pages 75–86 in *Grammata Demotika: Festschrift für Erich Lüddeckens.* Edited by Heinz-J. Thissen and Karl-T. Zauzich. Würzburg: Zauzich, 1984.

Hunt, A. S., and C. C. Edgar. *Select Papyri*. 2 vols. LCL 266, 282. Cambridge: Harvard University Press, 1932, 1934.

Huss, Werner. "Some Thoughts on the Subject 'State' and 'Church' in Ptolemaic Egypt." Pages 159–63 in *Life in a Multi-cultural Society: Egypt from Cambyses to Constantine and Beyond*. Edited by Janet H. Johnson. SAOC 51. Chicago: Oriental Institute, 1992.

Husson, Geneviève, and Dominique Valbelle. *L'Etat et les institutions en Egypte des premiers pharaons aux empereurs romains*. Paris: Armand Colin, 1992.

Jamieson-Drake, David W. *Scribes and Schools in Monarchic Judah: A Socio-archaeological Approach*. JSOTSup 109. Sheffield: Sheffield Academic Press, 1991.

Janssen, C. "Samsu-Iluna and the Hungry Nadtums." *Northern Akkad Project Reports* 5 (1991): 3–40.

Janzen, David. "The 'Mission' of Ezra and the Persian-Period Temple Community." *JBL* 119 (2000): 619–43.

Japhet, Sara. *I and II Chronicles*. OTL. Louisville: Westminster/John Knox, 1993.

———. *The Ideology of the Book of Chronicles and Its Place in Biblical Thought*. BEATAJ 9. Frankfurt am Main: Lang, 1989.

———. "The Relationship between Chronicles and Ezra-Nehemiah." Pages 298–313 in *Congress Volume: Leuven, 1989*. Edited by J. A. Emerton. VTSup 43. Leiden: Brill, 1991.

———. "The Supposed Common Authorship of Chronicles and Ezra-Nehemiah Investigated Anew." *VT* 18 (1968): 330–71.

Jelinková-Reymond, E. "Quelques recherches sur les reformes d'Amasis." *ASAÉ* 54 (1954): 251–87.

Jienitz, F. K. "Die saitische Renaissance." Pages 256–82 in *Die erste Halfte des I. Jahrhunderts of Die altorientalischen Reiche*. Vol. 3 of *Die altorientalischen Reiche*. Edited by Elena Cassin et al. Fischer Weltgeschichte 4. Frankfurt: Fischer, 1967.

Johnson, Janet H. "The Persians and the Continuity of Egyptian Culture." Pages 149–59 in *Continuity and Change: Proceedings of the Last Achaemenid History Workshop*. Edited by Heleen Sancisi-Weerdenburg, Amélie Kuhrt, and Margaret Cool Root. AH 8. Leiden: Nederlands Instituut voor het Nabije Oosten, 1994.

Junker, H. *Das Götterdekret uber Abaton*. Vienna, 1913.

Kalimi, Isaac. "Die Abfassungszeit der Chronik—Forschungsstand und Perspectiven." *ZAW* 105 (1993): 223–33.

Katary, Sally L. D. *Land Tenure in the Ramesside Period*. London: Kegan Paul, 1989.

Kees, Hermann. "Die Kopenhagener Schenkungsstele aus der Zeit des Apries." *ZÄS* 72 (1936): 40–52.

———. *Das Priestertum im ägyptischen Staat vom Neuen Reich bis zur Spätzeit*. Leiden: Brill, 1953–1958.

———. "Sesostris." Pages 1861–76 in vol. 2, second series of *Paulys Realencyclopädie der classischen Altertumswissenschaft*. Edited by G. Wissowa. 49 vols. Munich: Druckenmueller, 1980.

———. *Zur Innenpolitik der Saïtendynastie*. Nachrichten aus der Altertumswissenschaft I; Nachrichten von der Gesellschaft der Wissenschaften zu Göttingen. Philologisch-historische Klasse, N.F. Fachgruppe 1. Göttingen: Vandenhoeck & Ruprecht, 1935.

Kellermann, Ulrich. "Erwägungen zum Esragesetz." *ZAW* 80 (1968): 373–85.

Kent, R. G. *Old Persian: Grammar, Texts, Lexicon*. AOSM 33. New Haven, Conn.: American Oriental Society, 1953.

Kervran, M., et al. "Une statue de Darius découverte à Suse." *Journal asiatique* 260 (1972): 235–66.

Kippenberg, Hans G. *Die vorderasiatischen Erlösungsreligionen in ihrem Zusammenhang mit der antiken Stadtherrschaft*. Suhrkamp taschenbuch. wissenschaft. 917. Frankfurt am Main: Suhrkamp, 1991.

Kirkpatrick, Patricia G. *The Old Testament and Folklore Study*. JSOTSup 62. Sheffield: Sheffield Academic Press, 1988.

Klatt, Werner. *Hermann Gunkel: zu seiner Theologie der Religionsgeschichte und zur Entstehung der formgeschichtlichen Methode*. Göttingen: Vandenhoeck & Ruprecht, 1969.

Kleinig, John W. *The Lord's Song: The Basis, Function and Significance of Choral Music in Chronicles*. JSOTSup 156. Sheffield: JSOT Press, 1993.

Knauf, Ernst Axel. *Die Umwelt des Alten Testaments*. Stuttgart: Verlag Katholisches Bibelwerk, 1994.

Knoppers, Gary N. "Hierodules, Priests, or Janitors? The Levites in Chronicles and the History of the Israelite Priesthood." *JBL* 118 (1999): 49–72.

———. "Jehoshaphat's Judiciary and the Scroll of YHWH's Torah." *JBL* 113 (1994): 59–80.

———. "Reform and Regression: The Chronicler's Presentation of Jehoshaphat." *Bib* 72 (1991): 500–24.

———. "Sex, Religion, and Politics: The Deuteronomist on Intermarriage." *HAR* 14 (1994): 121–41.

———. "Sources, Revisions, and Editions: The Lists of Jerusalem's Residents in MT and LXX Nehemiah 11 and 1 Chronicles 9." *Textus* 20 (2001): 141–68.

———. "Treasures Won and Lost: Royal (Mis)appropriations in Kings and Chronicles." Pages 181–208 in *The Chronicler As Author: Studies in Text and Texture*. Edited by M. P. Graham and S. L. McKenzie. JSOT-Sup 263. Sheffield: Sheffield Academic Press, 1999.

Koch, Klaus. "Ezra and the Origins of Judaism." *JSS* 19 (1974): 173–97.

Kratz, Reinhard Gregor. *Translatio imperii. Untersuchungen zu den aramäischen Danielerzählungen und ihrem theologiegeschichtlichen Umfeld.* WMANT 63. Neukirchen-Vluyn: Neukirchener Verlag, 1991.

Kraus, F. R. *Ein Edikt des Königs Ammi-ṣaduka von Babylon.* Studia et Documenta ad Iura Orientis Antiqui Pertinentia 5. Leiden: Brill, 1958.

———. "Ein Zentrales Problem des Altmesopotamischen Rechtes: Was ist der Codex Hammu-rabi?" *Genava* 8 (1960): 283–96.

Kruchten, Jean-Marie. *Les annales des pretres de Karnak (XXI–XXIII dynasties) et autres textes contemporains.* OLA 32. Leuven: Departement Oriëntalistiek, 1989.

———. *Le Dékret d'Horemheb.* Brussels: University of Brussels, 1981.

Kuhrt, Amelie. *The Ancient Near East c. 3000—330 BC.* 2 vols. London: Routledge, 1995.

———. "The Cyrus Cylinder and Achaemenid Imperial Policy." *JSOT* 25 (1983): 83–97.

Kuhrt, Amelie, and Susan Sherwin-White. "Xerxes Destructions of Babylonian Temples." Pages 69–78 in *The Greek Sources: Proceedings of the Groningen 1984 Achaemenid History Workshop*. Edited by H. Sancisi-Weerdenburg and A. Kuhrt. AH 2. Leiden: Nederlands Institute voor het Nabije Oosten, 1987.

Lacau, Pierre. *Une stèle juridique de Karnak.* Cairo: IFAO, 1949.

Lacau, Pierre, and Henri Chevrier. *Une chapelle d'Hatshepsout à Karnak.* 2 vols. Cairo: IFAO, 1977–1979.

Lafont, Sophie. "Ancient Near Eastern Laws: Continuity and Pluralism." Pages 91–118 in *Theory and Method in Biblical and Cuneiform Law: Revisions, Interpolation, and Development.* Edited by B. M. Levinson. JSOTSup 181. Sheffield: Sheffield Academic Press, 1994.

Landsberger, Benno. "Die Babylonischen Termini für Gesetz und Recht." Pages 219–34 in *Symbolae ad Iura Orientis Antiqui.* Edited by T. Folkers et al. Leiden: Brill, 1939.

Lange, H.O., and H. Schäfer. *Grab- und Denksteine des mittleren Reiches.* 4 vols. Cairo: Institut français d'archéologie orientale, 1902–1925.

Lange, Kurt. *Sesostris, ein ägyptischer König im Mythos, Geschichte und Kunst.* Munich: Hirmer, 1954.

Laum, Bernhard. *Stiftungen in der griechischen und römischen Antike: Ein Beitrag zur antiken Rechtsgeschichte.* 2 vols. Leipzig: Teubner, 1914.

Leclant, Jean. "Fouilles et travaux en Égypte et au Soúdan, 1989–1990," *Or* 60 (1991): 159–273.

———. *Montouembat: Quatrième Prophète d'Amon, Prince de la Ville.* Cairo: IFAO, 1961.

Lecoq, Pierre. *Les inscriptions de la Perse achéménide.* Paris: Gallimard, 1997.

Leemans, W. F. "Aperçu sur les textes juridiques d'Emar." *JESHO* 31 (1988): 207–42.

———. "King Ḫammurapi As Judge." Pages 107–29 in vol. 2 of *Symbolae iuridicae et historicae Martino David dedicatae II.* Edited by J. A. Ankum et al. 2 vols. Leiden: Brill, 1968.

Lefebvre, Gustave. *Histoire des grands prêtres d'Amon de Karnak.* Paris: Geuthner, 1929.

Leighty, E. *The Omen Series Šumma Izbu.* TCS 4. Locust Valley, N.Y.: Augustin, 1970.

Lemaire, André. "Writing and Writing Material." *ABD* 6:999–1008.

Levinson, Bernard M. "The Human Voice in Divine Revelation: The Problem of Authority in Biblical Law." Pages 46–61 in *Innovation in Religious Traditions.* Edited by M. A. Williams, C. Cox, and M. S. Jaffee. Religion and Society 31. Berlin: de Gruyter, 1992.

————., ed. *Theory and Method in Biblical and Cuneiform Law: Revisions, Interpolation, and Development.* JSOTSup 181. Sheffield: Sheffield Academic Press, 1994.

Lichtheim, Miriam. "The Naucratis Stela Once Again." Pages 139–146 in *Studies in Honor of George R. Hughes.* SAOC 39. Chicago: Oriental Institute, 1976.

Lloyd, Alan B. *Herodotus Book II. A Commentary.* 3 vols. Leiden: Brill, 1975–1988.

————. "The Inscription of Udjaḥorresnet: A Collaborator's Testament." *JEA* 68 (1982): 166–180.

————. "The Late Period, 664–323 BC." Pages 279–348 in *Ancient Egypt: A Social History.* Cambridge: Cambridge University Press, 1983.

Lohfink, Norbert. "Gab es eine deuteronomistiche Bewegung?" Pages 313–82 in *Jeremia und die "deuteronomistische Bewegung".* Edited by W. Groß. BBB 98. Weinheim: Beltz Athäneum 1995 = pages 65–142 in vol. 3 of *Studien zum Deuteronomium und zur deuteronomistischen Literatur.* SBAB 20. Stuttgart: Katholisches Bibelwerk, 1995.

Lorton, David. "Legal and Social Institutions of Pharaonic Egypt." Pages 345–62 of vol. 1 in *Civilizations of the Ancient Near East.* Edited by J. Sasson. 4 vols. New York: Scribner, 1995.

————. "The Treatment of Criminals in Ancient Egypt through the New Kingdom." *JESHO* 20 (1977): 2–64.

Luft, U. "Zur Einleitung der Liebesgedichte auf Papyrus Chester Beatty I." *ZÄS* 99 (1973): 108–16.

Malaise, Michel. "Sésostris, pharaon de légende et d'histoire." *ChrEg* 41 (1966): 244–72.

Malinine, Michel. "Une affaire concernant un partage (Pap. Vienne D 12003 et D 12004)." *RdE* 25 (1973): 192–208.

————. *Choix de textes juridiques en hiératique anormal et en démotique.* Part 1. Paris: Librairie Ancienne Honore Champion, 1953.

Mannzmann, Anneliese. *Griechische Stiftungsurkunden: Studien zu Inhalt und Rechtsform.* Fontes et Commentationes 2. Münster: Aschendorff, 1962.

Manuelian, Peter Der. *Living in the Past: Studies in Archaism of the Egyptian Twenty-Sixth Dynasty.* London: Routledge, 1994.

Mariette, Auguste. *Abydos.* 2 vols. Paris: Imprimerie National, 1880.

Martin, Cary J. "The Child Born in Elephantine: Papyrus Dodgson Revisited." In *Acta Demotica*. Pisa: Giardini, 1994 = *EVO* 17 (1994).

Maspero, Gaston. *History of Egypt, Chaldea, Syria, Babylonia and Assyria*. 13 vols. London: Grolier Society, 1900.

Mattha, Girgis, and George R. Hughes. *The Demotic Legal Code of Hermopolis West*. Cairo: IFAO, 1975.

McDowell, A. G. *Jurisdiction in the Workmen's Community of Deir el-Medina*. Leiden: Nederlands Instituut voor het Nabije Oosten, 1990.

Meeks, Dimitri. *Annee lexicographique*. 3 vols. Paris: Librairie Cybele, 1980–1982.

Meiggs, R., and D. Lewis. *A Selection of Greek Historical Inscriptions to the End of the Fifth Century B.C.* Oxford: Clarendon, 1969.

Menu, Bernadette. "Les Actes de vente en Egypte ancienne, particulièrement sous les rois Kouchites et Saïtes." *JEA* 74 (1988): 165–81.

———. "Les Juges egyptiens sous les derniers dynasties indigenes." Pages 213–4 in *Acta Demotica*. Pisa: Giardini, 1994 = *EVO* 17 (1994).

———. *Récherches sur l'histoire juridique, économique et sociale de l'ancienne Égypt*. 2 vols. Versailles, 1982; Cairo: IFAO, 1998.

Metzger, Henri et al., eds. *Fouilles de Xanthos 6: La stéle trilingue du Létôon*. Paris: Klincksieck, 1979.

Meyer, Eduard. *Die Entstehung des Judenthums: Eine historische Untersuchung*. Halle: Niemeyer, 1896.

Mieroop, Marc Van De. *The Ancient Mesopotamian City*. Oxford: Clarendon, 1997.

———. "The Government of an Ancient Mesopotamian City." Pages 139–61 in *Priests and Officials in the Ancient Near East*. Edited by K. Watanabe. Heidelberg: Universitätsverlag C. Winter, 1999.

Miller, J. Maxwell, and John H. Hayes. *A History of Ancient Israel and Judah*. Philadelphia: Fortress, 1986.

Milgrom, Jacob. *Cult and Conscience: The Asham and the Priestly Doctrine of Repentance*. SJLA 18. Leiden: Brill, 1976.

Möller, George. *Hieratische Paläographie*. 3 vols. Leipzig: Hinrich, 1909–1912.

Montet, P. "Inscriptions de basse époque trouvés à Tanis." *Kêmi* 8 (1946): 29–126.

Moret, Alexandre. *Catalogue du Musée Guimet: Galerie égyptienne: Stèles, bas-reliefs, monuments divers*. Annales du Musée Guimet 32. Paris: Leroux, 1909.

Mosher, M., Jr. Review of U. Verhoeven, *Das saïtische Totenbuch der Iatesnakht. BO* 56 (1999): 636–39.

Mosis, R. *Untersuchungen zur Theologie des chronistischen Geschichtswerkes.* Freiburg: Herder, 1973.

Moursi, M. "Die Stele des Vezirs Re-hotep." *MDAIK* 37 (1981): 321–29.

Muffs, Yochanan. *Studies in the Aramaic Legal Papyri from Elephantine.* Leiden: Brill, 1969.

Muhs, B. "Demotic and Greek Ostraca in the Third Century B.C." Pages 249–52 in *Life in a Multi-cultural Society: Egypt from Cambyses to Constantine and Beyond.* Edited by Janet H. Johnson. SAOC 51. Chicago: Oriental Institute, 1992.

Murray, Oswyn. "Hecataeus of Abdera and Pharaonic Kingship." *JEA* 56 (1970): 141–71.

Nelson, Harold H. "Certain Reliefs at Karnak and Medinet-Habu and the Ritual of Amenophis I." *JNES* 8 (1949): 201–32, 310–45.

Neumann, Günter. *Neufunde lykischer Inschriften seit 1901.* Ergänzungsbände zu den Tituli Asiae Minoris 7. Vienna: Verlag der Österreichischen Akademie der Wissenschaften, 1979.

Nibbi, Alessandra. "Remarks on the Two Stelai from the Wadi Gasus." *JEA* 62 (1976): 45–56.

Niehr, H. "Religio-Historical Aspects of the 'Early Post-Exilic' Period." In *The Crisis of Israelite Religion: Transformation of Religious Tradition in Exilic and Post-Exilic Times.* Edited by B. Becking and M. C. A. Korpel. OTS 42. Leiden: Brill, 1999.

Nims, C. "The Term *ḥp,* 'Law,' 'Right,' in Demotic." *JNES* 7 (1948): 243–60.

North, R. "Civil Authority in Ezra." In *Studi in onore di Edoardo Volterra.* Vol. 6. Milan: Giuffré, 1971.

Noth, Martin. *A History of Pentateuchal Traditions.* Englewood Cliffs, N.J.: Prentice-Hall, 1972; Chico, Calif.: Scholars Press, 1981. Translation of *Überlieferungsgeschichte des Pentateuch.* Stuttgart: Kohlhammer, 1948.

———. *Das System der zwölf Stämme Israels.* BWANT 52. Stuttgart: Kohlhammer, 1930.

Obsomer, Claude. *Les campagnes de Sésostris dans Hérodote*. Brussels: Connaissance de l'Egypte ancienne, 1989.

Oeming, Manfred. *Das Wahre Israel: Die "Genealogische Vorhalle" 1 Chronik 1–9*. BWANT 128. Stuttgart: Kohlhammer, 1990.

Olmstead, A. T. "Darius As Lawgiver." *AJSL* 51 (1934/1935): 247–49.

———. *A History of the Persian Empire*. Chicago: University of Chicago Press, 1948.

Oppenheim, A. L. "The Babylonian Evidence of Achaemenian Rule in Mesopotamia." Pages 529–87 in *The Median and Achaemenian Periods*. Vol. 2 of *The Cambridge History of Iran*. Edited by Ilya Gershevitz. Cambridge: Cambridge University Press, 1985.

Otto, Eberhard. *Die biographischen Inschriften der ägyptischen Spätzeit: ihre geistesgeschichtliche und literarische Bedeutung*. Probleme der Ägyptologie 2. Leiden: Brill, 1954.

———. "Prolegomena zur Frage der Gesetzgebung und Rechtsprechung in Ägypten." *MDAIK* 14 (1956): 150–59.

Otto, Eckart. *Das Deuteronomium: politische Theologie und Rechtsreform in Juda und Assyrien*. BZAW 284. Berlin: de Gruyter, 1999.

———. "Kritik der Pentateuchkomposition." *TRu* 60 (1995): 163–91.

———. "Die nachpriesterschriftliche Pentateuchredaktion im Buch Exodus." Pages 61–111 in *Studies in the Book of Exodus. Redaction-Reception-Interpretation*. Edited by M. Vervenne. BETL 126. Leuven: Peeters, 1996.

———. Review of James W. Watts, *Reading Law: The Rhetorical Shaping of the Pentateuch*. *ZABR* 5 (1999): 353–57.

Otto, W. *Priester und Tempeln in hellenistischen Ägypten*. Leipzig, 1905.

Parker, Richard A. *A Saite Oracle Papyrus in the Brooklyn Museum*. Providence: Brown University Press, 1962.

———. *A Vienna Demotic Papyrus on Eclipses and Solar Omina*. Providence: Brown University Press, 1958.

Patrick, Dale. *Old Testament Law*. Atlanta: John Knox, 1985.

Patterson, Richard D. "Holding On to Daniel's Court Tales." *JETS* 36 (1993): 445–54.

Paul, Shalom. *Studies in the Book of the Covenant in the Light of Cuneiform and Biblical Law*. VTSup 18. Leiden: Brill, 1970.

Pedersen, Johann. *Israel: Its Life and Culture*. Vol. 3–4. Copenhagen: Branner, 1940.

Pestman, Pieter W. "Een juridisch 'Handboek' uit het Oude Egypte." *Phoenix* 25 (1979): 25–35.

Pestman, Pieter W. "L'origine et extension d'un manuel de droit égyptien." *JESHO* 26 (1983): 14–21.

Petersen, David L. "Israelite Prophecy: Change versus Continuity." Pages 191–203 in *Congress Volume: Leuven, 1989*. Edited by J. A. Emerton. VTSup 43. Leiden: Brill, 1991.

Petit, Thierry. *Satrapes et satrapies dans l'empire achéménide de Cyrus le Grand a Xerxes Ier*. Liège: Bibliothèque de la Faculté de Philosophie et Lettres de l'Université de Liège, 1990.

Pohlmann, K.-F. "Zur Frage von Korrespondenzen und Divergenzen zwischen den Chronikbüchern und dem Esra/Nehemia-Buch." Pages 314–30 in *Congress Volume: Leuven, 1989*. Edited by J. A. Emerton. VTSup 43. Leiden: Brill, 1991.

Poljakov, Fjodor B. *Die Inschriften von Tralleis und Nysa. Teil 1*. Inschriften griechischer Städte aus Kleinasien 36.1. Bonn: Habelt, 1989.

Porten, Bezalel. *Archives from Elephantine: The Life of an Ancient Jewish Military Colony*. Berkeley and Los Angeles: University of California Press, 1968.

———. "The Documents in the Book of Ezra and the Mission of Ezra" (Hebrew). *Shnaton* 3 (1978–1979): 174–96.

———. *The Elephantine Papyri in English: Three Millennia of Cross-Cultural Continuity and Change*. Leiden: Brill, 1996.

Porter, Joshua R. *Moses and Monarchy: A Study in the Biblical Tradition of Moses*. Oxford: Oxford University Press, 1963.

Posener, Georges. *Le Papyrus Vandier*. Cairo: IFAO, 1985.

———. *La première domination perse en Égypte*. Bibliothèque d'Étude 11. Cairo: IFAO, 1936.

Posener-Krieger, Paule. *Les Archives du temple funeraire de Neferirkare-Kakai*. Cairo: IFAO, 1976.

Posener-Krieger, Paule, and Jean Louis de Cenival. *The Abu Sir Papyri*. London: British Museum, 1968.

Postgate, J. N. *Early Mesopotamia: Society and Economy at the Dawn of History*. London: Routledge, 1992.

Quack, Joachim-Friedrich. "Der historische Abschnitt des Buches von Tempel." Pages 267–78 in *Literatur und Politik im pharaonischen und ptolemaischen Aegypten*. Edited by J. Assmann and E. Blumenthal. Cairo: IFAO, 1999.

———. "P. Wien 6319. Eine demotische Übersetzung aus dem Mittelägyptischen." *Enchoria* 19/20 (1992/1993): 124–29.

Quaegebauer, J. "Sur la 'loi sacrée' dans l'Égypte gréco-romaine." *Ancient Society* 11–12 (1980–1981): 227–40.

Quirke, Stephen. *The Administration of Egypt in the Late Middle Kingdom*. Whitstable: SIA, 1990.

Rad, Gerhard von. "The Form-Critical Problem of the Hexateuch." Pages 1–78 in *The Problem of the Hexateuch and Other Essays*. New York: McGraw-Hill, 1966. Translation of *Das formgeschichtliche Problem des Hexateuch*. BWANT 78. Stuttgart: Kohlhammer, 1938 = pages 9–86 in *Gesammelte Studien zum Alten Testament*. TB 8. Munich: Kaiser, 1958.

Randall-MacIver, David, and A. C. Mace. *El Amrah and Abydos*. London: Egypt Exploration Fund, 1902.

Ray, J. D. *The Archive of Hor: Texts from Excavations*. 2 vols. London: Egypt Exploration Society, 1976.

———. "Egypt 525–404 B.C." Pages 254–86 in vol. 4 of *The Cambridge Ancient History*. 2d ed. Cambridge: Cambridge University Press, 1991.

Redford, Donald B. "The Earliest Years of Ramesses II and the Building of the Ramesside Court at Luxor." *JEA* 57 (1971): 110–19.

———. *From Slave to Pharaoh: The Black Experience in Ancient Egypt*. Baltimore: Baltimore University Press, 2001.

———. *Pharaonic Kinglists, Annals and Daybooks: A Contribution to the Study of the Egyptian Sense of History*. Mississauga, Ont.: Benben, 1986.

———. "Scribe and Speaker." Pages 145–218 in *Writing and Speech in Israelite and Ancient Near Eastern Prophecy*. Edited by E. Ben Zvi and M. H. Floyd. SBLSymS 10. Atlanta: Society of Biblical Literature, 2000.

———. "Textual Sources for the Hyksos Period." Pages 22–24 in *The Hyksos: New Historical and Archaeological Perspectives*. Edited by E. Oren. Philadelphia: University Museum, 1997.

Reich, N. J. "The Codification of the Egyptian Laws by Darius and the Origin of the 'Demotic Chronicle'." *Mizraim* 1 (1933): 178–85.

Reisner, G. A. "Inscribed Monuments from Gebel Barkal." *ZÄS* 69 (1933): 73–78.

Rendtorff, Rolf. "Esra und das 'Gesetz'." *ZAW* 96 (1984): 165–84.

———. "Noch einmal: Esra und das Gesetz." *ZAW* 111 (1999): 89–91.

Reymond, E. A. E. *From Ancient Egyptian Hermetical Writings*. Part 2 of *From the Contents of the Suchos Temple in the Fayum*. Vienna: Hollinek, 1977.

Robert, Louis. "Décret d'une syngeneia carienne au sanctuaire de Sinuri." *Hellenica* 7 (1949): 59–68.

———. *Les inscriptions grecques*. Part 1 of *Le sanctuaire de Sinuri près de Mylasa*. Mémoires de l'Institut Français d'Archéologie de Stamboul 7. Paris: de Boccard, 1945.

———. "Une nouvelle inscription grecque de Sardes: Règlement de l'autorité perse relatif à un culte de Zeus." *CRAI* (1975): 306–30.

Robins, Gay, and Charles Shute. *The Rhind Mathematical Papyrus*. New York: Dover, 1987.

Rogerson, John W. *W. M. L. de Wette: Founder of Biblical Criticism: An Intellectual Biography*. JSOTSup 126. Sheffield: Sheffield Academic Press, 1992.

Römer, M. *Gottes- und Priesterherrschaft in Ägypten am Ende des Neuen Reiches*. Wiesbaden: Harrassowitz, 1994.

Römer, Thomas C., and Marc Z. Brettler. "Deuteronomy 34 and the Case for a Persian Hexateuch." *JBL* 119 (2000): 401–19.

Rose, Lynn E. "The Sothic Date from the Ptolemaic Temple of Isis at Aswan." *BO* 56 (1999): 14–34.

Rossler-Köhler, U. "Zur Textcomposition der naolphoren Statue des Udjahorresnet/Vatikan luv. Nr. 196." *GM* 85 (1985): 43–54.

Roth, Martha. *Law Collections from Mesopotamia and Asia Minor*. Atlanta: Scholars Press, 1997.

Rudolph, Wilhelm. *Chronikbücher*. HAT 21. Tübingen: Mohr Siebeck, 1955.

———. *Esra und Nehemia samt 3. Esra*. HAT 20. Tübingen: Mohr Siebeck, 1949.

Rundgren, F. "Zur Bedeutung von ŠRŠW—Esra vii 26." *VT* 7 (1957): 400–4.

Russmann, Edna R. *The Representation of the King in the 25th Dynasty*. New York: Brooklyn Museum, 1974.

Rüterswörden, Udo. "Die persische Reichsautorisation der Thora: Fact or Fiction?" *ZABR* 1 (1995): 47–61.

Ryholt, Kim. *The Story of Petese Son of Petetum*. Copenhagen: Casten Niebuhr Institute of Near East Studies, University of Copenhagen, Museum Tusculanum Press, 1999.

Sacchi, Paolo. *Storia del Secondo Tempio: Israele tra VI secolo a.C. e I secolo d.C.* Turin: Società Editrice Internazionale, 1994.

Şahin, M. Çetin. *Lagina, Stratonikeia und Umgebung*. Part 2.1 of *Die Inschriften von Stratonikeia*. Inschriften griechischer Städte aus Kleinasien 22.1. Bonn: Habelt, 1982.

Sancisi-Weerdenburg, Heleen. "Yaunā en Persai: Grieken en Perzen in een ander perspectief." Ph.D. diss., Leiden, 1980.

Sayed, R. el-. *Documents relatifs a Sais et ses divinites*. Cairo: IFAO, 1975.

Schaeder, Hans Heinrich. *Esra der Schreiber*. BHT 5. Tübingen: Mohr Siebeck, 1930.

———. *Der Mensch im Orient und Okzident*. Breslau [Wrocław]: Korn, 1940/1941; Munich: Kaiser, 1960.

Schams, Christine. *Jewish Scribes in the Second Temple Period*. JSOTSup 291. Sheffield: Sheffield Academic Press, 1998.

Scharff, Alexander, and Erwin Seidl. *Einfuhrung in die Ägyptische Rechtsgeschichte bis zum Ende des neuen Reiches*. Glückstadt: Augustin, 1957.

Scheil, V. *Mission en Susiane, Mélanges Épigraphiques*. Mémoires de la Mission Archéologique de Perse 28. Paris: Librairie Ernest LeRoux, 1939.

Schmitt, Hans-Christoph. "Die Suche nach der Identität des Jahweglaubens im nachexilischen Israel: Bemerkungen zur theologischen Intention des Pentateuch." Pages 259–78 in *Pluralismus und Identität*. Edited by J. Mehlhausen. Munich: Kaiser, 1995.

Schniedewind, William M. "King and Priest in the Book of Chronicles and the Duality of Qumran Messianism." *JJS* 45 (1994): 71–78.

———. *The Word of God in Transition: From Prophet to Exegete in the Second Temple Period*. JSOTSup 197. Sheffield: JSOT Press, 1995.

Schott, Siegfried. *Bücher und Bibliotheken in alten Ägypten*. Wiesbaden: Harrassowitz, 1990.

Schottroff, Wilhelm. "Zur Sozialgeschichte Israels in der Perserzeit." *VF* 27 (1982): 46–68.

Schramm, Brooks. *The Opponents of the Third Isaiah: Reconstructing the Cultic History of the Restoration.* JSOTSup 193. Sheffield: Sheffield Academic Press, 1994.

Seidl, Erwin. *Ägyptische Rechtsgeschichte der Saïten- und Perserzeit.* 2d ed. ÄF 20. Glückstadt: Augustin, 1968; 1st ed., 1956.

———. "Die Gottesentscheidungen der Saïten- und Perserzeit." Pages 59–65 in *Essays in Honor of C. Bradford Welles.* New Haven, Conn.: American Society of Papyrologists, 1966.

Sethe, Kurt. *Ägyptische Lesestucke.* Leipzig: Hinrichs, 1929.

———. *Sesostris.* Leipzig: Hinrichs, 1900.

Shaver, Judson R. *Torah and the Chronicler's History Work.* Atlanta: Scholars Press, 1989.

Shupak, N. "A New Source for the Study of the Judiciary and Law of Ancient Egypt: 'The Tale of the Eloquent Peasant'." *JNES* 51 (1992): 1–18.

Ska, Jean Louis. "Exode 19,3b–6 et l'identité de l'Israël postexilique." Pages 289–317 in *The Book of Exodus: Redaction-Reception-Interpretation.* Edited by M. Vervenne. BETL 126. Leuven: Peeters, 1996.

———. *Introduction à la lecture du Pentateuque. Clés pour l'interprétation des cinq premiers livres de la Bible.* Le livre et le rouleau. Paris: Cerf, 2000.

———. "Un nouveau Wellhausen?" *Bib* 72 (1991): 261–62.

———. "La scrittura era parola di Dio, scolpita sulle tavole (Es 32,16). Autorità, rivelazione e ispirazione nelle leggi del Pentateuco." Pages 7–23 in *Spirito di Dio e Sacre Scritture nell'autotestimonianza della Bibbia.* Edited by E. Manicardi and A. Pitta. Ricerche Storico-Bibliche 1–2. Bologna: Dehoniane, 2000.

Smend, Rudolf. *Deutsche Alttestamentler in drei Jahrhunderten.* Göttingen: Vandenhoeck & Ruprecht, 1989.

Smith(-Christopher), Daniel L. "The Mixed Marriage Crisis in Ezra 9–10 and Nehemiah 13: A Study of the Sociology of Post-Exilic Judaean Community." Pages 243–65 in *Second Temple Studies 2: Temple and Community in the Persian Period.* Edited by T. C. Eskenazi and K. H. Richards. JSOTSup 175. Sheffield: Sheffield Academic Press, 1994.

———. "The Politics of Ezra: Sociological Indicators of Postexilic Judaean Society." Pages 73–97 in *Second Temple Studies 1: Persian Period.* Edited by P. R. Davies. JSOTSup 117. Sheffield: Sheffield Academic Press, 1991.

Smith, H. S., and W. J. Tait. *Saqqara Demotic Papyri.* Vol. 1. London: Egypt Exploration Society, 1983.

Smith, M. "A Second Dynasty King in a Demotic Papyrus of the Roman Period." *JEA* 66 (1980): 173–74.

Smith, Morton. "Jewish Religious Life in the Persian Period." Pages 219–78 in *Introduction; The Persian Period.* Vol. 1 of *The Cambridge History of Judaism.* Edited by W. D. Davies and L. Finkelstein. Cambridge: Cambridge University Press, 1984.

————. *Palestinian Parties and Politics That Shaped the Old Testament.* New York: Columbia University Press, 1971.

Smith, W. Stevenson, and William Kelly Simpson. *The Art and Architecture of Ancient Egypt.* New Haven, Conn.: Yale University Press, 1983, 1998.

Smither, Paul C. "A Tax Assessor's Journal of the Middle Kingdom." *JEA* 27 (1941): 17.

Sokolowski, Franciszek. *Lois sacrées de l'Asie mineure.* École française d'Athènes. Travaux et mémoires 9. Paris: de Boccard, 1955.

Spalinger, Anthony. "Udjahorresnet." *LÄ* 4:822–824.

Spieckermann, Hermann. *Juda unter Assur in der Sargonidenzeit.* FRLANT 129. Göttingen: Vandenhoeck & Ruprecht, 1982.

Spiegelberg, Wilhelm. *Drei demotische Schreiben aus der Korrespondenz des Pherendates des Satrapen Darius' I., mit den Chnumpriestern von Elephantine.* SPAW. Berlin: Akademie der Wissenschaften, 1928.

————. *Die sogenannte demotische Chronik des Pap. 215 der Bibliothèque Nationale zu Paris.* Leipzig: Hinrichs, 1914.

Stamm, Johann Jakob. *Die akkadische Namengebung.* MVAG 44. Leipzig: Hinrichs, 1939.

Steck, Odil Hannes. *Der Abschluß der Prophetie im Alten Testament.* Neukirchen-Vluyn: Neukirchener Verlag, 1991.

Stern, Ephraim. "The Archeology of Persian Palestine." Pages 88–114 in *Introduction; The Persian Period.* Vol. 1 of *The Cambridge History of Judaism.* Edited by W. D. Davies and L. Finkelstein. Cambridge: Cambridge University Press, 1984.

Stern, Menachem. *Greek and Latin Authors on Jews and Judaism.* 3 vols. Jerusalem: Israel Academy of Arts and Sciences, 1974–1984.

Stolper, Matthew W. "Flogging and Plucking." Pages 347–50 in *Recherches récentes sur l'Empire achéménide*. Edited by M.-F. Boussac. Topoi Supplément 1. Paris: de Boccard, 1997.

Strübind, K. *Tradition als Interpretation in der Chronik: König Josaphat als Paradigma chronistischer Hermeneutik und Theologie*. BZAW 201. Berlin: de Gruyter, 1991.

Strudwick, Nigel. *The Administration of Egypt in the Old Kingdom*. London: Routledge, 1985.

Talmon, Shamaryahu. "Esra und Nehemia: Historiographie oder Theologie?" Pages 329–56 in *Ernton was man sät: Festschrift für Klaus Koch zu einem 65. Geburtstag*. Edited by D. W. Daniels et al. Neukirchen-Vluyn: Neukirchener Verlag, 1993.

Talshir, D. "A Reinvestigation of the Linguistic Relationship between Chronicles and Ezra-Nehemiah." *VT* 38 (1988): 165–93.

Tawfik, Sayed. "*ir·n·f m mnw·f* als Weihformel. Gebrauch und Bedeutung." *MDAIK* 27 (1971): 227–34.

Taylor, John H. *Egypt and Nubia*. London: British Museum, 1991.

Teixidor, Javier. "The Aramaic Text in the Trilingual Stele from Xanthus." *JNES* 37 (1978): 181–85.

Théodoridès, Aristide. "The Concept of Law in Ancient Egypt." Pages 291–322 in *The Legacy of Egypt*. Edited by J. R. Harris. Oxford: Oxford University Press, 1971.

———. "La 'Coutume' et la 'Loi' dans l'Egypte Pharaonique." *Recueils de la Societé Jean Bodin* (1990): 39–47.

———. "Dekret." *LÄ* 1:1037–43.

———. *Vivre de Maât: Travaux sur le droit égyptien ancien*. Brussels: Societe belge d'etudes orientales, 1995.

Thompson, D. J. *Memphis under the Ptolemies*. Princeton, N.J.: Princeton University Press, 1988.

Tod, Marcus N. *A Selection of Greek Historical Inscriptions*. 2 vols. Oxford: Oxford University Press, 1948.

Török, Lazlo. *The Kingdom of Kush: Handbook of the Napatan-Meroitic Civilization*. Leiden: Brill, 1996.

Tuplin, Christopher. "The Administration of the Achaemenid Empire." Pages 109–166 in *Coinage and Administration in the Athenian and*

Persian Empires. Edited by Ian Carradice. BAR International Series 343. Oxford: B.A.R., 1987.

Utzschneider, Helmut. *Das Heiligtum und das Gesetz: Studien zur Bedeutung der sinaitischen Heiligtumstexte (Ex 25–40; Lev 8–9).* OBO 77. Göttingen: Vandenhoeck & Ruprecht, 1988.

Vallat, F. "Les Inscriptions cunéiformes de la statue de Darius," *Cahiers de la délégation archéologique française en Iran* 4 (1974): 161–70.

———. "L'inscription trilingue de Xerxès à la porte de Darius." *Cahiers de la délégation archéologique française en Iran* 4 (1974): 171–80.

Vaux, Roland de. "The Decrees of Cyrus and Darius on the Rebuilding of the Temple." Pages 63–96 in *The Bible and the Ancient Near East.* Garden City, N.Y.: Doubleday, 1971. First published in *RB* 46 (1937): 29–57.

Vercoutter, Jean. *Textes biographiques du Sérapéum de Memphis.* Paris: Champion, 1962.

Verner, Miroslav. "Excavations at Abousir, Season 1988/89: A Preliminary Report." *ZÄS* 118 (1991): 162–67.

———. "La tombe d'Oudjahorresnet et le cimetière saïto-perse d'Abousir." *BIFAO* 89 (1989): 283–90.

Vittmann, Günter. *Der demotische Papyrus Rylands 9.* 2 parts. Agypten und Altes Testament 38. Wiesbaden: Harrassowitz, 1998.

———. "Eine misslungene Dokumentenfalschung: Die 'Stelen' des Peteese I (P. Ryl. 9, XXI–XXIII)." *EVO* 17 (1994): 301–15.

———. "Zu fremden und hellenisierten Ägyptern." Page 1238 in vol. 2 of *Egyptian Religion: The Last Thousand Years.* Edited by W. Clarysse. Leuven: Peeters, 1998.

Vleeming, Sven P. "Een lang uitgestelde benoeming." *Phoenix* 27 (1981): 82–91.

———. "The Tithe of Scribes (and) Representatives." Page 343 in *Life in a Multi-cultural Society: Egypt from Cambyses to Constantine and Beyond.* Edited by J. H. Johnson. Chicago: Oriental Institute, 1992.

Vogelsang, W. J. *The Rise and Organisation of the Achaemenid Empire: The Eastern Iranian Evidence.* SHANE 3. Leiden: Brill, 1992.

Vogt, Ernestus. *Lexicon Linguae Aramaicae Veteris Testamenti.* Rome: Pontifical Biblical Institute, 1971.

Volten, A. *Ägypter und Amazonen.* Vienna, 1962.

Waddell, W. G. *Manetho*. LCL. Cambridge: Harvard University Press, 1940, 1980.

Warburton, David A. *State and Economy in Ancient Egypt: Fiscal Vocabulary of the New Kingdom*. OBO 151. Fribourg: Universitätsverlag, 1997.

Watts, James W. *Reading Law: The Rhetorical Shaping of the Pentateuch*. Biblical Seminar 59. Sheffield: Sheffield Academic Press, 1999.

Weinberg, Joel P. *The Citizen-Temple Community*. JSOTSup 151. Sheffield: Sheffield Academic Press, 1992.

———. "Demographische Notizen zur Geschichte der nachexilischen Gemeinde in Juda." *Klio* 54 (1972): 45–59.

Weinfeld, Moshe. "Judge and Officer in Ancient Israel and in the Ancient Near East." *Israel Oriental Studies* 7 (1977): 65–88.

Wellhausen, Julius. *Prolegomena to the History of Israel*. Reprints and Translations Series. Atlanta: Scholars Press, 1994. Translation of *Prolegomena zur Geschichte Israels*. Berlin: Reimer, 1878; 3d ed., 1886.

Westbrook, Raymond. "Biblical and Cuneiform Law Codes." *RB* 92 (1985): 247–64.

———. "What Is the Covenant Code?" Pages 15–26 in *Theory and Method in Biblical and Cuneiform Law: Revision, Interpolation, and Development*. Edited by B. M. Levinson. JSOTSup 181. Sheffield: Sheffield Academic Press, 1994.

Westendorf, Wolfhart. *Koptisches Handwörterbuch*. Heidelberg: C. Winter Universitätsverlag, 1977.

Wette, Wilhelm Martin Leberecht de. *Dissertatio critica qua Deuterononium diversum a prioribus Pentateuchi libris, alius cuiusdam recentioris auctoris opus esse demonstratur*. Jena, 1805.

Wiedemann, Alfred. *Ägyptische Geschichte*. Gottha: Perthes, 1884.

Wiesehöfer, Joseph. *Ancient Persia from 550 BC to 650 AD*. London: I. B. Tauris, 1996.

———. "'Reichsgesetz' oder 'Einzelfallgerechtigkeit'? Bemerkungen zu P. Freis These von der Achämenidischen 'Reichsautorisation'." *ZABR* 1 (1995): 36–46.

———. "Zur Frage der Echtheit des Dareios-Briefes an Gadatas." *Reinisches Museum* 130 (1987): 396–98.

Willi, Thomas. *Juda-Jehud-Israel*. FAT 12. Tübingen: Mohr Siebeck, 1995.

Williams, R. J. Hebrew Syntax. 2d ed.; Toronto: University of Toronto Press, 1976.

Williamson, H. G. M. *Ezra, Nehemiah*. WBC. Waco, Tex.: Word, 1985.

————. *Israel in the Books of Chronicles*. New York: Cambridge University Press, 1977.

————. "Judah and the Jews." Pages 143–63 in *Studies in Persian History: Essays in Memory of David M. Lewis*. Edited by M. Brosius and A. Kuhrt. AH11. Leiden: Nederlands Instituut van het Nabije Oosten, 1998.

————. Review of Peter Frei and Klaus Koch, *Reichsidee und Reichsorganisation im Perserreich*. *VT* 35 (1985): 379–80.

Wilson, P. A *Ptolemaic Lexicon*. Leuven: Uitgeverij Peeters en Department Oosterse Studies, 1997.

Wilson, Robert R. "Israel's Judicial System in the Preexilic Period." *JQR* 74 (1983): 229–48.

Wörrle, Michael. *Stadt und Fest im kaiserzeitlichen Kleinasien: Studien zu einer agonistischen Stiftung aus Oinoanda*. Munich: Beck, 1988.

Wright, John W. "From Center to Periphery: 1 Chronicles 23–27 and the Interpretation of Chronicles in the Nineteenth Century." Pages 20–42 in *Priests, Prophets, and Scribes: Essays on the Formation and Heritage of Second Temple Judaism in Honour of Joseph Blenkinsopp*. Edited by E. C. Ulrich et al. JSOTSup 149. Sheffield: JSOT Press, 1992.

————. "Guarding the Gates: 1 Chronicles 26.1–19 and the Roles of Gatekeepers in Chronicles." *JSOT* 48 (1990): 69–81.

————. "The Legacy of David in Chronicles: The Narrative Function of 1 Chronicles 23–27." *JBL* 110 (1991): 229–42.

Young, T. Cuyler, Jr. "The Early History of the Medes and the Persians and the Achaemenid Empire to the Death of Cambyses." Page 94 in vol. 4 of *The Cambridge Ancient History*. 2d ed. Cambridge: Cambridge University Press, 1991.

Zauzich, K.-T. "Lesonis." *LÄ* 3:1008–9.

————. "Weitere Fragmente eines juristischen Handbuches in demotischer Schrift." *EVO* 17 (1994): 327–32.

Zenger, Erich. *Einleitung in das Alte Testament*. Stuttgart: Kohlhammer, 1995; 2d ed., 1996; 3d ed., 1998.

INDEX OF ANCIENT SOURCES

HEBREW BIBLE

ASIA MINOR

HELLENISTIC AND ROMAN AUTHORS

INDEX OF MODERN AUTHORS